Integrationism and the S

In recent years a set of challenging questions have arisen in relation to the status of animals; their treatment by human beings; their cognitive abilities; and the nature of their feelings, emotions, and capacity for suffering. This groundbreaking book draws from integrational semiology to investigate arguments around the rights of certain animals to be recognized as legal persons, thereby granting them many of the protections enjoyed by humans.

In parallel with these debates, the question of the legal personality of artificial intelligence (AI) systems has moved to the forefront of legal debate, with entities such as robots, cyborgs, self-driving cars, and genetically engineered beings under consideration. Integrationism offers a framework within which the wider theoretical and practical issues can be understood. Law requires closure and categorical answers; integrationism is an open-ended form of inquiry that is seen as removed from particular controversies. This book argues that the two domains can be brought together in a challenging and productive synthesis. A much-needed resource to examine the heart of this fascinating debate and a must-read for anyone interested in semiology, linguistics, philosophy, ethics, and law.

Christopher Hutton is Professor in the School of English at the University of Hong Kong.

Routledge Advances in Communication and Linguistic Theory

Series Editor: Adrian Pablé

Rethinking Linguistics
Edited by Hayley G. Davis & Talbot J. Taylor

The Written Language Bias in Linguistics
Its Nature, Origins and Transformations
Per Linell

Language and History
Integrationist Perspectives
Edited by Nigel Love

Language Teaching
Integrational Linguistic Approaches
Edited by Michael Toolan

Rationality and the Literate Mind
Roy Harris

Critical Humanist Perspectives
The integrational turn in philosophy of language and communications
Edited by Adrian Pablé

The Reflexivity of Language and Linguistic Inquiry
Integrational Linguistics in Practice
Dorthe Duncker

Integrationism and the Self
Reflections on the Legal Personhood of Animals
Christopher Hutton

For more information about this series, please visit https://www.routledge.com/Routledge-Advances-in-Communication-and-Linguistic-Theory/book-series/RACLT

Integrationism and the Self

Reflections on the Legal Personhood of Animals

Christopher Hutton

Routledge
Taylor & Francis Group
LONDON AND NEW YORK

First published 2019
by Routledge
4 Park Square, Milton Park, Abingdon, Oxon OX14 4RN
605 Third Avenue, New York, NY 10017

First issued in paperback 2021

Routledge is an imprint of the Taylor & Francis Group, an informa business

British Library Cataloguing-in-Publication Data
A catalogue record for this book is available from the British Library

Library of Congress Cataloging-in-Publication Data
Names: Hutton, Christopher, author.
Title: Integrationism and the self : reflections on the legal personhood of animals / by Christopher Hutton.
Description: New York, NY : Routledge, [2019] |
Series: Routledge advances in communication and linguistic theory |
Includes bibliographical references and index.
Identifiers: LCCN 2018059754
Subjects: LCSH: Persons (Law)—Philosophy. |
Animal rights—Philosophy. | Animals—Moral and ethical aspects. |
Animals—Law and legislation. | Artificial intelligence—Philosophy. |
Artificial intelligence—Law and legislation. | Integrational linguistics (Oxford school) | Semiotics.
Classification: LCC K625 .H88 2019 | DDC 342.08—dc23
LC record available at https://lccn.loc.gov/2018059754

ISBN 13: 978-1-03-209309-3 (pbk)
ISBN 13: 978-1-138-30879-4 (hbk)

DOI: 10.4324/9781315143132

Typeset in Galliard
by codeMantra

Contents

Acknowledgments vii
Note ix

Introduction 1

1 Bedrock concepts 6

2 The analysis of bedrock concepts within language studies 43

3 Integrationism and systems theory 67

4 Animals, personhood, and law 84

5 Litigating animal personhood 112

Conclusion: a personalist perspective 144

References 149
Index 175

Acknowledgments

I would like to thank the series editor, Adrian Pablé, for his encouragement and guidance of this project and many fruitful discussions about integrationism. I am grateful to my colleagues in the School of English and the Law and Humanities research group at the University of Hong Kong as well as to the members of the International Association for the Integrational Study of Language and Communication (IAISLC). I would like to thank Katie Peace and Samantha Phua of Routledge for their support throughout. This research was supported by the Research Grants Council of Hong Kong under its Prestigious Fellowship Scheme under the Humanities and Social Sciences (HKU 37600214) for the project entitled Defining Fundamental Concepts: The Legal Personhood of Animals. My gratitude goes to David Karlander, Sinead Kwok, and Jasper Wu for perceptive comments on earlier drafts.

Note

Key terms and concepts are given in italics. Word meanings or glosses are given in single inverted commas, as are quotations. Unless otherwise noted, cited italics are found in the original.

Introduction

> All concepts in which an entire process is promiscuously comprehended defy definition; it is only that which has no history which can be defined.
>
> (Friedrich Nietzsche, *On the Genealogy of Morals*)

This study emerges, albeit indirectly, from developments in animal law in the last 15 years (Sunstein and Nussbaum 2004), primarily in the United States. This new focus on animals reflects broader developments in animal studies or human-animal studies, where questions are raised about not only the status of animals in relation to humans but also the internal complexity of the category (non-human) *animal* itself (Calarco 2008: 2–3). The rise of a specific discourse of animal rights law is often traced to utilitarian philosopher Peter Singer's *Animal Liberation*, first published in 1975. Jeremy Bentham had written ([1823] 1879: 1), 'Nature has placed mankind under two sovereign masters, *pain* and *pleasure*, and thereby under the subjection of the *principle of utility*'. Writing in the context of a discussion of slavery, Bentham ([1823] 1879: 310 fn.) drew an analogy with the treatment of animals: 'The day may come, when the rest of the animal creation may acquire those rights which never could have been withholden from them but by the hand of tyranny'. The dividing line for such rights was conventionally the 'faculty of reason' or 'the faculty of discourse', but 'a full-grown horse or dog is beyond comparison a more rational, as well as a more conversable animal, than an infant'. So, the question was not 'Can they reason? Nor, Can they talk? But, Can they suffer?' ([1823] 1879: 310fn). Singer argued that animals' interests and suffering merited equal consideration to those of humans. To racism, sexism, homophobia, and ableism was added *speciesism* (see Godlovitch, Godlovitch and Harris 1971, Ryder 1975: 16).

Animal rights law is concerned with the basic framework required for the just treatment of animals by social systems (Nussbaum 2006), the categorization of animals as actual or potential property, and questions of rights and animal personhood (Regan and Singer 1976, Posner 2000, Wise 2000, 2002a, Cavalieri 2001, Regan 2001). For one practitioner, the distinctive feature of animal law is that animals, unlike other clients, are 'legal nonentities' (Wagman 2010: 202). As a consequence, animal rights activists have sought to persuade courts

DOI: 10.4324/9781315143132-1

that certain animals should be legally recognized as *persons*. The liberal model of the self, it is argued, can be extended to these animals. They possess individuality, creativity, free-will, and a rich emotional inner life. Certain animals are 'at the brink of the human mind' (see Savage-Rumbaugh and Lewin 1996, De Waal 2016). On YouTube one can watch a video entitled *Michael's Story, Where He Signs about His Family*, in which a gorilla offers a first-person sign-language narrative of the murder of his mother by bushmeat poachers (Zulueta 2015).[1]

Advocacy of animal rights essentially proposes to upgrade certain categories of animal to the level of human beings for some legal purposes, in this sense expanding rather than undermining the fundamental anthropocentricism of law. Yet for some critics, this humanization of certain animals risks 'perpetuating dehumanizing strategies against minorities' so that 'if a former slave and a donkey' gain equal protection, 'does that elevate the status of the donkey, demote the status of the person, both, or neither?' (Culbertson 2009, Boyle 2016: 170). A further objection to framing animals as quasi-human victims in this way is that it requires giving voice to the voiceless, raising the problem of 'speaking for the animal' (Suen 2015). Yet the analogy between animal and human oppression is a powerful one in the legal context (see Wise 2002b: 9ff., 2009), with case law offering models for widening the scope of judicial interventionism. Further, speciesism operates as a rhetorical device within discourses about human beings in the sense that oppression and genocide have been justified by the labelling of certain human groups as animals (Midgley 2011: 191–200, Adams 2014).

According to climate pessimists, the relative stability of the Holocene has given way to the Anthropocene as humans impact dramatically on the planet's overall ecological balance. Both a scientific and a polemical concept (Rull 2017), the Anthropocene has been dated to James Watt's invention of the steam engine in 1784 (Crutzen 2006) or as far back as the agricultural revolution (10,000 BCE). Agricultural civilization is seen as central to humanity's violent history (Nibert 2013), and it is the Capitalocene, a world system dominated by the multinational corporation, that has brought the planet to the point of crisis (Moore 2016). The concept of Anthropocene can be framed in distinctly anti-human terms. Tønnessen (2010: 98) talks of 'a global *colonial organism* of sorts', 'an ecological empire' which has provided a global breeding ground for species such as 'rats and doves to bugs and microbes of various sorts'. For some commentators we are in the midst of a *non-human turn* (Grusin 2015, Pennycook 2018). In his *Straw Dogs,* John Gray describes humanity as a 'plague animal' (2002: 12). For Gray, humanism is 'a secular religion thrown together from decaying scraps of Christian myth'. Within posthumanism, including anti-humanism and *ahumanism* (MacCormack 2014), consideration of animal interests opens the way to a fundamental critique of anthropocentric law (Wolfe 2010).

Law divides the world into three fundamental categories: *persona/res/acta* (Lamalle 2014: 305), a distinction which derives from Roman law: 'each law concerns persons, things, or actions' (Radin 1925: 207, Tellegen-Couperus 1993: 100, Pietrzykowski 2018: 9).[2] Law looks outwards to social conventions and natural ontologies as well as creating its own internally generated definitions, principles, and categories. *Person* is a natural as well as social category, and a specialized term of legal analysis. As an artificial category, it can refer to any entity, human or non-human, granted *personhood* in law:

> Does law seek to mirror life when it makes a legal person? Is it trying to capture some essence about a being (say, the capacity for reason, or perhaps humanity per se) when it turns someone into a rights-and-duty-bearing entity – a legal person?
>
> (Naffine 2011: 193)

The critique of humanism extends to law as one of the central institutions of modernity (Kammer 2017). Law 'entrenches the interests of humans over virtually all others and centres the reasonable human person as a main legal subject' (Deckha 2013: 784). Western law sees 'legal relations as a special kind of human relations – relations that can run between only men (or legal aggregates of men, such as corporations or the state)' (Morris 1964: 189).

One conclusion that has been drawn is that legal personhood is too deeply embedded in humanistic assumptions to be capable of reform: 'Personhood has historically been constituted as a charismatic gift to which humans are entitled only upon mastering their animalism' (Hamilton 2016: 321). In the same vein, the promotion of rights represents 'the harms that law both commits and tries to heal' (Douzinas and Gearey 2005: 188). Through personhood, the animal is defined in opposition to the human: 'The animal is always already necessary to, and yet still excluded from, the legal person' (Hamilton 2016: 321). If anthropocentrism is not tenable, then human beings are downgraded (from a humanistic perspective) to the level of naturalistic animals. The uniqueness of human beings as subjects in a world of objects is denied; the dualisms of nature/culture and mind/body are rejected.

In what follows, questions of law and personhood are approached through the framework of integrationism. Integrationism is a theory of language, communication, and the sign elaborated by Roy Harris and pursued by scholars within the International Association for the Integrational Study of Language and Communication (IAISLC). Harris rejected the reification of the language system within modern linguistics, diagnosing it as a reflection of the pervasive *language myth* in Western culture (Harris 1981). Integrationism assumes a sign-maker who acts autonomously and creatively, integrating past experience and present contingencies with expectations of the future: 'Signs are not *prerequisites* of communication, but its *products*' (Harris 2005: 110). Integrationism reflects humanism and modern liberalism, notably ideas of the autonomy of the individual, free speech, and individual creativity (Pablé 2017). Harris was much concerned with issues of free speech, in particular in academic discourse (Harris 2009a, Pablé 2012a).

Integrationism is a jealous god, along the lines of 'Thou shalt have no other theory of language before me'. It offers an unforgiving and intractable model of semiology since it puts a question mark against reification and generalization, and rejects mainstream theories of language and communication found in linguistics, psychology, and philosophy. Integrationism offers neither a methodology nor a mode of analysis. Yet it is also *lay-oriented*, suggesting openness to the varieties of human communicational practices and the beliefs that animate them: 'real people doing real things in real time' (Wolf 1997: 360). Integrationism recognizes that reification and generalization are intrinsic to *lay* linguistic behaviour whilst rejecting linguists' claims to special expertise and insight into language (Pablé 2012b). There is no third-person objective stance from which language can be studied as an autonomous, decontextual object (Harris 1981: 204, Wolf 1999: 27).

Integrationism sees language primarily as *acta* (Jones 2011). Speaking, writing, and interacting are *first-order* activities, and integration is a dynamic, contextual, time-dependent process (Love 1990, Cowley 2017: 47). Reifications of language are *second-order* constructs. Given their status as reifications, they are not straightforwardly potential objects of analysis. Integrationism insists on the indeterminacy of social action and rejects the authority of reductionist analysis (see Pablé and Hutton 2015: 37–39). If individual sign-making is the basis of semiology, it follows that both individuals and groups work against the moment-to-moment erosion of continuity and stability, and against the underlying momentum towards entropy. Social order must be *made* or *created* and is sustained against the indeterminacy of the signs with which it is made (Duncker 2018). Abstractions are second-order realities only, which means that the sense of certainty that they provide is always provisional (Hutton 1990). Human cultures require a ceaseless effort to counter indeterminacy, to create a sense of order and rhythm, and to frame social life as a set of recurrences marked by an overarching regularity. Religious, social, and political rituals serve both to mark the passage of time and, in appearance, to nullify life's contingences, discontinuities, and irregularities. Law from this point of view seeks to impose shape and order on an inchoate world. The rhetoric of law presents law as non-retroactive, largely predictable, objective, neutral, and relying substantially on the publicly shared and stable meanings of legal terms of art and ordinary language. Law rhetorically asserts the determinate status of ordinary meaning as one of its primary resources at the same time operating as a complex social practice designed to deal with uncertainty and contingency, including the indeterminacy of word meaning.

Integrationism engages with the legal personhood of animals at two distinct, though interrelated levels. First, *person* and *self* are abstract concepts, and integrationism is critical of intellectual models that rely on the definition and analysis of abstractions. These questions are discussed in relation to what are termed *bedrock concepts*, that is, fundamental concepts that cannot unproblematically be broken down into more basic components. If we assert that a dog has a *self* or argue that an orca in SeaWorld is a *slave*; if we seek *legal personhood* for a captive chimpanzee or proclaim that 'Parks are people too' (Gordon 2018: 50), there is an ambiguity as to whether this is a matter of the intrinsic qualities of the animals or entities concerned, when compared with humans, or of linguistic usage and the qualities that can be legitimately predicated of nouns such as *animal*, *whale*, *chimpanzee*, and *park*. Underlying this is the issue of proper attribution: of what kind of entity is a characteristic, such as thinking, intending, feeling, remembering, acting, loving, speaking, and having a self, predicated authentically, that is, non-metaphorically? Is it just human beings? Human beings of a certain cognitive status? God, corporations, human beings, and some animals? Or is this form of attribution always in some sense metaphorical? If calling a human being *good* and God *good* is held to invoke the same underlying meaning (even granted the vast gulf that separates the human and the divine realms), this is termed *univocity*. The medieval philosopher Duns Scotus (c. 1266–1308) argued that human beings can have knowledge of certain of God's attributes and therefore that religious language in some limited domains went beyond mere analogy (Barth 1965). The question of what it might mean to call an animal *good* or *kind* is at the heart of current debates.

Second, as noted, integrationism is broadly a humanistic philosophy. If it is pervasive as a process, how can notions such as *person* or *self* be abstracted or segregated from it? If the self is actively and constantly integrating, this might imply that it stands outside the stream of indeterminacy as a stable and self-identical agent. Yet if the self acts through integration, then it arguably also integrates itself. If signs are made and remade in contexts, so must the self be. If there is no autonomous human self, then integrationism is a variant of posthumanism. What integrationism sees as the creative agency of the speaker would be merely a mindless process of cybernetic adjustment. This nexus of problems means that if we wish to ask whether higher animals are persons or have selves, we have no unproblematic point of departure.

This book has a number of aims. Each chapter is relatively stand-alone. First, it explores the notion of *bedrock concept*, showing how questions of meaning and definition are open-ended and indeterminate, and that the cycle of tautology and circularity is only broken through stipulated definition (Chapters 1 and 2). In so doing, it offers what might be termed deep context for intellectual questions relating to animal personhood, focussing on the terms *person* and *self*. It then juxtaposes the humanism of integrationism with the anti-humanism of systems theory (Chapter 3). Moving onto law, it reviews legal approaches to personhood, both in terms of jurisprudence (Chapter 4) and of case law (Chapter 5). In conclusion, the case is made for integrationism as a form of *personalism*. The book stays largely within the confines of the Western tradition, given that even within this limited frame the amount of material is overwhelming. My hope is that by the end of the book the reader will have an analytical grasp of the intellectual landscape within which questions of legal personhood are set as well as the particular point of view that integrationism brings to bear both on questions of definition and on fundamental models of human identity.

Notes

1 See The Gorilla Foundation website, www.koko.org/michaels-story.
2 The Institutes of Gaius, c. 170 BCE, (I, s. 8), thelatinlibrary.com/law/gaius1.html.

1 Bedrock concepts

Introduction

Do chimpanzees (or gorillas or dolphins or whales) have *minds* or *selves*? Are they *people*? Is having a mind equivalent to having a self? Can a chimpanzee (or a gorilla or a whale) be considered a *person*? What are we to make of the title *Humankind: Solidarity with Nonhuman People* (Morton 2017)? Concepts such as *mind*, *self*, *person* are those that are difficult to break down into more fundamental ideas without circularity or tautology, yet which represent indispensable points of reference. They are termed here *bedrock concepts* (Hutton 2017b). Bedrock concepts are both the tool of reasoning and the object of definitional inquiry. They are both for thinking *with* and thinking *about*, and as a consequence are in general 'essentially contested' (Merrill 1998: 143). Bedrock or primitive categories are not necessarily indivisible or 'simple' (Ishiguro 1980: 65–66), but their status in this respect is problematic. It is much simpler – though still challenging – to offer decontextual definitions for mundane objects and functional institutions (*table*, *spectacles*, *nuclear power station*, *police station*) than for bedrock concepts which are implicated in fundamental ethical or philosophical debates.

Bedrock categories can be conveniently divided into heuristic classes: for example basic ontological categories, *thing*, *being*, *object*, *entity*, and *idea*, with their correlates, such as *to be* or *to exist*; basic existential categories, such as *human being*, *animal*, *man*, and *woman*; fundamental biosocial roles, *parent*, *mother*, *father*, and *child*; socially defined roles, such as *husband*, *wife*, *citizen*, and *employee*; mixed sociolegal concepts, notably *family*, *property*, *ownership*, *authority*, and *agency*; as well as the more straightforwardly legal bedrock concepts, *jurisdiction* and *sovereignty*. Many bedrock concepts express ontological, epistemological, moral, or analytical oppositions: *concrete* and *abstract*, *self* and *other*, *body* and *soul*, *truth* and *falsity*, *fact* and *fiction*, *living* and *dead*, *good* and *evil*, *right* and *wrong*, and *same* and *different*. Concepts related to the senses should also be included, such as basic categories of taste: *sweetness*, *sourness*, *saltiness*, *bitterness*, and *umami*. The concepts of *person*, *personhood*, and *personality* are entangled with *self* (or *selfhood*), *identity*, *autonomy*, *individuality*, and many others. Human beings are of course an animal species. Kemmerer (2006: 10–11) suggests

DOI: 10.4324/9781315143132-2

a neologism, *anymal*, to refer to animals excluding *Homo sapiens*. The Great Chain of Being schema, which underlies many of our ontological categories, envisages these within a comprehensive hierarchy of relative autonomy (Lovejoy [1936] 1964), from the absolute autonomy of God to the relative autonomy or bounded free-will of the human being, down through the animals to the relative passivity of the plant, and the absolute passivity of the rock. One source of this schema was Aristotle's *Historia Animalium* ([350 BCE] 1910: 588):

> Nature proceeds little by little from things lifeless to animal life in such a way that it is impossible to determine the exact line of demarcation, nor on which side thereof an intermediate form should lie.

Typically, intellectual questions about categories involve slippage between two distinct modes, namely *real* versus *verbal* or *nominal* definition (Mill 1843: 182–204, Harris and Hutton 2007: 37–58, Toolan 2009). Real definition characterizes an entity or a category in its essence, in terms of its primary or most significant characteristics. Verbal definition concerns word meaning or conceptual content. A real definition of *chimpanzee* might primarily invoke biological and taxonomic criteria but could also consider social organization, physical appearance, habitat, and a host of other details. However, this open-endedness means that the key characteristics for the purpose of comparison cannot emerge inductively. A verbal or nominal approach would focus on the meanings of keywords such as *animal, primate, chimpanzee, human being* and the resulting definition would depend on the sources chosen or the patterns of usage identified. C.S. Lewis (1898–1963) applied the real/verbal distinction in his entry on *life* in *Studies in Words* (1967: 269): 'It is for biologists and philosophers to discuss "what life is"; we have the less ambitious task of examining what people mean by the word *life*, or, more strictly, some of the different things they may mean'. From one point of view, it is odd to think that any substantive question could be solved by investigating the meanings of words alone. As Samuel Johnson (1709–1784) wrote in the preface to his dictionary (1766: para. 17):

> I am not yet so lost in lexicography, as to forget that *words are the daughters of the earth, and things are the sons of heaven*. Language is only the instrument of science, and words are but the signs of ideas: I wish, however, that the instrument might be less apt to decay, and that signs might be permanent, like the things which they denote.

To ask whether a chimpanzee is or could be a *person* is apparently a question about classes of entity, not the meanings of words. For example, a table is not plausibly to be seen as a person, but this is not directly apparent from the standard definitions of the words *table* and *human being*. If we turn our attention to the world of things, the disjunction between these two classes of entity, it might be argued, is evident. Yet it is hard to see much essential difference between asking how biologists understand the nature of life and analysing how biologists define and use the word *life* in specialist discourse. For any bedrock concept, the claim can be made that we are dealing with mere words, rather than any well-defined real entity: 'consciousness is not a thing, a place, or a cognitive process (whatever that is): it's only a word that we use in a variety of ways' (Schlinger 2008: 59).

Harris sees the Western tradition as concerned centrally with 'the relation between words and what they stand for' (1980: 33). He distinguishes between *reocentric surrogationism*, where words are understood to be primarily surrogates for things, and *psychocentric surrogationism*, where words stand primarily for ideas in the mind (Harris 1980: 44ff.). The tripartite distinction between word, thing, and idea was depicted in Ogden and Richards's *The Meaning of Meaning* as a triangular relation between *symbol*, *thought* (or *reference*), and *referent* (1923: 11). Surrogationism is rejected by integrationism: the sign 'integrates, it does not correlate with' (Wolf 1999: 27). In *The Semantics of Science*, Harris described Darwin's theory of evolution as 'an unprovable and patently *metaphysical* thesis', based on careful selection of evidence and linguistic usage (2005: 36). In the same vein, Harris pointed to 'a deliberate ambivalence between psychocentric and reocentric definition' in Einstein's thinking (2005: 139). So-called *supercategories* (art, science, law, religion, and history) reflect versions of the language myth (2005: xi). Propositions that appear to be about reality are actually embedded in a tangle of linguistic assumptions.

In what follows, key abstract concepts for thinking about animal personhood are analysed: *soul*, *person*, *self*, and *nature*. Some parts of the discussion are inevitably highly condensed. A full treatment would include a much wider set of interrelated terms, such as *body*, *brain*, *consciousness*, *identity*, *memory*, and *mind*.

Soul

The Western tradition moves between the extremes of animism (anthropomorphism) and either ontological idealism (immaterialism) or materialism. Edward Tylor (1832–1917) saw what he termed *animism* as the basis of all the religions of mankind. It involved belief in the 'souls of individual creatures, capable of continued existence after the death or destruction of the body' and 'in other spirits, upward to the rank of powerful deities' (1920: 426). Like many key concepts in the Western tradition, the modern notion of *soul* has its roots in classical antiquity. In Presocratic philosophy, an anthropomorphic model of the cosmos gave way to investigation into the grounds of being, notions of constancy and change, and the nature of the soul (Torchia 2008: 17–38). Plato's tripartite division of the soul or psychē into the rational, spirited, and desiring parts was a mirror of social organization (Ferrari 2005, Fukuyama 2018). In Aristotle's *De Anima* (c. 350 BCE), a series of fundamental questions are posed (Charlton 1980: 170):

> (1) To what logical kind of thing does soul belong? Does 'soul' signify a particular individual and a substance, or does it rather express a quality amount or the like? [...] (2) Is a soul a thing which exists in *dunamis* [potentiality]

> or rather a kind of entelecheia [actuality] (3) Is a soul a thing with parts? [...] (4) Is all soul the same in kind or are there different souls, the soul of a horse, the soul of a dog, the soul of a man, and so on? [...]

If one substituted *mind* for *soul* here, these questions arise in much the same way today. In scholarship on classical ideas of the soul, two basic views are distinguished: an *instrumental* one, in which 'the body serves the soul as instrument' and a *hylomorphist* one, where 'soul is form of the body' (King 2007: 322). Olshewsky sums up the Plato and Aristotle's views aphoristically as follows (1976: 391): 'On Plato's understanding, the soul is in the body; but Aristotle's account implies that the body is in the soul'.

The first philosophical reflection on the 'fundamental fact about the human mind that it is present to itself in such a way that it can be an object of its own awareness' has been attributed to Augustine (354–430) (Dutton 2016: 228). In mainstream Christian thought, the human soul is understood as 'an immaterial substance, distinct from the body' (Kagan 2012: 69). Possession of an immortal soul marked human beings out from all other earthly phenomena in the Great Chain of Being (Lovejoy [1936] 1964). The *scala naturae* itself can be traced back to Aristotle's (384–322 BCE) *Historia Animalium* (Heijnol 2017: 88). In a long and complex history, a set of contested questions arose in relation to the soul, such as whether and in what sense it was immortal (Duncan 1942, Young 1975), how it interacted with the body in dualist thinkers such as Plato and Descartes (Broadie 2001), whether animals might in some sense have souls (Brown 1998, Thomson 2010), and how non-Western and heretical philosophies should be understood, notably the possibility of reincarnation, or the transmigration of human souls into animals (Smith 1984).

With the scientific revolution of the seventeenth century, the divide between human beings and non-human animals became a matter of intense contestation. One possibility was that animals were organic machines in contrast to humans who were characterized by mind/body dualism; a second was that humans were like animals in being machines, though of a more sophisticated kind. The materialist philosopher, Julien Offray de La Mettrie (1709–1751) (La Mettrie [1747] 2003, Stock 2009) argued that neither human beings nor animals had souls in the Christian sense. A third view was that both animals and humans had souls, or at least shared a basic range of feelings (Spencer 2013). The view of animals as biological machines is commonly attributed to René Descartes (1596–1650 and Nicolas Malebranche (1638–1715) (Harrison 1992, Jolley 2000: 42). Descartes's view was that animals are soulless automata, that is, they are in essence 'biological machines without consciousness, who experience neither sensations nor emotions, though appearing to' (Grayling 2006: 25). The philosopher Mary Midgley ([1979] 1995: xxxii) criticized the persistence of this view: 'Animals are not machines. [...] Actually only machines are machines'. Descartes is the anti-hero of the animal rights movement, a rationalist counterpart to Thomas Aquinas (c. 1225–1274), whose hierarchical understanding of creation looked back to Aristotle (see Wade 2004).

While Darwinian evolution left no room for the Christian soul, it also proposed profound affinities between humans and higher animals (Darwin 1872). The term *soul* remained in scientific use however. The ethologist Eugène Marais (1937) used the terms *group psyche* or *group soul* to capture the collective mind of a termite nest. Marais's *Soul of the Ape* (1969), published posthumously, was one of the first accounts of primate life based on close observation. *Soul* in such contexts is an effective synonym for *mind*. Notions of the soul remain powerfully present in contemporary usage and thinking about human identity. Wittgenstein (1998: 178) evoked the intuitive sense that another human being is not an automaton. This was not a question of *belief* or *opinion*: 'My attitude towards him is an attitude towards a soul. I am not of the opinion that he has a soul'.

Soul is not a term used in mainstream philosophy of mind or naturalistic neuroscience: 'human capacities or facilities once attributed to the soul are now seen to be functions of the brain'. The brain is now seen as the *res cogitans* (Murphy 1997: 1) or 'the behavior of a vast assembly of nerve cells and their associated molecules' (Crick 1995: 3). Yet the complex of issues raised by the mind-body problem, and monadic versus dualistic accounts of how mind relates to body, reflect directly theological anthropology and continuing debates about the body-soul relation (Cooper 2015). Christian anthropology invokes the notion of the soul and personhood to resist the Darwinian naturalistic reduction of humanity to the status of higher animal (White 2013). Contrary to some understandings, Christianity does not necessarily deny embodiment. A notable theological voice on the centrality of human embodiment was Dietrich Bonhoeffer (1906–1945) (see Dahill 2012).

There is an apparent analogy between dualistic understanding of human beings (*mind* versus *body*) and dualistic understandings of language (*meaning* versus *form*). Yet Ullmann rejects the idea that the form-meaning relationship is analogous to that between body and soul (1966: 239):

> To compare the form of a word to the human body and its meaning to the soul is no more than a metaphor. [...] The distinction between form and meaning has nothing to do with metaphysics: it is simply an example of the duality inherent in any kind of sign and symbol. One could argue with just as much cogency that, in traffic lights, the green colour is the 'body' of the signal and the meaning: 'the traffic may proceed' is its soul.

Yet one need only refer to John 1: 14 to see the mystical analogy at work: 'And the Word became flesh and dwelt among us, and we beheld His glory, the glory as of the only begotten of the Father, full of grace and truth'. *Pace* Ullmann, theoretical approaches that deny the autonomy of mind also reject cognitive or mentalistic models of meaning. Behaviourism and systems theory are obvious examples. Similarly, mentalistic theories of meaning imply a mind/body duality.

Person

Person is a mundane linguistic category, a focus of theological and philosophical debate, and a legal term of art (Cameron 2007: viii). It has two plurals, *persons* and *people*, with *persons* having a theological or legalistic ring to it (Thomson 1997, Evnine 2008: 3). *Personalism* is a cover term for frameworks, both religious and secular, that put the human person at the centre, philosophically, methodologically, and ethically (Williams and Bengtsson 2018). Unlike secular humanism, personalism does not define itself in opposition to Christianity. Emmanuel Mounier (1905–1950) found the essence of the person 'in the living activity of self-creation, of communication and of attachment, that grasps and knows itself, in the act, as the movement of becoming personal' (1952: x). Personalism rejected individualism as atomistic but also collectivist and deterministic ideologies (Smith 2010: 98ff.). Smith defines *person* as (2010: 103):

> a conscious, reflexive, embodied, self-transcending center of subjective experience, durable identity, moral commitment, and social communication who – as the efficient cause of his or her own responsible actions and interactions – exercises complex capacities for agency and intersubjectivity in order to sustain his or her own incommunicable self in loving relationships with other personal selves and with the nonpersonal world.

What might be termed *impersonalism* is a key element of artistic modernism as well as a range of anti-humanist philosophical systems (see Esposito 2012).

As Dewey remarks, the intellectual and scientific history of Western Europe is reflected in the changing fortunes of the meanings of "persons" and "personality" (1926: 663). The concept of *person* accrued to itself over time the full onto-theological status of the human as the sole creature in the universe in possession of that divine spark, an immortal soul. Yet *person* is also in its origins a mask (von Balthasar 1986: 20). It is therefore the epitome of artifice and social surface, and of a disconnect between being and appearance. By way of orientation, one can distinguish four meanings of *person*: (i) mask, social role, status; (ii) God's image in humanity; (iii) human individual; and (iv) fictive or juridical entity. Simply put, the first is from ancient Greece; the second reflects Christian theology, the third represents the modern, secular notion, and the fourth personification by operation of law. Yet the notion of mask can be applied to explain corporate personality, or, going further, to explain the incorporation of the human individual into the legal order (Gaakeer 2016).

The first sub-division of the Oxford English Dictionary entry for *person* is headed 'A role taken by a person', that is (I):

> 1. A role or character assumed in real life, or in a play, etc.; a part, function, or office; a persona; a semblance or guise. Hence: any of the characters in a play or story.

Sub-division II is 'A human being, and related senses'. These are explicated in 2.a as 'An individual human being; a man, woman, or child'. In other words, the fictional *persona* is conceptually prior to *person* in the sense of 'human being'. Under 2.b, we find 'A man or woman of high rank, distinction, or importance; a personage'; under 2, we find 'a human being, as distinguished from an animal, thing, etc.' In later usage also, we find 'an individual regarded as having human rights, dignity, or worth'. A range of further general and technical meanings are given, including 2.5: 'In general philosophical sense: a conscious or rational being'. *Person* can be a synonym of both *self* and *personality* (II 3.a) 'The self, being, or individual personality of a man or woman, esp. as distinct from his or her occupation, works, etc.' *Person* can indicate 'body' as opposed to 'mind' (II 4.a): 'The living body or physical appearance of a human being; spec. (a) the body regarded as distinct from the mind or soul, or from its clothing, etc.; (b) the body regarded together with its clothes and adornments'.

The ordering of the entry reflects the etymology of *person*:

> classical Latin *persōna* mask used by a player, character in a play, dramatic role, the part played by a person in life, character, role, position, individual personality, juridical person, important person, personage, human being in general, grammatical person, in post-classical Latin also person of the Trinity [...].

On the evolution of the term, Trendelenburg (1910: 338) asks:

> how can 'person', *persona*, that is, the mask held before the face to indicate the role assumed, become the expression of the inmost moral essence, the expression of that [in Kantian terminology] which is most characteristic in man?

Adriano (2015: 367) offers metonymy as an explanation for this semantic evolution:

> From an etymological sense this word is derived from *personare*, a term that denotes *larva histrionalis*, meaning 'mask.' In this manner, the person acted as the mask covering the face of an actor who recited verses during a scene in a play because the purpose of the mask was to make the actor's voice resonant and loud. Later, people used the term 'person' in reference to the masked actor himself. In view of the above, it is quite understandable to associate the person as a natural being of the human species.

As noted, Roman law operated with three categories, *persona/res/acta*. Trendelenburg describes the Roman notion of *persona* as 'stripped of all particularity' so that it faded 'into the conception of man in general' (1910: 348). In Roman law one could be a person (human being) but not a legal person: '*Persona* is also used of slaves to denote them as human beings (*persona servi*, *servilis*) although legally they are treated as things (*res*) and therefore legal personality is denied them' (Berger 1953: 628). However this general meaning of *person* gradually gave way to the exclusive designation of freemen as persons, so that by Justinian's reign (527–565) 'the doctrine obtained that slaves were not persons'; slaves were things (Trendelenburg 1910: 356). While Roman law recognized corporate bodies, it did not use the term *persona* for them: 'A *persona* was simply a human being' (Buckland and McNair 1965: 54, see also Maitland 1900: xviii). The primary term for corporate body was *universitas* (Berger 1953: 751): 'A union of persons or a complex of things, treated as a unit (a whole) [...] distinguished from its members (*singuli*)'. It is contrasted with *societas*, a civil association or business partnership (Berger 1953: 17): 'The *societas* had no legal personality; the partners were liable for the debts of the societas, without regard to its funds, on the other hand the claims of the societas against its debtors were claims made of the partners'.

Turcescu (2005: 7) defines *person* in the Christian tradition as 'an indivisible, unique and therefore non-replicable unity in human existence'. This notion was elaborated by the Cappadocian fathers, notably Gregory of Nyssa (c. 335–395), and was unknown to the ancient Greeks: 'Hellenism [...] scorned the concept of the person' (McGuckin 2008: 187). In Christian theology, the emphasis is on the special dignity attached to the concept of personhood, in contrast to the status of mere individual: 'We see this in the animal kingdom where there are many individuals but no persons' (von Balthasar 1986: 18). Contemporary theologians argue that Christianity provides the basis for the Western notion of personhood (O'Callaghan 2016: 555–556): 'From the fact that in God there are three persons arises the possibility of applying the term "person" also to the human individual'.

The doctrine of the Trinity and the Christian concept of *person* co-evolved in complex ways, given that the Christian mainstream described each member of the Trinity as a person. This called for a definition of *persona* that was inclusive enough to cover both divine and non-divine persons, one that would be compatible with the underlying unity of the Trinity, and allow for the distinction between divine and human persons. Not surprisingly, the history of this definitional question is highly complex. According to Tertullian (c. 155–240), God was three persons but one substance (*tres personae, una substantia*). The use of *persona* pointed to a distinction, not a division: 'personae non substantiae nomine, ad distinctionem non ad divisionem' (Ayres 2010: 79). Augustine in his *De Trinitate* ([c. 412] 2002) preferred the term *essentia* ('essence') to *substantia* ('substance'), the equivalent to the Greek *ousia*. *Substantia* implied that a being was a substance that admitted of accidents (Ayres 2010: 201). The term *natura* was also commonly used instead of *substantia* (Ayres 2010: 79). In the fourth and fifth centuries the terminology for *person* was inchoate, with the gradual introduction of technical terms, such as *prosopon* and *hypostasis* (Thomas 2011: 411). The Council of Serdica in 343 'used the word *hypostasis* or "substance" (later equivalent to "person") as equivalent to *ousia*. It then went on to speak of the divine unity in terms of a single *hypostasis*' (Vaggione 2000: 71). During the period of these terminological debates, *ousia* and *hypostasis* were effective synonyms (Letham 2004: 115). As confirmed at the Council of Nicea (325 CE), God was one primary essence or substance (*ousia*), but three entities or persons (*hypostasis*) (Marshall 2004: 4). The term *prosopon* ('person', 'appearance', 'mask') was also widely used in debates about the Trinity (see Turcescu 1997). But one drawback with this usage was the suggestion that the persons of the Trinity were aspects, modes, or appearances of God (*modalism*), contrary to the mainstream view that the Trinity consisted of three coeternal persons (see Letham 2004).

An influential definition of *person* was provided by the philosopher Boethius (c. 477–524) (Marenborn 2004). Boethius wrote against both the monophysitic heresy of Eutyches and the dualistic heresy of Nestorius. To Eutyches of Constantinople (c. 380–456) is attributed the idea that Christ had only one nature and one will (Berti 2006: 63, Tannous 2014). Nestorianism is understood as the belief that there are two distinct persons in Christ, that is, Christ the human being and Christ the eternal Logos (however see Braaten 1963). In discussing the category *person*, Boethius lamented 'that the proper definition of Person is a matter of very great perplexity' (Boethius 1936: 81). In order for Boethius to demonstrate that Christ was one person in-and-of two natures, what was needed was a definition of *person* 'that applies to both the human and the divine' (Magee 2002: 223).

Of the several meanings of *nature*, the most relevant was 'the difference that gives form to anything' (Boethius 1936: 81). *Natura* was the more general category: 'For if every nature has person, the difference between nature and person is a hard knot to unravel; or if person is not taken as the equivalent of nature but is a term of less scope and range'. It followed that 'nature is a substrate of person, and that person cannot be predicated apart from nature'. *Person* was to be predicated of substances, not accidents (*white*, *black*, *size*). Substances came in many forms (Boethius 1936: 83):

> But of substances, some are corporeal and others incorporeal. And of corporeals, some are living and others the reverse; of living substances, some are sensitive and others insensitive; of sensitive substances, some are rational and others irrational. Similarly of incorporeal substances, some are rational, others the reverse (for instance the animating spirits of beasts); but of rational substances there is one which is immutable and impassible [incapable of suffering] by nature, namely God, another which in virtue of its creation is mutable and passible except in that case where the Grace of the impassible substance has transformed it to the unshaken impassibility which belongs to angels and to the soul.

It was clear that (Boethius 1936: 84–85):

> Person cannot be affirmed of bodies which have no life (for no one ever said that a stone had a person), nor yet of living things which lack sense (for

> neither is there any person of a tree), nor finally of that which is bereft of mind and reason (for there is no person of a horse or ox or any other of the animals which dumb and unreasoning live a life of sense alone), but we say there is a person of a man, of God, of an angel.

Person could not be applied to universals, but only 'to particulars and individuals'. *Persona* should be defined as 'rationalis naturae individua substantia' ('individual substance of a rational nature') (1936: 85). *Substantia*, as seen earlier, could be applied to both corporeal and incorporeal beings.

Like many other commentators, Boethius also explored the etymology of *persona* (Boethius 1936: 84–86, Otter 2010: 162):

> The name *persona* seems to have been transferred from elsewhere, namely from those 'personae' that in the comedies and tragedies represented those people of whom [the play] treats. *Persona* comes from *personare*, therefore, from the 'sound', because through the hollowness itself the sound necessarily had to become louder. The Greeks, too, call these *personae prosopa* from the fact that they are put on the face and cover the countenance before the eyes [of onlookers].

The underlying problem in making sense of these debates is that there were three basic levels of existence, but the terminology was used inconsistently. *Substantia* could be used as an equivalent for *ousia* ('being', 'nature') but also to define *hypostasis* ('person'). Boethius had derived his notion of *substance* from Aristotle's *substrate* (in Greek, *hypokeimenon*). This substrate was that of which universal concepts and their accidents were predicated, and which therefore could not itself be predicated of anything else (Berti 2006: 64):

> Since, in order to exist, both the universal and the accidental properties suppose the existence of a substrate on which they may be predicated or in which to inhere, this is termed not only *ousia* (literally 'being' in a strong sense, that is, permanent, lasting), which in Latin is translated as *substantia* (literally 'what is underneath', like the Greek *hypostasis*), but also 'primary' *ousia*, that is, preceding all others. On the contrary, species and genus, which do not exist 'in themselves', but only in the substrate, and nevertheless constitute its essence (that is, tell 'what it is'), are termed 'secondary' *ousia*.

Boethius's use of *substantia* allowed for equivocation between its meaning as primary *ousia* (God as undivided being) and as secondary *ousia* or *hypostasis* (God as a unity of three persons). Such equivocation was necessary since the Trinity is in essence a mystical idea. The underlying ontological question could not be given a definitive answer in terms of philosophically precise definitions.

To complicate matters further, Christological doctrine asserted that Jesus is both fully divine and fully human. This is known as the doctrine of hypostatic union or the 'two natures' of Christ existing in a single person (Lamont 2006). The Council of Chalcedon of 451 affirmed that Christ had two distinct natures. These were joined in one person (*prosopon*) and individual being (*hypostasis*) (Bradshaw 2009: 118, Price and Gaddis 2005: 204).According to Thomas Aquinas in the *Summa theologiae* (1265–1274) (Gorman 2000: 143):

> The person or hypostasis of Christ can be considered in two ways. One way is as something that exists in itself; in this way it is completely simple, as is the nature of the Word [*logos*]. The other way is as a person or hypostasis to which it is proper to subsist in some nature; in this way, the person of Christ subsists in two natures. Thus, although there is only one subsisting thing in this case, there are nonetheless two principles of subsistence. Thus he can be called a composite person, insofar as he is one thing subsisting in two ways.

The personhood of Christ cannot be simply equated to that of an ordinary human being (White 2015: 83):

> Rather, in Christ there is no autonomous human personhood or human personality. He is the person of the Son and Word made human, subsisting in a human nature. This hypostatic union then pertains to personal subsistence, but it is the personal subsistence not of a human person, but of God made man and of the person of the Son existing in human nature. He is particularly distinct, then, from other persons, because he is a divine person. Likewise, the conjoined instrument in this case is not a human body but the human body and soul of Christ. This body-soul composite is united to the person of the Son hypostatically.

These debates remain current within contemporary theology. However the modern, secular concept of *person* moved away from 'an integral, organic, and hierarchically structured religious worldview' situated in relation to God, towards 'a worldview that posits the independence and self-sufficiency of human nature in itself' (Lennan 1998: 45). At the heart of modern debates about personhood and self is the work of John Locke (1632–1704). For the liberal model of the self, the state ideally draws the limit of its powers at this private mini-sovereignty, a kind of self-owned and property-owning monad (Locke [1690] 1980: 19):

> Though the earth, and all inferior creatures, be common to all men, yet every man has a property in his own person: this no body has any right to but himself. The labour of his body, and the work of his hands, we may say, are properly his. Whatsoever then he removes out of the state that nature hath provided, and left it in, he hath mixed his labour with, and joined to it something that is his own, and thereby makes it his property.

This self stands outside nature and acts upon it; through its labour it annexes to itself personal property.

Locke distinguished between human beings and animals in terms of what constituted their continuity ([1690] 1975: 333):

> An Animal is a living organized Body; and consequently, the same Animal, as we have observed, is the same continued Life communicated to different Particles of Matter, as they happen successively to be united to that organiz'd living Body.

In the case of the word *man*, 'ingenious observation puts it past doubt, that the *Idea* in our Minds, of which the sound *Man* in our mouths is the Sign, is nothing else but of an Animal of such a certain Form' (Locke [1690] 1975: 333). The human being was a body joined to a rational being ([1690] 1975: 335):

> For I presume 'tis not the *Idea* of a *Man* in most Peoples Sense; but of a Body so and so joined to it; and if that be the *Idea* of a *Man*, the same successive Body not shifted all at once, must as well as the same immaterial Spirit go to the making of the same *Man*.

Person was defined as ([1690]1975: 335)

> a thinking intelligent Being, that has reason and reflection, and can consider it self as it self, the same thinking thing in different times and places; which it does only by that consciousness, which is inseparable from thinking, and, as it seems to me, essential to it: It being impossible for any one to perceive, without perceiving that he does perceive.

Personhood and self were mutually constituting:

> And as far as this consciousness can be extended backwards to any past Action or Thought, so far reaches the Identity of that *Person*; it is the same *self* now it was then; and 'tis by the same *self* with this present one that now reflects upon it, that that Action was done. (Locke [1690] 1975: 335)

The human *self* was understood as ([1690] 1979: 341):

> that conscious thinking thing, (whatever Substance made up of whether Spiritual or Material, Simple or Compounded, it matters not), which is sensible, or conscious of Pleasure and Pain, capable of Happiness or Misery, and so is concern'd for it *self*, as far as that consciousness extends.

This notion of continuity is the basis for holding the individual to account as a moral and juridical being: 'In this personal identity is founded all the right and justice of reward and punishment' ([1690] 1975: 341).

If a finger were to be amputated, and consciousness went along with it, then ([1690] 1979: 341):

> Upon separation of this little Finger, should this consciousness go along with the little Finger, and leave the rest of the Body, 'tis evident the little Finger would be the *Person*, the *same Person*; and *self* then would have nothing to do with the rest of the Body.

What makes sameness of personhood and 'the inseparable self' over time is the consciousness that 'goes along with the Substance' ([1690] 1975: 341):

> That with which the *consciousness* of this present thinking thing *can* join itself, makes the same *Person*, and is one *self* with it, and with nothing else; and so attributes to it *self* and owns all the Actions of that thing, as its own, as far as consciousness reaches, and no further; as everyone who reflects will perceive.

Barresi and Martin (2011: 34–25) point out that Locke at one point equates *self* and *person*: *Person*, as I take it is the name for this *self*', [1690] 1975: 346), though when he explicitly defines these terms he makes a distinction. Personhood operates at a higher degree of reflexivity than self, though both definitions share a reliance on continuity of identity over time as grounded in consciousness. The previous quotation continues ([1690] 1975: 346):

> Wherever a Man finds, what he calls *himself*, there I think another may say is the same *Person*. It is a Forensick Term appropriating Actions and their Merit; and so belongs only to intelligent Agents capable of a Law, and Happiness and Misery.

Continuity of identity is the basis of accountability and self-ownership:

> This personality extends it *self* beyond present Existence to what is past, only by consciousness, whereby it becomes concerned and accountable, owns and imputes to it *self* past Actions, just upon the same ground, and for the same reason, that it does the present.

Balibar puts consciousness at the centre of Locke's theory of identity, together with the notion of self-ownership. There is 'a parallelism of responsibility and property; of self-consciousness and "property in oneself"'. The psychological and the juridical are joined in self-ownership: the individual is the proprietor of the self (Balibar 2013: 101).

Modernity affirmed the authenticity and centrality of the psychological self and located that self as an inner reality within the social person or *persona*. Ideally the inner self, while in tension with social *persona* or *personae* and the associated set of social obligations and roles, was nonetheless generally reconciled to a form of social contract in which extreme self-seeking was tempered by the benefits of sociality, conformity, and compromise. This socialized self submitted to legal and ethical constraints, and occupied the various social roles demanded of it since these were ultimately beneficial in terms of the acquisition of status and power. Civility required 'the bifurcation of private affect from public demeanor' (Cuddihy 1974: 13).

However this model was subject to intellectual erosion from its inception. The *self-persona* dichotomy became a focus of analysis and critique. This critique came from emergent theories of evolution and racial struggle (social Darwinism), notions of class struggle (Marxism), and the discontents of modern civilization (psychoanalysis), as played out in the interplay of *id (Es)*, *ego (Ich)*, and *superego* (*Über-Ich*) (Freud 1923, 1930). It was Carl Gustav Jung who formalized the notion the psychoanalytical notion of *persona*, understood as 'a more or less accidental or arbitrary slice of the collective psyche'. This seeming individuality was a fashioned social role (Jung 1928: 164–165):

> Whereas it is, as its name tells us, only a mask of the collective psyche, a mask that is a substitute for individuality, intending to make others as well as oneself believe one is individual. In reality it is only a role that is played; it is, as it were, the collective psyche speaking.

The *persona* represents 'a compromise between the individual and society' so that the *persona* 'is a semblance, a two-dimensional reality' (1928: 165).

This intellectual tension is found across the social sciences. Marcel Mauss (1872–1950) pointed to the dynamic evolution of the concept *person* ([1938] 1985: 22):

> From a simple masquerade to the mask, from a 'role' (*personnage*) to a 'person' (*personne*), to a name, to an individual; from the latter to a being possessing metaphysical and moral value; from a moral consciousness to a sacred being; from the latter to a fundamental form of thought and action - the course is accomplished.

The American sociologist Charles Cooley (1864–1929) emphasized that society was a produced imaginary (1902: 84–85): 'Society exists in my mind as the contact and reciprocal influence of certain ideas named "I," Thomas, Henry, Susan, Bridget, and so on. It exists in your mind as a similar group, and so in every mind'. It followed that (Cooley 1902: 86) 'Persons and society must, then, be studied primarily in the imagination'. In this sense, 'persons who have no corporeal reality' such as the dead, fictional characters, gods, etc. were part of society, and 'a corporeally existent person is not socially real unless he is imagined' (1902: 88–89). The person was not a 'separate material form', rather 'the social person is a fact of the mind' (1902: 89–90).

There is an underlying tension here between the etymological-metonymical understanding of *person* and an explanation of *person* in terms of metaphor.

The metonymy arises as a link between the original meaning, 'mask', and the extended meaning of 'its bearer', just as the term *hat* is used in organizational jargon to refer to a specific task or role. In the metaphor, the underlying non-figurative meaning is that of 'human being' and the metaphorical extension is to the social and fictional roles that human beings occupy and through which they enter into social relations. This metaphor informs the famous lines from Shakespeare's *As You Like It* (II: vii):

> All the world's a stage,
> And all the men and women merely players;
> They have their exits and their entrances,
> And one man in his time plays many parts,
> His acts being seven ages.

The etymological meaning, 'mask', returns here as the metaphorical explanation.

A similar double movement underlies Erving Goffman's *The Presentation of Self in Everyday Life*. Social existence is presented as in essence a performance. The performer generally seeks not just to persuade others of the authenticity of the role performed, but ultimately constitutes the self through this (more or less reflexively self-aware) performance (1956: 10):

> At one extreme, we find that the performer can be fully taken in by his own act; he can be sincerely convinced that the impression of reality which he stages is the real reality. When his audience is also convinced in this way about the show he puts on – and this seems to be the typical case – then for the moment, anyway, only the sociologist or the socially disgruntled will have any doubts about the 'realness' of what is presented.

Goffman cites Robert Park's *Race and Culture* (1950: 249): it is 'probably no mere historical accident that the word person, in its first meaning, is a mask'. The word's original meaning is 'a recognition of the fact that everyone is always and everywhere, more or less consciously, playing a role'. Further, these roles tell us not only how other people are but also about ourselves:

> In a sense, and in so far as this mask represents the conception we have formed of ourselves – the role we are striving to live up to – this mask is our truer self, the self we would like to be. In the end, our conception of our role becomes second nature and an integral part of our personality. We come into the world as individuals, achieve character, and become persons.

On the one hand, the mask can be plausibly seen as the artifice that overlays or conceals the true person behind it; yet, on the other hand, the metaphor suggests that we are only truly human in our sociality and our performance of various social roles. The biological being becomes authentically a human being only through participation within a symbolic order.

Goffman's sociology of the modern persona denies the existence of an underlying authentic self. Each individual wears many masks and has many roles. These are understood to be linked by a fiction to a single, underlying self. The authentic self is a fiction that animates the person and is for some purposes (e.g. accountability for moral consistency in conduct) retrospectively constituted out of those performances. The notion of a true, inner self is a secularized product of religious notions such as the soul or spirit.

Hannah Arendt (1906–1975) had a slightly different take on the double meaning of *persona* as mask, in the context of the centrality of theatre metaphors for the study of politics (Arendt 1973: 106, Horsman 2016): 'The mask as such obviously had two functions: it had to hide, or rather to replace, the actor's own face and countenance, but in a way that would make it possible for the voice to sound through'. In Rome, there was a distinction between a private individual and a Roman citizen, in that the latter 'had a *persona*, a legal personality, as we would say'. This meant that the law had assigned that individual 'the part he was expected to play on the public scene, with the provision, however, that his own voice would be able to sound through'. The right-and-duty-bearing person who appears before the law is the person created by law (Arendt 1973: 107):

> Without his persona, there would be an individual without rights and duties, perhaps a 'natural man' - that is, a human being or homo in the original meaning of the word, indicating someone outside the range of the law and the body politic of the citizens, as for instance a slave - but certainly a politically irrelevant being.

Resistance to any potential depersonification of the human individual frequently rests on the uniqueness that is held to attach to the status of person (Barker 1934: xvii):

> Persons [...] have infinity or extension in the sense that, *sub specie aeternitatis*, each of them is 'a living soul' (as nothing but the individual person is or can be), with an inner spring of spiritual life which rises beyond our knowledge and ends beyond our ken.

Collectivities just do not have this special combination of qualities: groups might be 'organisations of persons, or schemes of personal relations', but not persons.

On *person* as grammatical category, Émile Benveniste elevated the duality of *I/You* into an almost mystically immanent feature of language (1971: 220):

> Since [these pronouns] lack material reference, they cannot be misused; since they do not assert anything, they are not subject to the condition of truth and escape all denial. Their role is to provide the instrument of a conversion that one could call the conversion of language into discourse. It is by identifying himself as a unique person pronouncing *I* that each speaker sets himself up in turn as the 'subject'.

The third person is not a true pronoun since it is an impersonal mode. In some languages we find that the third person 'is indeed literally a "nonperson"' (1971: 221). Human selves are constituted through language: 'It is in and through language that man constitutes himself as a *subject,* because language alone establishes the concept of "ego" in reality, in *its* reality which is that of the being' (1971: 224). Language should not be viewed primarily as an instrument since that would suggest a disassociation of language from humanity. In the polarity of I/*You* emerges consciousness of self since only through contrast can the self be experienced:

> I use *I* only when I am speaking to someone who will be a *you* in my address. It is this condition of dialogue that is constitutive of *person,* for it implies that reciprocally *I* becomes *you* in the address of the one who in his turn designates himself as *I.*

Benveniste took up a radical position, based on an ontological reading of grammatical person as authentic personhood (1971: 217):

> It must be seen that the ordinary definition of the personal pronouns as containing the three terms, *I, you,* and *he,* simply destroys the notion of 'person.' 'Person' belongs only to *I/you* and is lacking in *he*. This basic difference will be evident from an analysis of *I.*

Both *I* and *You* are dependent on the contingent moment of discourse for their referent (1971: 119): 'these "pronominal" forms do not refer to "reality" or to "objective" positions in space or time but to the utterance, unique each time, that contains them, and thus they reflect their proper use'. This dialectical intersubjectivity is the basis of sociality and 'makes linguistic communication possible' (1971: 230). There is a parallel between Benveniste's *I/You* and Martin Buber's (1878–1965) *Ich und Du* ('I and thou') (see Buber 1937, Coetzee 1992: 69–90, Clarkson 2009). Similarly, the psychiatrist R. D. Laing lamented that psychiatry treats individuals as isolates ([1959] 1990: 19): 'Instead of the original bond of I and You, we take a single man in isolation and conceptualize his various aspects into "the ego", "the superego", and "the id"'.

In *What are We?* (2007), Olson insists on the referential nature of the pronoun *I,* dismissing philosopher Elizabeth Anscombe's (1975) claim that, in his paraphrase, 'the word "I" in "I am walking" no more purports to refer to something that walks than the word "it" in 'it is raining' purports to refer to something that rains'. Wittgenstein ([1922] 2009: 130e) had stipulated that:

> "I" doesn't name a person, nor "here" a place, and "this" is not a name. But they are connected with names, names are explained by means of them. It is also true that it is characteristic of physics not to use these words.

Olson argues that if this were correct,

> then I am not the thing I refer to when I say "I", for I don't refer to anything when I use that word. But it doesn't follow from this claim that I don't exist, or that there is nothing here speaking that could be referred to.
> (Olson 2007: 11)

I or personal names must be referring expressions, given Olson's insistence that there is a correct answer, a metaphysical truth, to the question of human identity: 'There *must* be some sort of thing that we are, if we exist at all' (Olson 2007: 14).

If we turn to look at non-human animals, common sense tells us that a chimpanzee (or a gorilla or a dolphin or a whale) is not a *person*. The word *person* seems to exclude non-human animals as a matter of definition, whereas thinking hard about whether a chimpanzee has a self depends on the criteria adopted. Yet the category of *personhood* is currently being treated as one that is open for new admissions. Herzing and White make the case for dolphins as a *who* not a *what*, based on awareness of the world and experiences (1998: 65): 'In particular, persons are aware of the fact that *they are aware*, that is, they have some sort of *self*-awareness and reflective consciousness'. They list a set of criteria so that a person is a being who is 'alive' and 'aware', 'feels positive and negative sensations', 'has emotions', 'has a sense of self', 'controls its own behaviour', 'recognizes other persons', and 'has a variety of sophisticated cognitive abilities' (Herzing and White 1998: 65). While these criteria are not without problems, including the human-centred nature of the category, they argue that 'dolphins evidence all of the necessary traits to enough of a degree that they should be regarded as persons', that is, as 'members of the community of equals' (1998: 67, 80; see also White 2007). By contrast, Scott (1990: 102) rejects the idea that personhood can be an honorary or bestowed status. Even if we bestow personhood on Caligula's horse, 'we would be unable to explain and predict its behavior in anything like the manner in which we can do for authentic persons'. Not all environmental ethicists would argue for animal personhood. Paul Taylor defines *personhood* so as to exclude animals, arguing that only a being with a sense of life purpose, self-respect in relation to rights, autonomy and rationality, and a value system can qualify (see Taylor 1986, Kemmerer 2006: 145ff.). In contrast, Gray attacks what he describes as the 'cult of personality', that is, the idea 'that only *persons* have any kind of intrinsic worth'; Gray would see no merit in ascribing personhood to animals. Absent faith in Christianity, 'the very idea of the person becomes suspect' (2002: 58–59).

Self

Self is both a psychological-philosophical concept and a key socio-political term. The Western model of the autonomous, agentive self, it has been argued, is historically and ideologically contingent (Taylor 1989, Dumont 1992, Siedentop 2014). This self is a creature with a complex intellectual lineage, traceable to Greek concepts of rationality, the Christian notion of the soul, and seventeenth century liberal political theory, notably John Locke. One can start its history in antiquity (Remes and Sihvola 2008) or find its origin in early modernity (Seigel 2005). The modern self is generally seen as the bearer of rights and duties. Struggles for equality within modern societies have concerned the extension of such rights to hitherto marginal or oppressed groups, notably children, women, and slaves. In this sense, a particular liberal model of the self underlies contemporary understandings of legal personhood. The modern concept of the human self reflects two dialectically interacting forms of identity, often termed the *I* and the *me*. There is the distinct quality of being an individual with a subjective existence, what might be termed *first-person* sentience, the reflexivity or consciousness that one exists (Baker 2007: 203): 'The first-person perspective is, well, first-personal; it is the perspective from which one thinks of oneself as oneself without the aid of any third-person name, description, demonstrative or other referential device'. Second, the self emerges relationally through its recognition by others as distinctive and autonomous (the *third-person* view). It is seen as possessing continuity and an individual personality, reflecting its unique status within the fabric of interpersonal relations and social institutions.

Following the rise of scientific empiricism in the seventeenth century, the intellectual space was opened up to consider a whole range of issues in relation to both human and animal selves, including whether animals were organic machines, whether they might have souls, and the nature of human ethical responsibilities in relation to animals, if any. Science as an empirical endeavour led to systematic doubt about the concept of the human soul since the soul could not be observed. The autonomous, agentive self emerged out of this as a secular reconfiguration of the soul. Even as the human self was enthroned as the liberal political subject, the same science that cleared a space for it was also undermining it (Barresi and Martin 2011: 55):

> The self was recruited to take [the soul's] place, including providing unity and direction to the human person, as well as being the vehicle for persistence both during life and after bodily death. In effect, science took the I, as soul, out of heaven and in the guise of a unified self brought it down to earth.

The sceptical momentum was unstoppable: 'What had been real became fiction. And what had been a source of explanations became itself in need of explanation. Analysis has been the self's undoing'.

René Descartes's (1596–1650) famous 'Je pense donc je suis' ('I think therefore I am') paradoxically grounded epistemological certainty in the human subject's own self-awareness (Descartes 1637). This was in preference to the Aristotelian definition of man as *rational animal* (Descartes [1642] 1680: 14):

> What therefore have I heretofore thought my self? A Man, But what is a man? shall I answer, a Rational Animal? By no means; because afterwards it may be asked, what an Animal is? and what Rational is? And so from one question I may fall into greater Difficulties; neither at present have I so much time as to spend it about such Niceties.

The *cogito* raised a series of further questions as to the nature of the inference and the status of the *I* (see Williams 2005). For Descartes, there appears to be an agent doing the thinking and an action, thinking, which led to the conclusion that the self can know of its own existence. But can the inference get us from subjective awareness to the *I* to the *self* and then to *identity* and to *personality* (Spaemann 2006: 111ff.)? From the contemporary point of view, this Cartesian self is both disembodied and 'a profoundly asocial phenomenon' (Bakhurst and Sypnowich 1995: 3).

Descartes's reasoning can be seen as an artefact of his view of language. The separation of the actor from the action, it has been argued, reflects the pronoun plus verb structure, or, in the case of Latin *cogito*, the verb inflection. Georg Christoph Lichtenberg (1742–1799) commented on the Cartesian *cogito* as follows (1994: 412):

> We are aware of certain representations which are not dependent upon us; others are of the view that we at least are dependent upon ourselves. But where is the dividing line? We only know of the existence of our sensations, representations, and ideas. *There's thinking* [Es denkt], one should say, just as one says *There's lightening* [Es blitzt]. To talk of the *cogito* is to go too far, once one translates it as *I think*. To presume the *I*, to postulate it, is a practical necessity.[1]

Hobbes took issue with Descartes's conclusion that the *cogito* gave grounding to an independent, non-material, self-observing self. Hobbes accepted that it followed from the experience of thinking that there was something doing the thinking, 'for whatever Thinks cannot be Nothing' (appendix, Descartes [1642] 1680: 117). However Hobbes denied that this thinking was necessarily done by a mind, soul, understanding, or reason: 'for it does not seem a Right Consequence to say, I am a Thinking Thing, therefore I am a Thought, neither, I am an Understanding Thing, therefore I am the Understanding'. By analogy, the fact that 'I am a Walking Thing' would imply that 'therefore I am the Walking it self' ([1642] 1680: 117–118). Where do we get the knowledge of the proposition 'I think', from which is derived the certainty that 'I am'? Only from the fact that 'we cannot conceive any Act without its subject, as dancing without a Dancer, knowledge, without a Knower, thought without a thinker' ([1642] 1680: 119).

Hobbes found in this the suggestion that the 'thinking Thing' was a 'Corporeal Thing' since acts are carried out by material entities, as in the example of a piece of wax which remains the same underlying substance whilst being transformed in terms of shape, colour, consistency, etc. (appendix to Descartes [1642] 1680: 119–120):

> But I cannot conclude from another thought that I now think; for tho a Man may think that he hath thought (which consists only in memory) yet 'tis altogether impossible for him to think that he now thinks, or to know, that he knows, for the question may be put infinitely, how do you know that you know, that you know, that you know? &c. Wherefore seeing the Knowledge of this Proposition I am, depends on the knowledge of this I think, and the knowledge of this is from hence only, that we cannot separate thought from thinking matter, it seems rather to follow, that a thinking thing is material, than that 'tis immaterial.

It follows that the self 'is imaginary, simply a construct arising from our inability to conceive of thinking without a thinker to do it' (Tuck 1989: 43).

David Hume (1711–1776) struggled with the nature of personal identity ([1738] 1888: 1, IV, 252):

> There are some philosophers who imagine we are every moment intimately conscious of what we call our *self*; that we feel its existence and its continuance in existence; and are certain, beyond the evidence of a demonstration, both of its perfect identity and simplicity.

Individuals were, however, 'nothing but a bundle or collection of different perceptions, which succeed each other with an inconceivable rapidity, and are in a perpetual flux and movement' (Hume [1738] 1888: 1, IV, 252). Hume proposed a famous metaphor for mind as 'a kind of theatre, where several perceptions successively make their appearance; pass, re-pass, glide away, and mingle in an infinite variety of postures and situations' ([1738] 1888: 1, IV, 253). The point of the metaphor was the succession of perceptions; it was these that 'constitute the mind'. The theatre itself was obscure: 'nor have we the most distant notion of the place, where these scenes are represented, or of the materials, of which it is composed' ([1738] 1888: 1, IV, 253). While Locke defended the idea of a self constituted over time through continuity of consciousness and memory (Thiel 2011), for Hume the opposite was true: 'The identity, which we ascribe to the mind of man, is only a fictitious one, and of a like kind with that which we ascribe to vegetables and animal bodies' ([1738]1888: 1, IV, 254–255).

Hume also compared the *soul* or the mind to a republic 'in which the several members are united by the reciprocal ties of government and subordination' and where dynamic change was the only constant ([1738] 1888: 1, IV, 261): 'in like manner the same person may vary his character and disposition, as well as his impressions and ideas, without losing his identity'. Elsewhere Hume talks of the *soul* or *self* as fictions that confer a sense of identity masking the variability and non-continuity of objects ([1738] 1888: 1, IV, 255):

> Thus the controversy concerning identity is not merely a dispute of words. For when we attribute identity, in an improper sense, to variable or interrupted objects, our mistake is not confined to the expression, but is commonly attended with a fiction, either of something invariable and uninterrupted, or of something mysterious and inexplicable, or at least with a propensity to such fictions.

In a posthumously published essay, Hume attacked arguments for the immortality of the soul (Hume [1777] 2007b). His grounding of human reason in the emotions, and his insistence on an analogy between human and animal reasoning, transformed the divide between human beings and animals into a continuum (Hume [1777] 2007a: 77):

> Animals, therefore, are not guided in these inferences [as to regularities in nature] by reasoning: Neither are children: Neither are the generality of mankind, in their ordinary actions and conclusions: Neither are philosophers themselves, who, in all the active parts of life, are, in the main, the same with the vulgar, and are governed by the same maxims.

Immanuel Kant (1724–1804), in part provoked by his reading of Hume, is associated with the assertion of human personhood as a unique status. As a member of a natural species, the human being (*homo phaenomenon, animal rationale*) has no special value, but a *person* ('der Mensch als *Person*') ([1797] 1991: 230)

> as the subject of a morally practical reason, is exalted above any price; for as a person (*homo noumenon*) he is not to be valued merely as a means to the ends of others or even to his own ends, but as an end in himself, that is, he possesses a *dignity* (an absolute inner worth) by which he exacts *respect* for himself from all other rational beings in the world.

Kant's account of self, mind, and personhood is philosophically complex. It is grounded in a basic distinction between the transcendental self, a formal locus which must create synthesis out of the disorder of inputs, and a second, experiential and moral self which is self-aware and morally accountable. Mead describes this first self (1936: 66–67) as 'that unifying power which holds together, constructs our percepts, makes them different from bare sensations, and gives unity to them'. For Kant, it is 'a self that must be constantly postulated and that cannot be known'; it must exist in order for there to be ownership of inner experience ([1798] 2006: 32):

> The 'I' of reflection contains no manifold in itself and is always one and the same in every judgment, because it is merely the formal element of

> consciousness. On the other hand, *inner experience* contains the material of consciousness and a manifold of empirical inner intuition, the 'I' of *apprehension* (consequently an empirical apperception).

Kant's moral position on personhood is correlated with the unity of the self ([1798] 2006: 15):

> The fact that the human being can have the 'I' in his representations raises him infinitely above all other living beings on earth. Because of this he is a *person*, and by virtue of the unity of consciousness through all the changes that happen to him, one and the same person – i.e., through rank and dignity an entirely different being from *things*, such as irrational animals, with which one can do as one likes. This holds even when he cannot yet say 'I,' because he still has in its thoughts, just as all languages must think it when they speak in the first person, even if they do not have a special word to express this concept of 'I.' For this faculty (namely to think) is *understanding*.

Paradoxically, there must be two distinct aspects to self in order for it to be unified: in effect there is an apersonal or impersonal self underlying a personal self.

One way out of the Kantian intellectual maze, and the 'ontological insecurity' of late seventeenth-century intellectual discourse (Rzepka 1986: 10), was to exploit the uncertain line between self and world as a stimulus to the active, creative imagination. Mead argues that the apersonal Kantian self was transformed into a Romantic self (Mead 1936: 67). In Romanticism, questions of subjectivity and authenticity were appealed to both in terms of the individual self, in particular the self-fashioning of the artist, and the collective self, in terms of culture, homeland, nationhood, or people. Bode (2008) uses the term *self-modelling* in relation to English Romantic poets; in the German context, organicist Romantic political theory was based on a rejection of the French Revolution and Enlightenment universalism (Fichte 1808). In this sense one can think of Hegel as a Romantic, in that the Hegelian self is formed reflexively out of exchange and confrontation with other selves in a dynamic process of self-realization (Hegel [1807] 2018: 102ff, Pippin 2010).

It was Darwinism that threatened definitively to rupture the link between personhood and the self, suggesting as it did the animal features behind the human mask. Following Charles Darwin's *Origin of Species* (1859), intellectual developments challenging the model of an autonomous self gathered pace. This took place across a range of disciplines, in particular psychology, psychoanalysis, evolutionary biology, semiotics, structural linguistics, economics, philosophy, and general systems theory. *Avant-garde* modernism attacked the Romantic model of the self and the artist: one of modernism's central themes is *impersonality* (Cameron 2007, Farbman 2016, Volpicelli 2016). Artistic modernism envisaged the self as fragmented, divided, or dislocated (Brown and Theodore 1989), in part as a reflection of hyper-reflexivity and hyper-self-consciousness, attacking

Romantic ideas of authentic self-expression yet foregrounding an individual sensibility at odds with modern mass society (Bahun 2013: 46):

> On the one hand, modernists treated the fragment as a marker of the loss of 'totality' or continuity between the subject and the object/world/home. At the same time, the modernist fragment was poised to liberate the subject precisely from the shackles of 'totality'.

Rimbaud's famous line, 'Je est un autre' ('I is an other'), sums this up perfectly since the self is both foregrounded (hyper-present) and, presumptively, liberated through its objectification.[2]

The psychologist William James (1842–1910) emphasized the instability of the self, and a dialectical movement between an *I*, the underlying continuous ego, and a *me*, made up of the material self, the social self, and the spiritual self. James used the metaphor of a *river* or *stream* to capture consciousness (1890: 239):

> Consciousness, then, does not appear to itself chopped up in bits. Such words as 'chain' or 'train' do not describe it fitly as it presents itself in the first instance. It is nothing jointed; if flows. A 'river' or a 'stream' are the metaphors by which it is most naturally described. *In talking of it hereafter, let us call it the stream of thought, of consciousness, or of subjective life.*

In relation to the material self, James noted (1890: 291), 'Certainly men have been ready to disown their very bodies and to regard them as mere vestures, or even as prisons of clay from which they should some day be glad to escape'. The body was 'a fluctuating material' with no single relationship to the self: 'The same object being sometimes treated as a part of me, at other times as simply mine, and then again as if I had nothing to do with it at all'. In its widest sense (1890: 291–292),

> *a man's Self is the sum total of all that he* CAN *call his*, not only his body and his psychic powers, but his clothes and his house, his wife and children, his ancestors and friends, his reputation and works, his lands and horses, and yacht and bank-account. All these things give him the same emotions.

This posits a self which is extended and of uncertain boundaries, defined primarily in terms of ownership and possessions (Belk 1988). This is both a psychological and a juridical notion, as in Locke's model, one that might be termed 'property for personhood' (Radin 1992).

Cooley argued that self and other were not 'mutually exclusive social facts' (1902: 92). While there was an instinctual basis to the 'emotion or feeling of self' (1902: 139), the social self might be termed 'the reflected or looking-glass self', in that it was made up of how the self imagined it was perceived, how it imagined it was judged by others, and the 'self-feeling' that arose (1902: 152).

If this social reflexivity is constitutive of the self, then this would tend to suggest a divide between animals and humans, even granted similarities at other behavioural or instinctual levels. George Herbert Mead (1863–1931) saw the human self as constituted by a dialogic relation between the *I* and the *me*. He stressed the human ability to reflect back on oneself (Mead [1934] 1962: 137fn.):

> Man's behavior is such in his social group that he is able to become an object to himself, a fact which constitutes him a more advanced product of evolutionary development than are the lower animals. Fundamentally it is this social fact – and not his alleged possession of a soul or mind [...] – that differentiates him from them.

In using the faculty of reason, the self demonstrated not just consciousness but self-consciousness (Mead [1934] 1962: 138): 'Reason cannot become impersonal unless it takes an objective, non-affective attitude toward itself; otherwise we have just consciousness, not *self*-consciousness'.

The lack of this interplay of *I* and *me* meant that the attribution of personality to domestic animals was false since they lacked the prerequisites for it – namely language ([1934] 1962: 183):

> We put personalities into the animals, but they do not belong to them; and ultimately we realize that those animals have no rights.

There was no wrong in killing an animal ([1934] 1962: 183) since animals do not have a future to lose:

> he has not the 'me' in his experience which by the response of the 'I' is in some sense under his control, so that the future can exist for him. He has no conscious past since there is no self of the sort we have been describing that can be extended into the past by memories.

This point was emphasized repeatedly: 'our conduct which implies selves in domestic animals has no rational justification' ([1934] 1962: 290).

With its roots in the phenomenology of Edmund Husserl (1859–1938) and Alfred Schütz (1899–1959) and symbolic interactionism, social constructionism has been centrally concerned with the status of the self (Berger and Luckmann 1966: 68, 73, 90–91). In the post-Second World War era, the target of constructionist polemic was essentialist models of identity, especially in relation to sex/gender, race, and disability. Sociocultural orders were held to be products of social, institutional, and political processes, rather than grounded in universal evolutionary, in particular, biological processes. Society was seen as a complex weave of discursive construction reflecting dominant ideologies, rather than as the reflection of deeply entrenched biological drives. Social constructionism squared off against evolutionary psychology and sociobiology in a conflict that continues to this day (Baron-Cohen 2010, Fine 2010). It was intertwined with identity politics, and related notions of authenticity, self-definition, and self-realization, prioritizing the first-person individual (or group) perspective and rejecting claims to academic objectivity in relation to identity. *Identity* first emerged definitively in its current popular social science sense in the 1950s (Gleason 1983). Locke's use of the term *personal identity* was primarily a philosophical one ([1690] 1975: 335).

In terms of the status of the self, this political stance implied a tangled mix of reification and dereification since some identity beliefs, for example, belief in the deterministic relationship between sex and gender, might be rejected, whereas others were to be affirmed on political grounds through self-labelling or self-categorization. In social theory, *reflexivity* took on two distinct meanings. In one sense, 'reflexivity is a defining characteristic of all human action. All human beings routinely "keep in touch" with the grounds of what they do as an integral element of doing it' (Giddens 1990: 36). Martin and Bickhard make a contrast with animals (2012: 2): 'Unlike the members of other animal species, persons are not understood only in terms of their corporeal and adaptive attributes and capacities, but also in terms of their own self interpretations and ascriptions'. In modernity, reflexivity of a distinct kind is systemic, being 'introduced into the very basis of system reproduction, such that thought and action are constantly refracted back upon one another'. Given this, 'social practices are constantly examined and reformed in the light of incoming information about those very practices, thus constitutively altering their character' (Giddens 1990: 38). It follows that 'the construction of the self becomes a reflexive project' (1990: 114).

The self is seen as a relational social construct, the ongoing product of performativity, or defined by a narrative, but also a potential site of personal or collective authenticity. Abstractions such as languages or identities are understood as processes, not products. Hence the proliferation of terms such as *negotiating*, *(de)constructing*, *constituting*, *(re)inventing*, *(re)imagining*, *(re)producing* (Anderson 1983, Makoni and Pennycook 2006, Hakala 2016). Social constructionism, as a form of open-ended anti-foundationalism, can be used to deessentialize or undermine any given category (Hacking 1999). Alternatively, it can be used to ground or explicate a concept like the self in terms of its discursive production or dynamic process of becoming (Stetsenko and Arievitch 1997). These processes may happen simultaneously, as in human attempts at deep identification with animals across the species divide (Foster 2016) or in cases of performed animal or *furry* identities (Carlson 2011). The human is deconstructed in service of a constructed kinship or empathetic identification with the animal.

This post-structuralist turn framed the self as attenuated or virtual, taking from psychoanalysis the self's blindness towards its own inner drives and rationales. The status of this constructed self in relation to notions of autonomy and agency was particularly problematic, especially from a Foucauldian point of view (Gergen 2011: 644). Ahearn (2001: 118) defines agency provisionally as 'the socioculturally mediated capacity to act'. One view might be that constructionism opens up the possibility of self-fashioning, self-invention, and self-realization, yet if there is no human nature and no true self, there is also no site for authentic agency. The self is in this sense at the mercy of social construction: it is produced, maintained, and perhaps nurtured but also in some contexts undermined, divided, or even destroyed. In anti-psychiatry the genesis of psychiatric illness was located in social context, the family, or institutions. The self was constructed and regulated through social feedback mechanisms, and if these were in conflict they could result in a *double-bind* triggering schizophrenia (Bateson et al. 1956).

Influence from non-Western philosophical systems, understood as arguing that the self is ultimately fictional or illusory, can be traced throughout the nineteenth and twentieth centuries. Arthur Schopenhauer (1788–1860), whose engagement with Buddhism and Hinduism interacted with his contrapunctal reading of Kant's transcendental idealism (Janaway 1989, Zöller 1999, Cross 2013), argued that higher animals showed a form of cognition and morality, yet ([1841] 2009: 162):

> Because [...] Christian morals give no consideration to animals, they are at once free as birds in philosophical morals too, they are mere 'things', mere means to whatever ends you like, as for instance vivisection, hunting with hounds, bull-fighting, racing, whipping to death in front of an immovable stone-cart and the like[.]

Lacking reason, animals had been wrongly excluded from the Kantian moral system. In Schopenhauer, the naturalization of the human self, the attempt to free the self from the demands of the will, and compassion for animals are closely interconnected.

Any questioning of the reality of the individual, autonomous self opens up the possibility of non-anthropocentric universalism, either because the individual self is a derivative of God (Spinoza) or because all of creation is suffused with some form of mind. This position is known as *panpsychism*: 'the view that all things have mind or a mind-like quality' and 'an ancient concept, dating back to the earliest days of both Eastern and Western civilizations' (Skrbina 2005: 2). Adherents of panpsychism have 'no reason to limit mind to humans and (perhaps) higher animals; in fact, they have reasons – both intuitive and rational – to claim that mind is best conceived as a general phenomenon of nature' (Skrbina 2005: 2). One inference might be that certain animals, no less than humans, are 'aware of themselves as distinct individuals' (Mathews 2003: 144). Alternatively, neither humans nor animals have core, stable selves.

Ideas about *anatta* 'no-self' go in and out of fashion in the West (Blackmore 1999: 230). Alan Watts (1915–1973) described the first stage in Zen training as a process of untying the knot of the self: 'And when that tense knot vanishes there is no more sensation of a hard core of selfhood standing over against the rest of the world' (1957: 166). The notion of *anatta* finds its counterpart in naturalistic discourse. The philosopher Daniel Dennett (1992) described the self as a narrative device or fiction, a 'center of narrative gravity' or 'benign user illusion'. Hofstadter (2007: 362) uses the term *mirage*:

> You and I are mirages who perceive themselves, and the sole magical machinery behind the scenes is perception – the triggering, by huge flows of raw data, of a tiny set of symbols that stand for abstract regularities in the world.

The *I* we posit 'does such a good job of explaining our behavior that it becomes the hub around which the rest of the world seems to rotate'. However this notion was 'just a shorthand for a vast mass of seething and churning of which we are necessarily unaware'. Dennett presents consciousness as the product of memes (1991: 207, cited in Blackmore 1999: 230):

> The haven all memes depend on reaching is the human mind, but a human mind is itself an artefact created when memes restructure a human brain in order to make it a better habitat for memes.

Richard Dawkins employs the term *illusion*: 'Each of us knows that the illusion of a single agent sitting somewhere in the middle of the brain is a powerful one' (2000: 283–284). Metzinger (2003: 1) speaks of a *self-model*:

> Nobody ever *was* or *had* a self. All that ever existed were conscious self-models that could not be recognized *as* models. The phenomenal self is not a thing, but a process – and the subjective experience of *being someone* emerges if a conscious information-processing system operates under a transparent self-model.

Belief in the self arises from a confusion or illusion, generated internally by an information-processing system, that is, a naturalistic system. Gray (2002: 70–71) enlists Eastern thought in his attack on Christianity and humanism: 'Recent cognitive science and ancient Buddhist teachings are at one in viewing this ordinary sense of self as illusive'. For Gray, animals differ from humans, however, 'in lacking the sensation of selfhood' (2002: 61). One dissenting voice is that of Mary Midgley, who sees reductionalist notions of the self as reflecting 'residual cartesian dualism' (2011: 99): 'But "self" is in fact a highly complex idea with many different uses. Nothing can be gained by trying to shoot it down in favour of this tinpot successor'. The reflexive self and the personhood which it underwrites are obstacles in the way of a scientistic dream of *consilience*, that is, the unification of all knowledge within a scientific framework (Wilson 1999).

The question of animal selfhood depends, of course, on what we understand by *having a self*. Turner (2013) speaks of selfhood in terms of attribution, self-awareness, intersubjectivity, self-concept/reflexivity, and narration. But his conclusion in relation to animals is equivocal. Rose lists terms 'that cluster around it - autonomy, identity, individuality, liberty, choice, fulfilment' (Rose 1998: 1). He also points to the 'specificity of our modern Western conception of a person' according to which 'the person is construed as a self, a naturally unique and discrete entity, the boundaries of the body enclosing, as if by definition, an inner life of the psyche' (Rose 1998: 22). Smith (2003: 33) asserts that human personhood is always grounded in a moral order, a quality that makes human beings unique. Morality is related to self-consciousness, and from this point of view personhood and selfhood are interdefining and human beings construct standards beyond their own personal interests (2003: 42). In reaction to humanistic model of the self, ***animalism*** emphasizes that human beings and non-human animals share a common identity, that of 'being an animal'. It rejects Locke's contention that the conditions of identity over time for a human self were quite distinct from the bodily continuity that constituted an animal's mode of being (Blatti and Snowden 2016: 3), offering in effect a naturalistic reduction of claims for human uniqueness.

The *haecceity* ('thusness') of consciousness represents a profound intellectual challenge. In an essay entitled 'What is it like to be a bat?' (1974), Thomas Nagel argued that we have no way of knowing the quality of the experience of being a bat since consciousness was irreducibly subjective and not susceptible to explanation within an 'objective, physical theory' (1974: 427). While consciousness was found 'at many levels of animal life', it was 'very difficult to say in general what provides evidence of it' (1974: 436). On this point, the Cambridge Declaration of Consciousness (July 7, 2012) concludes with the following statement:

> the weight of evidence indicates that humans are not unique in possessing the neurological substrates that generate consciousness. Nonhuman animals, including all mammals and birds, and many other creatures, including octopuses, also possess these neurological substrates.[3]

Having the prerequisites for consciousness says nothing definitive about the quality of that consciousness. The question about animal selves could also be posed in terms of possession of ***mind*** (Morell 2013) or ***identity*** (Atkins-Sayre 2010). The otherness of, say, cephalopods, suggests the possibility of a radically incommensurable form of mental complexity or inner life (Godfrey-Smith 2016). Complex beings such as cetaceans can be understood to have complex social forms and 'cultural lives' (Whitehead and Rendell 2014). While philosophers such as Dennett (1991) restrict consciousness to human beings, others use *sentience* to argue for communality between human beings and animals (Singer 1975, Balcombe 2016). Expressing a view that can be traced back to Jeremy Bentham ([1789] 1879), the animal rights philosopher Peter Singer equates the ability to suffer with consciousness, awareness, or sentience (Singer 1975, Griffin 1976, Varner 2012, Ratamäki 2014). Reflexivity or metacognition offers another intellectualist way to frame the question of difference between humans and animals (Smith 2009).

Within the broad camp of anti-humanism, human consciousness, experienced in the form of a unitary and autonomous self, is a fiction, that is, an epiphenomenon of real, non-fictional systems, and of no explanatory value: 'This idea of humanism cannot continue. Who would seriously and deliberately want to maintain that society could be formed on the model of a human being, that is, with a head at the top and so on?' (Luhmann 1996: 213). Further, there is no such referent (Luhmann 1994: 371): 'Everyone knows, of course, that the word "human being" is not a human being. We must also learn that there is nothing in the unity of an object that corresponds to the word'. For Luhmann, social subsystems are functionally differentiated and organizationally closed. Communication between subsystems (e.g. ecological activism, politics, and law) is haphazard and resistant to conscious steering. Society itself as a system cannot predict or direct its actions towards the natural environment, precisely because the environment's interaction as the 'outside' of a system with society is not knowable or transparent to any central agentive consciousness (Luhmann 1989). The self is epiphenomenal to the system.

The category *fiction* and its near-synonyms, deployed by Hume and other sceptics of the self, represents a source of considerable intellectual temptation. In designating one concept as *real*, others in the same domain must be dereified as *fictional* in order to evade the dense network engendered by near-synonymous bedrock concepts. Strawson (1996: 87–116) argues for 'the primitiveness of the concept person'. This allows the analysis of consciousness or ego-substance 'as a secondary, non-primitive concept'. He argues that 'the concept of person is logically prior to that of an individual consciousness' and that of 'a particular human body'. While it makes sense to ascribe predicates of consciousness as well as predicates of corporeal characteristics to the concept of person, this is not to say that a person is the union of two kinds of entity: 'The concept of a person is not to be analyzed as that of an animated body of an embodied anima' (1996: 103, Ishiguro 1980). Similarly, for Harré (1998), there is no such entity as the (human) self: 'the singularity we feel ourselves to be is not an entity'; it is rather 'a site from which a person perceives the world and a place from which to act': 'There are only persons. Selves are grammatical fictions, necessary characteristics of person-oriented discourses' (1998: 3–4). But one might just as easily argue the reverse: selves are real, whereas persons are grammatical fictions, the mediated construction of personal pronouns, or other linguistic devices. What Harré offers are merely stipulated definitions, allowing the relegation of one category in order to elevate another.

Gordijn (1999) suggests eliminating the concept of *person* from bioethical debate, citing the overlapping definitions and frameworks derived primarily from Locke. Gordijn points to Wiggins's (1987: 56) comment that it is difficult to keep in focus: '(a) the idea of a person as object of biological, anatomical, and neurophysiological inquiry; (b) the idea of the person as subject of consciousness; and (c) the idea of the person as locus of all sorts of moral attributes and the source or conceptual origin of all value'. The complexity of the ordinary use of *person* leads to an eliminativist approach, such as that of Gordijn (Taylor and Vickers 2017) or to the use of stipulation (Teichman 1985). Teichman concludes that *person* is not the name of a natural species nor of a 'broad natural kind', given that it refers both to artificial persons and bodiless gods and angels. Summing up the modern progress of the self, Brinkmann sees it as increasingly elusive (2005: 43): 'A classical tradition seems to have been exhausted as the modern self gives way to its postmodern signifiers'.

Nature and the human

Nature, often understood in opposition to *culture*, has been described as 'perhaps the most complex word in the [English] language' (Williams 1983: 219).[4] As Delaney (2003: 15) points out, ***nature*** 'can be used to signify order and disorder, determinacy and indeterminacy'; it can name 'both what we want to overcome or escape and what we need to respect, stay within, or aspire to'. Williams gives three basic meanings for the term: '(i) the essential quality and character of something; (ii) the inherent force which directs either the world or human beings or both; (iii) the material world itself, taken as including or not including human beings'. Theologically, human beings are part of God's creation, creatures of the natural world, yet in virtue of being created in God's image and placed at the pinnacle of creation under God, and in virtue of their possession of an immortal soul, human beings are set apart. The attempt to understand that apartness or difference is the central theological and, subsequently, scientific, challenge of the Western tradition.

For the pioneers of the scientific revolution, the rigorous observation and investigation of nature, being the close study of God's handiwork, was in some sense a devotional activity. Francis Bacon (1561–1626), generally regarded as the original philosopher of scientific empiricism (Henry 2002), explained objective or unbiased inquiry into nature in his *Sylva Silvarum* as reflecting 'humility towards the creator' and 'reverence and esteem of his works' ([1627] 1733, III: 5). This implied a deep compatibility between religion and science. Bacon urged mankind to set aside its 'preposterous, fantastic and hypothetical philosophies' which have held 'experience captive and childishly triumphed over the work of God' ([1627] 1733, III: 5). A mind purged of 'opinions, idols and false notions' could peruse the book of creation and find that it is written in 'the language which has gone out to all ends of the earth, unaffected by the confusion at Babel' ([1627] 1733, III: 5):

> this is the language that men should thoroughly learn, and not distain to have its alphabet perpetually in their hands: and in the interpretation of this language they should spare no pains; but strenuously proceed, persevere and dwell upon it to the last.

The language of nature is the master language, to which, by implication, human language is a secondary system. Human language should be constrained by vigilance as to the reality of nature to which language must ultimately refer.

Bacon stressed the distinction between the knowledge displayed in Adam's naming of the animals and the cause of the expulsion from Eden. In his piece *Valerius Terminus of the Interpretation of Nature* ([1603] 1838: 219), he distinguished between ***natural knowledge*** and ***moral knowledge***. The former was innocent in the fall. It was 'not pure light of natural knowledge, whereby man in paradise was able to give unto every living creature a name according to his propriety, which gave occasion to the fall'. This universal naming system, this 'pure knowledge of Nature and universality' ([1603] 1838: 2), is, presumptively, that to which science aspires since the names given by Adam were bestowed 'according unto their properties' ([1603] 1838: 2). In the relationship between nature's real categories and language, it is language that is the weak point, as the punishment at Babel demonstrated. Science sought to recapture the real referentiality of the Adamic language. Commenting on Ecclesiastes, Bacon declared that 'God hath framed the mind of man as a mirror or glass'. In this natural order, man has dominion over nature 'being in his creation invested with sovereignty of all inferior creatures'. When compared with animals, human beings shared 'perpetuity by generation'. However 'memory, merit, and noble works are proper to men' ([1625] 1883: 46).

For Bacon's philosophy, the Adamic language remains a latent potentiality, accessible through the application of the inductive methods of empirical science and a real language of description, rather than a process of mystical decoding. Nature can be described objectively, using a language which is not personal to the speaker: 'Science must not only penetrate beyond the appearances of things, but construct *a new language* in which the findings of science may be correctly reported' (Harris 2009b: 26). Insistence on the unique place of human beings when set against a reified, distinct *nature*, as opposed to a theological understanding of man's dominion over nature, emerged with the beginnings of modern empirical science. René Descartes (1596–1650) in particular is associated with early modern arguments for the uniqueness of human beings, a view elaborated in part in polemics against Michel de Montaigne (1533–1592) (Melehy 2006):

> The difference between the *res cogitans* and the *res extensa* that Descartes elaborates in the *Meditations* ([1642] 1680) is the same as that between a human soul, of the same nature as God, and a body, between that which is in possession of reason and that which is not.
>
> (Melehy 2005: 265)

Latour (1993) argues that the clash between the scientist Robert Boyle (1627–1691) and the political philosopher Hobbes (1588–1679) typifies the object-subject distinction that modernity sets out but which it cannot sustain in pure form. The objective study of nature is seen as a domain entirely separate from the study of human beings as political animals. In this way, Boyle and Hobbes invented the modern world: 'a world in which the representation of things through the intermediary of the laboratory is forever dissociated from the representation of citizens through the intermediary of the social contract' (Latour 1993: 27). The separation of these two domains, what Latour refers to as the 'two halves of the modern Constitution' (1993: 46), is what sustains them (1993: 27):

> The representation of non-humans belongs to science, but science is not allowed to appeal to politics; the representation of citizens belongs to politics, but politics is not allowed any relation to the nonhumans produced and mobilized by science and technology.

While this separation operates at the conceptual level or ideal type, modernity is replete with hybrids (Latour 1993 49–50):

> When the only thing at stake was the emergence of a few vacuum pumps, they could still be subsumed under two classes, that of natural laws and that of political representations; but when we find ourselves invaded by frozen embryos, expert systems, digital machines, sensor-equipped robots, hybrid corn, data banks, psychotropic drugs, whales outfitted with radar sounding devices, gene synthesizers, audience analyzers, and so on, when our daily newspapers display all these monsters on page after page, and when none of these chimera can be properly on the object side or on the subject side, or even in between, something has to be done.

The modern constitution 'guaranteed Nature its transcendent dimension by making it distinct from the fabric of Society', thus running counter to 'the continuous connection between the natural order and the social order found among the premoderns' (1993: 139). This separation allowed human beings as citizens to imagine themselves 'totally free to reconstruct it artificially', again in contrast 'to the continuous connection between the social order and the natural order that kept the premoderns from being able to modify the one without modifying the other' (1993: 139). This double separation allowed in practice for 'the mobilization and construction of Nature', at the same 'made it possible to make Society stable and durable'. The domains were held separate: 'Nature will remain without relation to Society; Society, in turn, even though it is transcendent and rendered durable by the mediation of objects, will no longer have any relation to Nature' (1993: 139). A crossed-out God 'made it possible to stabilize this dualist and asymmetrical mechanism by ensuring a function of arbitration, but one without presence or power'. In spite of this constitutive ordering, modernity generates or proliferates 'quasi-objects' and 'quasi-subjects' and it is these that should be represented rather than repressed (1993: 139). As summarized by Lash (1999):

> Now in fact, as distinct from in law, what this constitutional dualism permits and encourages is the invention and innovation of a host, a proliferation of quasi-objects, of hybrids that totally violate modernity's categories and guarantees. The point in time has come now, Latour says, where these quasi-objects, these monsters, like gene technologies, thinking machines and ozone layers, have become so omnipresent that we can no longer deny their existence. Hence we should recognize now that we are not modern and that we never have been.

The separation of nature into its own autonomous domain by modern science lends retrospective unity to what has been termed 'the emblematic worldview'. This is 'the belief that every kind of thing in the cosmos has myriad hidden meanings and that knowledge consists of an attempt to comprehend as many of these as possible' (Ashworth 2008: 142). For premodern and early modern understandings, the idea that there was a pure non-metaphorical nature to be found beyond the walls of human society would have been incoherent. In modern terms, there was no fact-value distinction to be made in relation to animals and other natural phenomena. Further, the notion that an animal should be studied purely in terms of 'anatomy, physiology, and physical description, was a notion completely foreign to Renaissance thought' (Ashworth 2008: 142). By the early seventeenth century 'there was available a cornucopia of animal allegories and symbolism' so that to know about the peacock was to know (Ashworth 2008: 142)

> not only what the peacock looks like but what its name means, in every language; what kind of proverbial associations it has; what it symbolizes to both pagans and Christians; what other animals it has sympathies or affinities with; and any other possible connection it might have with stars, plants, minerals, numbers, coins, or whatever.

In emblematic thinking, animal figures are not drawn from a pre-existing non-metaphorical nature in order to represent culture (Cuneo 2017). Discussing legal emblems in the Renaissance, Goodrich explains (2014: 20) that emblems, which include 'doors, gates, flags, sails, windows, books, masks, clouds, and screens as also colors, animals, birds, precious metals, and stones':

> are hieroglyphs, enigmas of law, esoteric symbols of erudite meanings. They have to be translated as well as interpreted so as to reconstruct the visible law as it transmits custom and norm, moral and caution through visual depictions that accompany but are not reducible to their verbal explanations.

Heraldic art implies 'the proper order of colours, metals, stones, and animals'; drawn from 'a simple lexicon of the visual signs of a highly regulated manifest social, military, ecclesiastical and legal hierarchy' (Goodrich 2014: 65).

With the overturning of the emblematic worldview, nature came to be seen as an autonomous domain with its own objectively determinable order. This reductive understanding led to the great taxonomic projects of the eighteenth century, such as that of Carl Linnaeus (1707–1778) and his *Systema Naturae* (1735), Georges-Louis Leclerc, Comte de Buffon (1707–1788), whose *Histoire naturelle, générale et particulière* was published between 1749 and 1804, and Georges Cuvier (1769–1832) whose *Le Règne Animal* first appeared in 1817. These projects were based on close comparative observation and entailed the engineering of a system of precise and unambiguous nomenclature. Linnaeus's category of *anthropomorpha* included both human beings (the genus *Homo* and its sub-categories, see Vermeulen 2015: 367) and primates (*Simia*). The uncertain boundary might be seen as the symptom of a new, secular modesty about the place of human beings in nature alongside all other animals, or as part of a racially inflected continuum between white Europeans at one end and higher primates at the other (see Cribb, Gilbert and Tiffin 2014: 30–57).

Under criticism for grouping *Homo* together with *Simia*, Linnaeus responded as follows (letter to Georg Gmelin, cited in Vermeulen 2015: 366):

> It is not pleasing that I placed humans among the *anthropomorpha* [primates], but man knows himself (*homo noscit se ipsum*). Let us get the words out of the way. It matters little to me what words we use. But I ask you and the whole world, [to show me] a generic difference between man and ape, one that is in accordance with the principles of Natural History. I certainly know of none. If only someone would indicate one to me! But, if I called man an ape, or vice versa, I would have brought together all the theologians against me. It may be that as a naturalist I ought to have done so.

This marks the beginning of a vexed and unresolved discussion of the relationship between humans and animals within these new taxonomic orders.

In relation to scientific taxonomy, Dupré (1999) advocates what he terms *promiscuous realism*, according to which 'there are many, perhaps very many, possible ways of classifying naturally occurring objects that reflect real divisions among the objects. But not just any arbitrary classification will reflect such divisions'. 'Good classifications' reflect 'natural kinds', but these should not be understood in terms of essentialism and are not mutually exclusive; rather they should be understood in relation to the purposes for which they are devised and for which they are applied. It is not that nature provides no natural divisions, as suggested by constructivists, but that it provides too many (Dupré 1999: 473, Dupré 2002). A more sweeping rejection of the authority of scientific taxonomy forms part of the counter-Enlightenment, within which arguably Michel Foucault is the dominant figure (Foucault [1966] 1989).

Beginning with Romanticism, intellectuals have sought to heal the alienation from nature created by industrial and urban modernity, proposing models of interconnectedness, symbiosis, oneness, deep unity, and harmony. Modern science, in radically separating society and culture from an external objectified nature, pushed the emblematic model to the intellectual margins. This model thrived, however, in mythical and literary domains, within the polemics of counter-Enlightenment thinking, modern New Age thinking, and some strands of ecological thinking. Comparative anthropology represented non-modern societies as invested in complex yet non-rational forms of identification with animals and plants. An analogous idea was presented in terms of *identification* (Jung 1921) or *mystic participation* found in non-rational beliefs systems and their understanding of the relation of humans to the natural world (Lévy-Bruhl 1910, 1922). Natural objects such as trees, rocks, rivers, and mountains, as well as animals, are outward manifestations of the divine or the supernatural. From a rationalist point of view, animism is a symptom of the over-attribution of agency (Talbot and Wastell 2015). Nature as a whole may be understood as a *persona*. Williams gives this analysis of what he terms 'the very early and surprisingly persistent personification' of singular Nature as a goddess (Williams 1983: 221):

> This singular personification is critically different from what are now called 'nature gods' or 'nature spirits': mythical personifications of particular natural forces. Nature herself is at one extreme a literal goddess, a universal directing power, and at another extreme (very difficult to distinguish from some non-religious singular uses) an amorphous but still all-powerful creative and shaping force. The associated 'Mother Nature' is at this end of the religious and mythical spectrum.

In Gaia theory, named after the Greek goddess of the Earth, the earth is viewed as an integrated set of self-regulating systems, as a living organism akin to a vast single body, or even as a deity which has the potential 'to take revenge' on human beings for the harm they are causing to the equilibrium of systems on which the planet is based (Harding 2006, Lovelock 2006, Latour 2017). If the earth itself is a complex organism or even a kind of person (Lovelock 1979), then human beings are an increasingly toxic subsidiary system within it. In this way humanity is depersonified, while in some understandings of Gaia, nature is personified within a 'pseudo-religion' (Bondi 2015):

> Nature acquires features that are denied, at the same time, to the single man. In fact the human being, in this conceptual framework, is only a part of the Great Whole, the Mother Nature; he cannot be 'her' guardian at all, he has to abandon any pretense of ontological superiority and to 'believe' in the infinite potential of Gaia, who always finds a way to restore the threatened balance.

Deep ecology rejects the 'man-in-environment' model for 'the relational, total-field image', though arguably deep ecology, with its desire to cure 'the alienation of man from himself', remains within the Romantic tradition (Naess 1973: 95, 96). *Dark ecology* begins with a rejection of the category of nature itself: 'Putting something called Nature on a pedestal and admiring it from afar does for the environment what patriarchy does for the figure of Woman. It is a paradoxical act of sadistic admiration' (Morton 2017: 5). Anti-Romantic, hypermodern ecologies beyond nature or 'without nature' (Morton 2007) envisage radical reconfigurations of the human-nature (subject-object) dichotomy, from a cyborg future (Haraway 1991), Latour's *parliament of things* (1993), Morton's *Severing* (2017: 23), and many other iterations. The aim is to reorder the concept of the human self. Latour uses the political language of representation and delegation, fusing ecology with politics and law (1993: 138): 'Humanism can maintain itself only by sharing itself with all these mandatees. Human nature is the set of its delegates and its representatives, its figures and its messengers'.

Conclusion

In relation to fundamental concepts, Francis Bacon rejected definitional solutions ([1620] 2000: 48): 'For the definitions themselves consist of words, and words beget words'. The notion of foundational concepts relies on a particular second-order metaphorical framing, the idea that certain concepts are historically prior, more concrete, more simple, and that these build the world of concepts from the bottom up. Bedrock meanings exist only, if at all, as fictions of folk linguistics, in the way that speakers view *tree* as the name of a naturally given object found in the external world. For the integrationist, definitions and related reductionist accounts of meaning, of which there are many kinds, are second-order reifications or constructs (Love 1990, Cowley 2017: 47). Problems of circularity, tautology, and the blurred boundary between real and verbal (nominal) definition are symptoms of the intense difficulty we experience in thinking clearly in a reflexive way in relation to bedrock concepts. On the one hand, *self* can be sharply distinguished from *person*. Alternatively, 'being a self (with some degree of self-awareness)' is understood as 'a necessary element of being a person in the full sense' (Moran 2017: 4).

Once the intellectual spotlight turns on fundamental concepts, the attempt to ground a definition or achieve conceptual clarity through an explicit analysis often succeeds only in making the familiar strange, in alienating the analyst from the intuitive certainty that was there at the outset and which the analysis is intended to place on a solid intellectual foundation. What is ideally involved in philosophical analysis is *real* rather than *nominal* or *verbal* definition, an investigation of things rather than of word meanings or concepts since meanings can always be seen as culture-bound, subjective, and subject to a regress of explanation (since meanings are always given in words). Given that there are no languageless propositions (Harris 2011: 93, Pablé 2011: 554–557), the attempt to achieve clarity at this level of inquiry, and to avoid circularity or tautology, involves a form of cognitive dance, whereby some meanings are momentarily held fixed in order that others may be interrogated, at the same time as the inquiry is understood to look beyond the surface structure of language to matters of philosophical substance or ontology. Stipulative definition is a fundamental technique for countering this disorientation and alienation.

Notes

1 The structure *es blitzt* 'It is lightening') or *es regnet* ('it is raining') is extended by analogy from agentless weather to the human being.
2 Letter from Rimbaud to Georges Izambard, 13 May, 1871, available at: fr.wikisource.org/wiki/Lettre_de_Rimbaud.
3 See: fcmconference.org.
4 See now the Keywords Project, keywords.pitt.edu.

2 The analysis of bedrock concepts within language studies

Introduction

The Western tradition is suffused with a deep sense of linguistic displacement, decline, and loss. Two traumatic events dominate: the expulsion from Eden, and the confounding of languages at Babel. In Genesis the origin of language is depicted as follows (2:19):

> And out of the ground the Lord God formed every beast of the field, and every fowl of the air; and brought them unto Adam to see what he would call them: and whatsoever Adam called every living creature, that was its name.

Harris observes that the Adamic language is founded on the 'one-to-one principle', in that 'Adam never bestows two names on the same animal' (2009b: 28). For Archbishop Trench, Genesis showed that man 'is not a mere speaking machine'. God did not teach Adam as one teaches a parrot. Speech had both a divine and a human origin (1853: 15). However the 'confusion of tongues' at Babel suggested that linguistic diversity was divine punishment. Language became an unstable category, suspended, like humanity, between the divine and the natural. The corollary to loss is a search for foundations. If somehow a secure basis could be found for language, the world will be seen aright. This idea is often expressed quite subtly, as when we feel that a certain usage is alienated from the norm. To call an animal, a *person*, or animals, *people*, is one such context. If we retort, 'But animals are simply not people', this locates a norm in established linguistic practice correlated in the imagination with a related set of common-sense ontological distinctions. But if we go further and ask about the status of this linguistic practice or the grounding of our common-sense ontologies, then all that is solid melts into air.

Etymological thinking

Etymological thinking reflects the idea that the essence of a word meaning is locatable in its origin. In the *Cratylus* of Plato (c. 360 BCE), the issue was whether

DOI: 10.4324/9781315143132-3

names (i.e. proper names and nouns) are properly understood to be natural or conventional. In the course of the exchanges, the figure of Socrates embarks on a series of fanciful etymological discussions, one of which offers an answer as to why human beings are called *anthropos* (ανθρωπος). Noting that in language, 'we often pull in and pull out letters and words, and give names as we please, and change the accents', Socrates comments (Jowett 1875: 221):

> The name ανθρωπος [*anthropos*], which was once a sentence, and is now a noun, appears to be a case just of this sort, for one letter, which is the α, has been omitted, and the acute en on the last syllable has been turned to a grave.

In response to Hermogenes's request for clarification, Socrates continues (Jowett 1875: 221):

> I mean to say that the word 'man' implies that other animals never examine or consider, or look up at what they see, but that man not only sees (ὄπωπε) but considers, and looks up at that which he sees, and hence he alone of all animals is rightly called ανθρωπος, meaning ἀναθρῶν ἃ ὄπωπε.

As glossed by Barney (2001: 67), 'the name anthrôpos is correct because alone of the animals a human "observes closely" [*anathrei*] "what he has seen" [*ha opôpe*]'.

Later in the dialogue, Socrates complains that many 'original names' have 'long been buried and disguised by people sticking on and stripping off letters' and that 'time may have had a share in the change'. This means that 'names will too easily be made, and any name may be adapted to any object' (Jowett 1875: 238). It is only the 'ancient form' that 'shows the intention of the giver of the name' (1875: 242). A third factor in rendering a form indecipherable may be that it is a foreign borrowing (1875: 245). The inquiry may come to a stop once 'names which are the elements of all other names and sentences' are identified, for these presumably 'cannot be supposed to be made up of other names' (1875: 246). The word *good* (*agathon*) can be understood as a combination of *admirable* (*agastos*) and *swift* (*thoos*). Probably *thoos* 'is made up of other elements, and these again of others'.

The end must be reached at some point: 'But if we take a word which is incapable of further resolution, then we shall be right in saying that we have at last reached a primarily element, which need not be resolved any further' (1875: 246). The 'principle of primary names' is that '[a]ll the names we have been explaining were intended to indicate the nature of things' (1875: 246). Following this, Socrates offers a mode of explanation for these primary elements based on the natural meanings of sounds, that is, a form of non-arbitrariness or mimesis (1875: 248ff.). The analogy is drawn and discussed in relation to the image: 'primitive nouns may be compared to pictures' (1875: 256). The dialogue does not come to any clear conclusion, circling back on itself in the closing sections.

For Harris and Taylor (1989: 18–19), the point of the dialogue is to insist that 'language demands our recognition of truth as independent and non-illusory'. If this were not the case, Socrates would have sacrificed his life in vain.

Ultimately, *Cratylus* privileges real definition: 'is there any better way of framing representations than by assimilating them to the objects as much as you can' (Jowett 1875: 259). These are 'sempiternal realities whose existence supplies the ultimate foundation for all human knowledge' (Harris and Taylor 1989: 19). The search for the ultimate constituents of language, suggestive though it may be, is insufficient. Even original names might be a contrivance attributed to divine help (Jowett 1875: 250); the legislator of names 'may be good or he may be bad' (Jowett 1875: 257). Plato stages the inadequacy of verbal (nominal) definition, showing that 'the task faced by etymology is virtually impossible' (Joseph 2000: 86). The *Cratylus* shows at the very outset of the Western tradition that real and verbal definition cannot be aligned.

Etymology as a technique of verbal definition, in the form of small-scale narratives about word meaning, found its culmination in the *Etymologiae* of Isidore, Bishop of Seville (c.560–636), a popular compilation drawing on a wide range of classical and Christian sources (Lindsay 1911, Barney et al. 2006). The term *homo* represents a metonymy, whereby the body stands for the union of body and soul (Brehaut [1912: 213] 2003:139):

> Homo is so named because he is made of *humus* (earth), as it is told in Genesis: 'Et creavit Deus hominem de humo terrae.' And the whole man made up of both substances, that is, of the union of soul and body, is termed *homo* by an abuse of the word. [...] Man is two-fold, the inner and the outer. The inner man is the soul (*anima*); the outer man, the body.

For Isidore, 'the road to knowledge was by way of words'. These were to be 'elucidated by reference to their origin rather than to the things they stood for' (Brehaut [1912] 2003: 18). 'The task of the etymologist was to identify original meanings. These would then attach themselves to the general scheme of truth' (Brehaut [1912] 2003: 18). For Isidore, etymology was a technique for presenting knowledge in encyclopaedic form. Isidore's investigations are locked within the received circle of etymological theorizing, that is, remain restricted to a specific form of verbal (nominal) definition.

Renaissance Humanism, with its emphasis on classical learning, reoriented intellectual energy towards issues of textual criticism and translation, in particular in relation to the Bible. St Jerome's Latin translation (the Vulgate), which had become canonical in western Christendom, was supplanted by more philologically informed renditions, such as those of Erasmus (1466–1536). Vernacular translation domesticated and transformed sacred texts in complex ways, further complicating the notion of literal meaning in its tension with allegorical interpretation. Erasmus was fond of citing, 'The Spirit gives life, but the flesh is of no use', finding there license for non-literal interpretation. But he was critical of its use as a justification for deviation from the frame of the text (MacCulloch

2005: 102). The leader of the reformation in Switzerland, Huldrych Zwingli (1484–1531) applied this text in rejecting what he saw as Luther's literal-minded understanding of the Eucharist and Christ's words at the Last Supper (MacCulloch 2005: 147). In Matthew 26:26–328 it is reported:

> And as they were eating, Jesus took bread, and blessed it, and brake it, and gave it to the disciples, and said, Take, eat; this is my body. And he took the cup, and gave thanks, and gave it to them, saying, Drink ye all of it; For this is my blood of the new testament, which is shed for many for the remission of sins.

The emergent Protestant denominations were deeply divided on this and other fundamental theological questions. The unitary interpretative authority of the Church was replaced by an uncertain mix of philology, close-reading, and a renewed emphasis on faith.

The rise of humanism, even within the framework of the Church, opened up questions of historicity, philological method, and interpretative authority. The early modern paradigm of universal history relied on etymology for tracing the descent and history of nations (Parsons 1767). In his *English Etymologies* (1847: vii), H. Fox Talbot (1800–1877) claimed that etymology could cast light on the general history of nations, 'their manners and customs', and 'ancient migrations and settlements'. Talbot was at the tail end of this historical paradigm. In the nineteenth century, a clear duality emerged between a professionalized academic discipline and an unruly, rebellious and imaginative form of mythical etymologizing. Walter Skeat (1835–1912) asserted that etymology 'depends no longer on barefaced and irresponsible assertion, but has been raised to the dignity of a science' (1912: 1). He poured scorn on Talbot's *English Etymologies* (Skeat 1912: 2, Talbot 1847).

Reviewing this history, Malkiel noted that etymology had always meant something like 'original meaning' (1993: 1). For example, the 'core meaning of a word' can be understood as 'something wholly independent of the passage of time and endowed with magic messages or mystic overtones' (1993: 1). With the rise of 'time-dominated disciplines, principally history', etymology was equated with 'previous meaning', 'earlier actually attested meaning', or 'earliest reconstructable meaning' rather than some primeval, pristine meaning. It became a 'strictly identificational discipline' where words were 'divested of any residual magic' (1993: 2). Etymology in this modern sense is about the past, that is, the 'shape the word at issue once possessed', rather than being concerned with telling people 'what to do at present or what to expect from the future' (1993: 2).

The divergence between these two kinds of etymology can be traced to Nietzsche (1844–1900), a classical philologist who turned etymology into a creative counter-discourse (Porter 2000, Pollack 2009). In his *On the Genealogy of Morals* ([1887] 2013: 17) Nietzsche discusses the origin and development of the opposition between *good* and *bad*, rejecting the assumed origin of these terms in a morality of usefulness or selflessness:

> What put me on the *right track* was this question: what is the true etymological meaning of the various terms for the idea 'Good' which have been

> coined in various languages? I then found that they all led back *to the same evolution of the same idea* – that everywhere 'aristocrat', 'noble' (in the social sense) is the root idea out of which necessarily developed 'good' in the sense of 'with aristocratic soul', 'noble' in the sense of 'with a noble soul', 'with a privileged soul' – a development which inevitably runs parallel with that other evolution, in which 'vulgar', 'plebian', 'low' are transformed finally into 'bad'.

Both Christianity ('slave mentality') and modern-democracy ('plebianism') were rejected, and the original caste nature of the distinction affirmed.

For Nietzsche, it is through the uncovering and reanimation of lost or obscured meanings that we grasp the vital essence of the *good*. Language is capable of seducing our understanding, through 'the fundamental fallacies which have become petrified within it' ([1887] 2013: 33). In relation to human action, it can lead us to believe that there is an agent who acts or a subject who wills, when there is just 'those very phenomena of impelling, willing, acting' ([1887] 2013: 32). Action in the world needed to be seen without false abstractions ([1887] 2013: 33):

> Now just as people distinguish between lightning and its flash, and, so interpret the latter as the *action* which is performed by a subject called lightning, so also does popular morality distinguish strength from the expression of strength, as though behind the strong man there existed some indifferent neutral substratum which enjoyed the freedom to express strength or not.

These misconceptions pervade even the language of science, which is 'a dupe of the tricks of language'. They persuade us that it is possible for the strong to act in a weak manner, and that we should blame birds of prey for following their own nature ([1887] 2013: 33). Action, process, and movement are prior to, or more fundamentally real than, the reified or artificial categories of actor, agent, or abstraction. To speak of an entity called lightening in the abstract is to suggest falsely that there exists such an entity independently of lightening events.

In a famous passage from the *Nachlass*, written in 1873 (Nietzsche 1954), Nietzsche's mistrust of language extends to an attack on the notion of literal meaning and the associated notion of truth (Hinman 1982). There is an unbridgeable gap between language and the real (Nietzsche 1954: 46):

> Every concept originates through our equating what is unequal. No leaf ever wholly equals another, and the concept 'leaf' is formed through an arbitrary abstraction from these individual differences, through forgetting the distinctions; and now it gives rise to the idea that in nature there might be something besides the leaves which would be 'leaf' – some kind of original form after which all leaves have been woven, marked, copied, colored, curled, and painted, but by unskilled hands, so that no copy

> turned out to be a correct, reliable, and faithful image of the original form.

In this sense all linguistic usage is metaphorical (1954: 46–47):

> What, then, is truth? A mobile army of metaphors, metonyms, and anthropomorphisms – in short, a sum of human relations which have been enhanced, transposed, and embellished poetically and rhetorically, and which after long use seem firm, canonical, and obligatory to a people: truths are illusions about which one has forgotten that this is what they are; metaphors which are worn out and without sensuous power; coins which have lost their pictures and now matter only as metal, no longer as coins.

Since language cannot literally represent reality, the real can best be represented by a dynamic and unfettered rhetoric, which challenges and breaks stale habits of language and mind.

One can trace the line of etymological thinking, wordplay and punning through literary modernism (James Joyce), psychoanalysis and the interpretation of dreams, slips of the tongue, etc. (Freud 1904) to Martin Heidegger's 'etymological web' (Eiland 1982) on to post-structuralism and literary deconstruction (Jacques Derrida, Paul de Man), where etymological play likewise plays a foundational if largely undertheorized role (see Paulhan 1953, Syrotinski 2011). Etymological play is held to break down verbal habits and illuminates deeper, more authentic or more dynamic relationships. For Ullmann (1966: 240, drawing on Wandruszka 1958), Heidegger's drawing of an etymological link between *Zeichen* ('sign') and *zeigen* ('to show'), *hell* ('clear') and *hallen* ('to resound') was illegitimate. The noun *Entschlossenheit* ('resoluteness') is even read as 'openness, opening up' since the prefix *ent* means to remove or take away and *schliessen* means 'to close'. Radical etymological thinking sees in reconfiguring language the potential for revitalization, as a means of re-energizing or even superseding worn-out linguistic categories. For the Nietzschean etymologist, we must go back to the roots of things in order to go forward, freed of the shackles of the accumulated language of false reification.

Atomism and compositionality

Atomism or atomic theory can be traced to ancient Greece as an account of the building-bricks of matter (Berryman 2016). It was revived in the seventeenth century in the form of ***mechanical atomism*** (Chalmers 2014: s.1). Robert Boyle (1627–1691) referred to the smallest units of matter as ***minima naturalia*** or ***prima naturalia*** (Chalmers 2014: s.1). If reality were formed out of ultimate elements, then an ideal language of real description would mirror that compositionality. The scientific revolution required a stable, universal, and systematic language of representation. This reflected 'a philosophical view of nature originally articulated by Aristotle' (Slaughter 1982: 3). In his *Essay towards a Real*

Character, and a Philosophical Language (1668), John Wilkins (1614–1672) set out the most famous of the universal languages (Emery 1948), though not the first (DeMott 1958). George Delgarno (1616–1687) in his *Ars Singorum* (1661) devised a generic conceptual language based on 1068 monosyllabic roots (Cram and Maat 2001). Wilkins sought to provide 'a distinct sign for each human notion, with the ideal of systematicity as with Dalgarno, but also with the ideal of exhaustiveness'; Dalgarno's aim was 'to provide not a taxonomy of human notions but the minimal set of elements and rules whereby those notions might be expressed' (Cram 1992: 198). Leibniz (1646–1716) proposed an *alphabetum cognitationum humanarum*, an 'alphabet of human thoughts' (Leibniz [1677] 1960), which did not represent the absolutely definitive simple or primitive ideas but was the best that humanity could do given its cognitive limitations (Poser 2016: 96).

Plans for ideal languages tend to falter once they are confronted with the problem of definition at bedrock level. In *Logic or the Art of Thinking*, the Port-Royal philosophers Antoine Arnauld (1612–1694) and Pierre Nicole (1625–1695) concluded that the attempt to define terms about which people were in agreement was pointless, if the term could be connected to 'a clear and distinct idea' ([1662] 1996: 64). For example, an intellectual definition of *time* distracted from the everyday understanding, one which was shared by both the 'learned and the ignorant alike', as when, for example, they are told 'that a horse takes less time to travel a league than a tortoise does'. Their conclusion was that not every word could be defined ([1662] 1996: 64):

> For in order to define a word it is necessary to use other words designating the idea we want to connect to the idea being defined. And if we wished to define the words used to explain that word, we would need still others and so on to infinity. Consequently, we necessarily have to stop at primitive terms which are undefined.

Hobbes grappled with the problem of defining basic terms, given that 'it was common to all sorts of method to proceed from known things to unknown' ([1640] 1999: 194). The problem was that conceptual analysis required 'that the terms of the definition are more simple and universal than the terms being defined', leaving a problem in the case of 'the most simple and universal' (Zarka 1996: 64–65). If ideas were not innate and universal, they must be derived from experience. Knowledge derived from the senses, however, gave superior knowledge of the whole than the parts, 'as when we see a man, the conception or whole idea of that man is first more known, than the particular idea of his being *figurate* ['of a determinate form'], *animate*, and *rational* (Hobbes [1655] 1839: 66–67). Hobbes's materialism led him to reject certain collocations as self-contradictory: '*Substance* and *Body*, signifie the same thing; and therefore *Substance incorporeall* are words, which when they are joined together, destroy one another, as if a man should say, an *Incorporeall Body*' ([1651] 1909: 303).

Compositionality in modern philosophy and its critics

The seventeenth century dream of a real language of science became once again a serious intellectual goal in the early twentieth century. Twentieth-century analytic philosophy was concerned with establishing stable links between literal meaning and reality (Klement 2016, Russell [1911] 2003: 94):

> The philosophy I espouse is *analytic*, because it claims that one must discover the simple elements of which complexes are composed, and that complexes presuppose simples, whereas simples do not presuppose complexes.

These components were free-standing or autonomous, and not changed by their interaction with other components when combined into complexes ([1911] 2003: 94):

> Many philosophers believe that the constituent of a complex, as such, is not exactly the same as what it is in itself, but is changed in becoming a constituent. This seems to me to rest on a confusion between the practical identity of people and things in everyday life, and logical identity.

There were 'simple beings in the universe', which formed relations within complexes. While 'every simple entity' was an atom, these were not physical objects but 'purely logical' entities. There were two classes of simples, namely *particulars* and *universals*. The ultimate aim was a logically perfect language that would correctly depict reality, stripped of metaphysical clutter (Russell 1918: 197):

> It is exceedingly difficult to make this point clear as long as one adheres to ordinary language, because ordinary language is rooted in a certain feeling about logic, a certain feeling that our primeval ancestors had, and as long as you keep to ordinary language you find it very difficult to get away from the bias which is imposed upon you by language.

Joseph (1996) refers to this as the 'metaphysical garbage' view of the relation of language to reality.

The logical positivism of the Vienna Circle sought a unification of the sciences and a universal language. Ordinary language had to be purged of its metaphysics in order to serve in the unification of knowledge. Otto Neurath (1882–1945), a member of the Vienna circle, was engaged in attempts to create an international picture language and in the design of a language-neutral visual system for conveying statistical and other information, involving what he termed *isotypes* (Neurath 1936, 1937). Neurath expressed the challenge facing the systematizer when dealing with the interlocking and interdefining nature of bedrock concepts (Neurath 1921, cited and translated in Nemeth and Stadler 1996: 35–36):

> That we always have to do with a whole network of concepts and not with concepts that can be isolated, puts any thinker in the difficult situation of having unceasing regard for the whole mass of concepts that he cannot even survey at once. […] We are like sailors who on the open sea must reconstruct their ship but are never able to start afresh from the bottom. Where a beam is taken away a new one must at once be put there, and for this the rest of the ship is used as support. In this way, by using the old beams and driftwood the ship can be shaped entirely anew, but only by gradual reconstruction.

It was not possible for the human intellect to question simultaneously the foundation of key concepts of ordinary language. One set of such concepts must be held constant in order for others to be brought into sceptical focus.

Compositionality as discussed in contemporary linguistics and linguistic philosophy is a feature of linguistic structure and a matter of verbal definition only. The principle of compositionality has been defined as follows (Kamp and Partee 1995: 135): 'The meaning of a complex expression is a function of the meanings of its parts and of their syntactic mode of combination'. This 'nearly uncontroversial' notion requires among other things a specification of 'the nature of the meanings of the smallest parts-that is, a theory of lexical semantics' (1995: 135). Szabó (2017) declares bluntly, 'Anything that deserves to be called a language must contain meaningful expressions built up from other meaningful expressions'. Central to compositionality is the notion of literal meaning as an ideal neutral reference point (see Toolan 1996), bracketed by etymological meaning (point of origin) and figurative meaning (extension through metaphor or other semantic process).

In Wittgenstein's *Tractatus*, the opening proposition is that ([1922] 1981: 1) 'The world is everything that is the case'. The world is made up of atomic facts of which things (*Dinge*) are constituent parts (1.1–2.012). The relationship between language and the world is envisaged as iconic, as a picture: 'The picture is a model of reality' (1981: 2.12). It follows that there is no systematic place for human subjectivity: 'The thinking, presenting subject; there is no such thing' (5.631) and 'The subject does not belong to the world, but it is a limit of the world' (5.632). Philosophy requires 'a non-psychological I' (5.641) so that 'The philosophical I is not the man, not the human body or the human soul of which psychology treats, but the metaphysical subject, the limit – not part of the world' (5.641). The ideal of an austere and transparent language requires a compositional syntax (5.45):

> If there are logical primitive signs a correct logic must make clear their position relative to one another and justify their existence. The construction of logic *out of* its primitive signs must become clear.

The tone of the *Tractatus* reflects a cultish impersonality.

In the *Philosophical Investigations*, Wittgenstein took up both a relativist and a contextualist stance (Wittgenstein [1953] 2009). The grounding of language, now seen as an activity, is in community. As Ernst Gellner expressed it, the *Tractatus* envisages a 'world without culture', in that beneath the surface of individual languages there is uniformity: 'genuine referential content has the same form in all of them' (Gellner 2004: 68). The dramatic turn represented by the later Wittgenstein was to embrace an entirely contrary notion, namely that 'human thought and language' were 'embodied in systems of social custom, each tied to the community which employs it, and each logically ultimate, self-validating, and beyond any other possible validation' (Gellner 2004: 72). This can be seen in the dependence of words and their meanings on *language games* within *forms of life*: 'Here the term "language-*game*" is meant to bring into prominence the fact that the *speaking* of language is part of an activity, or of a form of life' ([1953] 2009: 15e). The meanings of words arise within, and are dependent on, distinct forms of life (*Lebensform*). In linguistics, this became the idea that '[w]e dissect nature along lines laid down by our native language' (Whorf 1956: 213). Joseph (1996) terms this the 'magical key' view of language, in that, through an analysis of a particular language, we can discern the reality that culture or group constructs for itself.

The early Wittgenstein proposed an individualistic and atomistic vision of knowledge, based on '[s]eparation, segregation, analysis, and independence'. The later Wittgenstein, by contrast, evokes an organic or collectivist understanding of knowledge, in which elements can only be understood in their relation to one another: 'the constituent elements form a system, whose parts are in intimate and intricate relation with each other. Separation of all separables is not the heart of wisdom, but of folly' (Gellner 2004: 4–6). In a compositional system, such as that of the *Tractatus,* the model is generated bottom-up, in that the primary units of meaning (and their corresponding objects) exist independently of their assimilation into more complex structures. In a model such as that of the *Philosophical Investigations*, what appear to be bedrock or primitive terms are generated by the community and arise out of its holistic or *Gestalt* nature. If we look for a stable semantic core in the meaning of a word like *game*, we will not find it (Wittgenstein [1953] 2009: 36e–38e):

> Consider, for example, the activities that we call 'games'. I mean board-games, card-games, ball-games, athletic games, and so on. What is common to them all? – Don't say: 'They *must* have something in common, or they would not be called "games"' – but *look and see* whether there is something common to all. For if you look at them you won't see something that is common to *all*, but similarities, affinities, and a whole series of them at that.

This could be read as a plea for real definition over verbal (nominal) definition, in that we are enjoined to look past the assumption that a word has a core of stable meaning to the range of activities that it refers to. In so doing we can observe that these activities do not have a common feature or features, but rather display a network of criss-crossing affinities. But this raises the further question as to why we would look at just those activities designated by the word *game*, that is, why we would frame our looking at the world through the lens of word *game*, as if there was nonetheless an intuitive coherence to the set of activities designated by the word, rather than these being merely a motley set of arbitrarily grouped forms of behaviour. This is the classic nominalist objection to abstract categories.

New Semantic Metalanguage

Contemporary universalist approaches to meaning parallel in some respects seventeenth-century universal language schemes, as well as modern attempts to devise and introduce artificial or auxiliary languages such as Basic English, Esperanto, Volapük, and Gestuno (a sign language variety). Post-Second World War, there was considerable excitement about machine translation, based on identifying an underlying set of universal concepts that could mediate between languages (Hutchins 1995). Within linguistics proper, one atomic approach to meaning was componential analysis, a form of structural semantics. The aim was to identify a set of binary components or features for semantic analysis, a technique that was also applied in the study of kinship structures in anthropology (Lamb 1965, Burling 1964). Semantic analysis dealt with 'the conceptual units out of which the meanings of linguistic utterances are built' (Goodenough 1956: 196). Common examples of such features are +MALE or +ADULT in defining *man*, and +ABSTRACT for ideas or concepts. These components were held to be language-independent, in that they were abstract features realized in patterns of presence and absence in different languages. An optimal system would allow for the fewest possible features compatible with the complexity of the phenomenon being analyzed: 'the greatest possible conceptual economy with the greatest possible explanatory and descriptive power' (Katz and Fodor 1963: 190). Any metatheory for semantics 'must be a theory which represents semantic universals' (Katz and Fodor 1963: 208). These components were to provide criteria for semantic anomalies, such as the phrases *female uncle* or *spinster insecticide* (Warmbrōd 1974), and for setting out the folk classifications as part of *ethnoscience*. A question like 'What "things" (in this culture, using its language) are considered animals?' would be used as input to a structural model of the culture (Werner 1972: 273).

This dream of a universal set of language-neutral components is generally expressed more cautiously today (Immler 1991, Fintel and Matthewson 2008). The theory of semantic universals is now associated in particular with the publications of Anna Wierzbicka, beginning in the 1970s with a work entitled *Semantic Primitives* (Wierzbicka 1972), and of Cliff Goddard (Goddard 2011). This approach is known as the *Natural Semantic Metalanguage* (NSM) approach. A further element of the NSM programme is the promotion of Minimal English. This is 'an English version of the common core of all (or nearly all) languages which has come to light through a decades-long program of cross-linguistic and intralinguistic investigations undertaken in the NSM approach to language and culture' (Goddard and Wierzbicka 2011: 2). Semantic primitives are explained as themselves inexplicable (Wierzbicka 1997: 25):

> The elements which can be used to define the meaning of words (or any other meanings) cannot be defined themselves; rather, they must be accepted as 'indefinibilia', that is, as semantic primes, in terms of which all complex meanings can be coherently represented.

Meaning 'cannot be described without a set of semantic primitives', that is, without the use of semantic primes 'in terms of which all complex meanings can be coherently represented' (1997: 25). Examples of semantic primes include (Wierzbicka 2015: 385):

> I, YOU, SOMEONE, SOMETHING~THING, PEOPLE, BODY (substantives); KIND, PART (relational substantives); THIS, THE SAME, OTHER~ELSE (determiners); ONE, TWO, MUCH~MANY, LITTLE~FEW, SOME, ALL (quantifiers); GOOD, BAD (evaluators); BIG, SMALL (descriptors); KNOW, THINK, WANT, DON'T WANT, FEEL, SEE, HEAR (mental predicates); SAY, WORDS, TRUE (speech); DO, HAPPEN, MOVE, TOUCH (actions, events, movement, contact).

The NSM lexicon is derived from empirical research into individual languages (Wierzbicka 2006: 1):

> Results to date strongly support the original hypothesis that all languages share a universal core, both in their lexicon and in their grammar; a core which constitutes the bedrock of human understanding, communication, and translation.

NSM involves 'paraphrase without circularity', avoiding the entanglement of explanation in definitional circularity: an 'ideal metalanguage for the purpose of semantics would consist of words which are simple and easy to understand' (Goddard 2017: 3.1.1).

Animal is explained as follows: '[X is an animal.] = There are many kinds of living things that can feel and can move when they want. X is one of these'.[1] One level of analysis for such concepts is termed a *semantic template*, a mode originally developed for 'artefact and natural terms'. Animal terms are defined in relation to certain sections: [a] CATEGORY, [b] HABITAT, [c] SIZE, [d] BODY, [e] BEHAVIOR, [f] SOUND, [g] RELATION TO PEOPLE. These descriptions are intended to capture what is psychologically real from the point of view of the native speaker, rather than the objective qualities of the referent (Goddard 2010: 469–470). In other words, NSM is concerned with verbal (nominal) rather than real definition.

NSM takes an interesting stance in relation to the bedrock concepts *self* and *person*. In a 1993 article, Wierzbicka analyzed debates about the universality of the concept *self.* Lutz (1985) had critiqued the Anglocentric bias of ethnopsychology, but, as Wierzbicka notes, even critical approaches are dependent for their key reference points on the English expressions *self* and *emotion* (1993: 205). Kondo (1990: 42) had pointed to the difficulty of separating anthropological investigations from 'the semantic load of the word "self", when agency, boundedness, and fixity are indelibly inscribed in the sedimented linguistic history of the term'. *Self* was often presented as if it were 'divorced from specific historical, cultural, and political contexts', and therefore as embodying 'the notion of some abstract essence of selfhood we can describe by enumerating distinctive features'. To invoke 'culture and self', 'a concept of self' or a 'notion of person' connects to 'static, essentialized global traits' (Kondo 1990: 36). This dismantling of the unitary model of the self would rule out any cross-cultural analysis, leading to the *reductio ad absurdum* that 'all science is ethnoscience' (Spiro 1984: 327, cited Wierzbicka 1993: 207). Universals are identifiable through their lexicalization, in that 'a word provides tangible evidence for the existence of a concept' (1993: 209). A concept which is not lexicalized systematically across languages is a weak candidate for universal status (Wierzbicka 1993: 209):

> When someone suggests, for example, that 'self' may be a universal human concept, which just happens to be lexically embodied in English but not in other languages of the world, and that, therefore, it is legitimate to use 'self' as a conceptual tool for analyzing languages and cultures, this is little more than a thinly veiled form of anglocentrism: why should 'universal human concepts' just happen to be lexically embodied in English, rather than in Ifaluk, Ilongot, or Pitjantjat-jara?

Kondo had expressed similar scepticism about the universality of the concept of *person* (1990: 34–35):

> Are the terms 'self' and 'person' the creations of our own linguistic and cultural conventions? If 'inner' processes are culturally conceived, their very existence mediated by cultural discourses, to what extent can we talk of 'inner, reflective essence' or 'outer, objective world' except as culturally meaningful, culturally specific constructs?

Wierzbicka, however, draws a key distinction between *self* and *person. Self* was culturally specific, whereas *person* was not (1993: 210):

> Because (as evidence suggests) all languages distinguish lexically between 'someone' and 'something,' between 'who' and 'what,' the idea that the notion of 'person' ('someone') is the product of Western culture is simply not tenable.

Unlike *self, person* has 'referential solidity' and 'essential unity'; *person* should also not be equated with *I* (a mistake made by Marcel Mauss [1938] 1985): 'In fact, "person" and "I" are two distinct concepts, which (as far as we know) are both (separately) lexicalized in all languages of the world' (1993: 211). *Mind*, however, is 'a rather unique creation of the English language, without equivalents in the other languages of the world' (1993: 212). If, as Bruner (1990: 39) suggests, personhood is itself 'a constituent concept of our folk psychology', this is true across cultures since 'the idea of a "person" who "thinks," "wants," "feels," and "knows" (as well as "says" and "does" various things) appears to be universal' (Wierzbicka 1993: 213).

Wierbicka notes that Clifford Geertz (1984: 126) had defined the Western concept of person as 'bounded, unique, more or less integrated motivational and cognitive universe, a dynamic center of awareness, emotion, judgement, and action organized into a distinctive whole'. However, this formulation could cover the universal understanding of person, the cultural differences that overlay it notwithstanding (Wierzbicka 1993: 214). The quotation continued: 'But at least some conception of what a human individual is, as opposed to a rock, an animal, a rainstorm, or a god, is, so far as I can see, universal' (Geertz 1984:126). It is not the notion of 'human individual' that is universally lexicalized, but rather the concept of *people*: 'the latter is, therefore, presumably more basic, and more salient, than the former' (1993: 220).

Cognitive linguistics and metaphor

Within the Western tradition, the problem with metaphorical language is that it is literally false and therefore potentially misleading. The *locus classicus* for this view is found in Aristotle's *Poetics* ([c. 335 BCE] Bernadette and Davis 2002: 51):

> Metaphor is the application of a word belonging to something else either from the genus [*genos*] to a species [*eidos*], or from the species to the genus, or from species to a species, or according to analogy.

Metaphor transgresses against the normative hierarchy of categories expressed in *per genus et differentiam* definition, as expounded in Aristotle's *Categories*, whereby *man* is defined as 'a rational animal'. The *genus* is the category of *animal* and the distinguishing feature is rationality (Ackrill 2002). As Harris points out, Aristotle's discussion assumes that there is a pre-existing correlation in place between words and their meanings, which metaphor then disrupts. Further, the different sub-types of metaphor all involve analogy, rather than being separate and distinct types of metaphor as Aristotle suggests (Harris 1998a: 90). Fear and mistrust of metaphor is a pervasive component of logophobia, a recognizable theme from Bacon and Locke (see Harris and Hutton 2007: 27), and from Orwell ([1946] 1969) to Chomsky – in his political writings (Chomsky 2002). Noting that what one person called *wisdom,* another called *fear*, what some saw as *cruelty*, other viewed as *justice,* Hobbes warned that 'such names can never be true grounds of any ratiocination'. The same was true of metaphor and other figurative usage, though 'these are less dangerous, because they profess their inconstancy; which the other do not' ([1651] 1909: 32).

Personification is often the target of logophobic criticism since it appears to blur a fundamental ontological divide between beings that possess free-will and agency, and the rest of creation. The *Oxford English Dictionary* (OED) defines personification as:

> The attribution of human form, nature, or characteristics to something; the representation of a thing or abstraction as a person (esp. in a rhetorical figure or a metaphor); (*Art*) the symbolic representation of a thing or abstraction by a human figure.

Interestingly, this definition identifies personification as operating primarily to reconceptualize or reframe objects or abstractions. *Anthropomorphism* by contrast, as defined in the OED, involves the 'attribution of human form, character, or attributes to God or a god' or the 'attribution of human personality or characteristics to something non-human, as an animal, object, etc.' Hobbes remarked in *Leviathan* ([1651] 1909: 86) that in matters of religion, which concern *powers invisible,* 'there is almost nothing that has a name that has not been esteemed amongst the Gentiles, in one place or another, a god or devil; or by their poets feigned to be animated, inhabited, or possessed by some spirit or other'. In the context of psychology, anthropomorphism has been defined as a way of conceptualizing non-human, agentive behaviour: '[i]mbuing the imagined or real behavior of nonhuman agents with humanlike characteristics, motivations, intentions, and emotions' (Epley, Waytz and Cacioppo 2007: 864). Through anthropomorphism, different animal species are given human-like qualities, with foxes being *wily* or *crafty*, owls *wise*, bees *industrious*, and lions *regal* in their role as *king of the jungle* or the masters of the *animal kingdom*.

Hume [1757] 2007c: 127) understood anthropomorphism as a response to the unknowability of fate: 'There is an universal tendency among mankind to conceive all beings like themselves, and to transfer to every object, those qualities, with which they are familiarly acquainted, and of which they are intimately conscious'. In the case of *idolatry*, the human possessor of an idol becomes in effect the possessed (Lamb 2011: 78). Treating language as having autonomy, power and agency can itself be seen as a kind of idolatry. Bacon's termed *idols of the Marketplace* confusions created by words ([1620] 2000: 48):

> For men believe that their reason controls words. [...] And words are mostly bestowed to suit the capacity of the common man, and they dissect things along the lines most obvious to the common understanding. And when a sharper understanding, or more careful observation, attempts to draw those lines more in accordance with nature, words resist.

For Charles Ogden, language was 'essentially the creation of savages', who, for all their merits, held 'less advanced views on the subtler aspects of science and jurisprudence' (1932: cxxi). *Word-magic* was the ultimate target of Ogden and Richards's *The Meaning of Meaning* (1923, Hutton 1995). For Ernst Cassirer (1874–1945), this view was found in the works of Max Müller and Herbert Spencer who saw mythical thinking as a disease of language (Cassirer 1946: 22): 'The worship of conspicuous objects, conceived as persons, results from linguistic errors'.

Within the cognitivist framework, 'the essence of metaphor is understanding and experiencing one thing in terms of another' (Lakoff and Johnson 2003: 5). Cognitive linguists reject the notion that metaphor is misleading or mere stylistic adornment, emphasizing the centrality of concrete domains (spatial orientation, the human body and its senses, the earth's landscape) in our conceptual make-up, with these understood as mapping onto abstract domains. Abstract ideas are given form by their expression in terms of concrete objects (Lakoff and Johnson 2003: 34):

> we conceive of our experiences in terms of objects, substances, and containers in general, without specifying exactly what kind of object, substance, or container is meant [...]. In general, ontological metaphors enable us to see more sharply delineated structure where there is very little or none.

The distinction between *literal* and *non-literal* (i.e. *figurative*) meaning is fundamental within metaphor studies but also highly problematic. As noted by Saeed (2003: 15), many semantics textbooks assume the distinction 'but attempting to define it soon leads us into some difficult and theory-laden decisions'. At first sight it is a 'common-sense' distinction, distinguishing 'between instances where the speaker speaks in a neutral, factually accurate way, and instances where the speaker deliberately describe something in untrue or impossible terms in order to achieve special effects' (Saeed 2003: 15). However 'the vocabulary of language is littered with fossilized metaphors' and 'this continuing process [of fossilization] makes it difficult to decide the point at which the use of a word is literal rather than figurative' (2003: 15). At one level, Lakoff and Johnson (2003) reject the distinction, seeing 'metaphor as an integral part of human categorization: a basic way of organizing our thoughts about the world' (Saeed 2003: 15). Nonetheless Lakoff and Johnson's model relies on a binary distinction between *source* and *target* domain. Typically the more concrete domain provides the source for the more abstract, implying a mapping from a more concrete to a less concrete meaning.

When cognitive metaphor theorists use the term *personification*, they start from the well-defined sociobiological being, the human person, attributes of which are projected onto objects, animals, processes, and ideas. For Lakoff and Johnson (2003: 34), personification is 'a general category that covers a very wide range of metaphors' having in common that 'they are extensions of ontological metaphors' which 'allow us to make sense of the phenomena in the world in human terms–terms that we can understand on the basis of our own motivations, goals, actions, characteristics'. This viewpoint implies comprehension of the human, from the *inside* as it were, as offering a secure foundation for the challenge of grasping processes and actions (2003: 34):

> The INFLATION IS AN ADVERSARY metaphor [...] gives rise to and justifies political and economic actions on the part of our government; declaring war on inflation, setting targets, calling for sacrifices, installing a new chain of command, etc.

Personification has its counterpart in depersonification within the ladder of being (Lakoff and Turner 1989: 192–193):

> Sometimes we understand people in terms of animals or other lower-order forms of being. Sometimes we understand those lower-order forms of being in terms of people. [...] There we have well-elaborated schemas characterizing what animals are like, and we usually understand these characteristics, metaphorically, in terms of the characteristics of human beings.

For Lakoff and Turner (1989: 194), while metaphors create mergers between the distinctions on the Great Chain of Being, the underlying distinctions themselves are well defined and stable:

> Animals act instinctively, and different kinds of animals have different kinds of instinctive behavior. We comprehend their behavior in terms of human behavior, and we use the language of human character traits to describe such behavior. [...] It is so natural for us to understand nonhuman attributes in terms of our own human character that we often have difficulty realizing that such characterization of animals are metaphorical.

Thus, dogs are not really loyal, and cannot display courage, since animals lack 'a moral sense and a capacity for moral judgment' and act out of instinct (1989: 194). In a phrase like 'Achilles is a lion', the metaphor relies on the metaphorical understanding of what is an instinctive trait in animals 'in terms of a character trait of humans'. The steadfastness of Achilles is seen as 'unchanging and reliable as if it were an animal instinct' and the idea that courage is the quintessential feature of lions is mapped onto Achilles (1989: 195–6).

One objection might be that this model is essentially static, reliant as it is on the reification of meanings that are 'read off' decontextual examples. The relation of metaphorical or figurative meaning to non-metaphorical or literal meaning is fundamentally obscure. Literal meaning blurs into etymological meaning, especially when close semantic description is accompanied by morphological analysis: *to undermine* can be literally or etymologically understood as *under* + *mine*, and the activity in question as destroying the foundations of an opinion or a person's self-esteem by digging beneath its surface and causing a collapse. If we talk of the *family* of a lion or the *society* of a beehive, is this metaphorical language? Do animals have *parents* and *children* in the same way that human beings do? Can a dog be literally a *family member*? (Gaita 2003: 19–20) Do human emotional terms (*anger, frustration, love, hate, humour*) apply to animal behaviour?

According to metaphor theory, the basic understanding of personhood is extended only metaphorically to animals, objects, weather systems, social processes, and abstractions of various kinds. The implication is that personification is a device that creates or affirms fictional entities, what has been referred to as 'metaphysically impossible entities'. This is a controversial position (see Nolan 2015, Bourne and Bourne 2018), suggesting as it does a kind of conceptual (rather than philosophical or religious) animism. Personhood or personality is an explanatory mode, linking the known or knowable to the less known, or to the difficult or impossible to grasp. Personhood is held constant as a known quantity in order to make sense of other phenomena. But in the case of *person* and therefore *personification*, the cognitive linguistics model breaks down since mask and self are mutually constituting (or, at least, neither is logically or conceptually prior to the other), given that the literal meaning in some sense is 'mask'. Put another way, cognitive linguistics represents a form of etymological reasoning, in which the literal is both historically and conceptually prior to the metaphorical, and therefore it cannot accommodate the kind of ambiguity of priority found in *person*.

Cognitive linguistics defines itself against what it terms an *objectivist* theory of meaning, that is, one that treats meaning 'as a relation between sentences and objective (mind-independent) reality' (Johnson 1987: 173). A non-objectivist or cognitive semantics draws on three key notions: understanding, imagination, and embodiment. Against arguments that these must be transcended 'in order to guarantee the possibility of objectivity', Johnson argues that 'at the very least, image-schematic structures and their metaphorical projections have a shared, public character'. There exist 'meaning gestalts related to structures of bodily experience that we all can share' (1987: 175). As Toolan observes (1996: 87), the rejection of abstract objectivism in cognitive linguistics represented 'in no way a rejection of collective categorization itself, but rather as emphasis on different roots of categorization (experience in the body) and a different kind of categorization (prototypical etc. rather than absolute)'.

Metaphor, personification, and religious language

The notion that religious language is a distinct linguistic domain is a product of secular modernity. In contemporary theology, language has become, as a consequence, a key focus and source of anxiety. Logical positivism saw religious language as not false but meaningless since it did not express propositions that could be empirically verified (Ayer 1946, Carnap 1974). Yet if human beings as sign-makers make meaning, then religious language is no more or less meaningful than any other kind of discourse. Nonetheless, in relation to language, 'religions face chronic dilemmas posed by the tensions between transcendence and the situated and concrete nature of verbal practices' (Keane 1997: 49). Religious language can be described as a medium through which 'the presence and activity of beings that are otherwise unavailable to the senses can be made presupposable, even compelling, in ways that are publicly yet also subjectively available to people as members of social groups' (Keane 1997: 49). In *Metaphorical Theology*, Sally McFague related the problem of religious language to the secular reality which forms the basis of daily experience, consequent on the disappearance of the 'sacramental universe' (1982: 1): 'For most of us, it is not a question of being sure of God while being unsure of our language about God. Rather, we are unsure both at the experiential and the expressive levels'. For McFague, religious language is inevitably shaped by its historical and cultural context: to treat the Biblical text literally is to make an idol of Scripture (1982: 4). Biblical language consists of images and metaphors, just as theological language consists of models. At the same time there is the recognition 'that when we try to speak of God there is nothing which resembles what we can conceive when we say that word' (Simone Weil, cited McFague 1982: 194).

Given this uncertainty in relation to religious language, metalinguistic labels such as *metaphor*, *personification*, and *anthropomorphism* are themselves of uncertain status. Theologically, one might argue that the notion of God as personal is not a case of personification or of anthropomorphism since God is the ultimate personal being, and humans are imperfect beings whose personhood is derivative: 'So God created man in his own image, in the image of God created he him; male and female created he them' (Genesis 1: 26). As we have seen, *person* does not have a literal meaning in any straightforward sense, and therefore the personhood of God, on one view, is not derived analogically or metaphorically from the human quality. Rather, human personhood is derivative from God as a personal being.

The attribution of personhood to God, and the nature if any of that personhood, is a matter of theological controversy, given the mainstream view that it is the members of the Trinity who are persons. The personhood of God 'is not a kind of eternal substance that somehow splits itself into three modes of being, but God is in essence *personal*'. In contradistinction to Boethius's individualistic definition of personhood ('an individual substance of a rational kind'), personhood should be understood as relational, as 'being-in-communion with others' (van der Kooi and van den Brink 2017: 259). If a person at all, God is generally characterized as a *person without a body*. However, in relation to the Hebrew Bible, Sommer (2009) argues that God is, contrary to a widespread assumption, understood as literally embodied.

In contemporary Christian debate, the status of the phrase *person without a body* is controversial. Swinburne (1979) has argued that God is a unique class of person, that is, person without a body. Herrmann (2004: 111) denies that this is a meaningful proposition:

> The word 'body' is empirically grounded, and is also true of the word 'person'. The phrase 'person without a body', on the other hand, is not empirically grounded, if we leave aside legal persons. (In the case of legal persons,

> the empirical ground is an organization, company, association, or similar). If we leave aside the legal sense of the word 'person' then the usual meaning of 'person' – as opposed to the meaning philosophers speak about – refers to a human being with a body.

Herrmann has been criticized, in turn, for employing a positivist theory of how language relates to reality (Kraal 2014).

The Catholic commentator Edward Feser (2014) labels the view that God is a person without a body *theistic personalism*, seeing in it a reduction of God to 'an instance of a kind', that is, of the genus *person*, albeit a unique kind of person, and entailing reduction to the status of creature rather than creator. God should be seen as 'pure actuality, subsistent being itself, absolutely simple, immutable, and eternal'. To the criticism that this renders God *impersonal*, Feser responds:

> It is also simply false to imply [...] that Thomists and other critics of theistic personalism regard God as 'impersonal.' When classical theists [...] say that God is not 'a person,' they do NOT mean that God is impersonal, an 'it' rather than a 'he.' On the contrary, most classical theists, including all Thomists, would say that among the divine attributes are intellect, will, omniscience, freedom, and love. Naturally then, they regard God as personal rather than impersonal, since nothing impersonal could intelligibly be said to possess these attributes. As I have said many times, the problem with the thesis that 'God is a person' is not the word 'person,' but rather the word 'a'.

In the background is a profound tension between the Greek ontological categories and Christian personalism: 'The word *hypostasis* signified not only persons, but things' (Letham 2004: 321).

Personhood is also a theological issue in relation to the devil. Historically the devil is the personification of evil (Russell 1987). This gives rise to the question of whether Satan is properly referred to as a *person* (van der Kooi and van den Brink 2017: 333–4):

> God is person in *optima* forma, and we are persons in an imperfect way as bearers of the image of God. God is therefore the original person (*analogans*); all other persons can be viewed as such only in a secondary sense (as being similar, or *analogata*). God is the ultimate person who, as the Giver of life, makes us into persons, into responsive and responding beings. This view makes personhood a meaningful theological and salvific concept. The figure of Satan falls far short of this concept of personhood. [...] The devil is 'unperson' or 'antiperson'.

The exact status of Satan is not determinable by human beings: 'As creatures, we are unable to provide an exact ontological definition of the opposite of God as the Giver of life'.

When the language of human description is applied to God, this must, in some sense, be received or interpreted as anthropomorphic since God, while *personal* (or even the 'personal being *par excellence*', Letham 2004: 374), is not an individual human being. One distinction made is between ascriptions of *bodily predicates* (as when the 'the Son sits on the right hand of the Father'), which are almost universally conceived of as purely metaphorical, and *mentalistic predicates* (statements such as 'God knows' or 'God loves'), which some theologians treat as literally true (Kenny 2014). The question becomes that of understanding this anthropomorphic language, with the awareness that it does not necessarily imply a direct parallel between an individual human being and God. When God created the world, as described in Genesis I, it was done through utterances, that is, acts of speaking and naming. God is described not only as creating but also as moving and evaluating. God displays emotions such as anger, in addition to love, as well as being spoken of as having a physical body (Exodus 33: 21–23):

> And the LORD said, Behold, there is a place by me, and thou shalt stand upon a rock: And it shall come to pass, while my glory passeth by, that I will put thee in a clift of the rock, and will cover thee with my hand while I pass by: And I will take away mine hand, and thou shalt see my back parts: but my face shall not be seen.

The question of *univocity of being* in relation to personhood is one of the most complex in the history of Christianity. The classical view of the Trinity emphasizes the doctrines of 'divine aseity, immutability, impassibility, simplicity, eternity, and the substantial unity of the divine persons'. Relational or social trinitarianism takes the Trinity as a model of community and, to varying degrees, sees God as involved in a mutual process of *becoming* together with humanity (Dolezal 1982: 1ff.). Social Trinitarians see the personhood of the Trinity as univocal with human personhood.

Phrases like *God the Father* raise issues of theologio-linguistic personification, as well as facing challenge from feminist theologians (McFague 1993, Ramshaw 1995, DesCamp and Sweetser 2005). The western Christian church rejects any suggestion of subordination or of temporal sequence in the relationship of God the Father to the Son, reflecting a denial of univocity at least in this domain. Yet if Jesus is the *Son of God*, what kind of metaphor is that, if *metaphor* is the correct term? And if we do not use human beings as a reference point for personhood, how are we to orient ourselves in contemplating the divine persons? The theological dilemma reflects the extremes of total ineffability on one side and misleading analogy on the other. The *love* of God for humanity is presumptively a different entity from the love that humans have for one another, and that might be said to differ again from the love that a pet dog shows for its puppies or for human beings. This also raises an important translation question in relation to Greek terms for *love*. The three most important are *agape* ('ideal or unconditional love', 'charity'), *eros* ('sexual love'), and *philia* ('friendship').

Crystal argues for a *signpost* view of descriptions of God (1965: 136):

> The anthropomorphic language suggests a point of immediate comparison, so that human understanding can be channelled in the right direction rather than not at all; the comparison is not intended to be complete or precise. God is never given a specific one-to-one correlation with the human condition.

Alston (1989: 64–66) sums up the way God has been described in terms of increasing fundamental otherness: '(A) Incorporeality (B) Infinity. […] (C) Timelessness. (D) Absolute simplicity. No composition of any sort. (E) Not a being (God is rather "Being-itself")'. Alston considers a number of ways in which 'creaturely terms' can be used to talk about God. He argues that 'common possession of abstract features is compatible with as great a difference as you like in the way in which these features are realized' so that we can call a meeting and a train of thought 'orderly'. So if we ascribe the same property or activity to a person and to God, there remains an abstract feature in common, even though for God to *make something* is quite different from what it means for a human being: 'It is something like the way in which a man and a wasp may both be *trying to reach a goal*, even though what it is for the one to try is enormously different from what it is for the other'.

Rowan Williams denies that religious language is distinctive in its reliance on metaphor (2008: x):

> Metaphor is omnipresent, certainly in scientific discourse (selfish genes, computer modelings of brain processes, not to mention the magnificent extravagances of theoretical physics), and its omnipresence ought to warn us against the fiction that there is a language that is untainted and obvious for any discipline.

Religious metaphor has been defended in terms of collective meaning-making in the face of the 'utter inability to comprehend God' (Soskice 1985: x). The Christian, like the scientist, 'makes claims on the basis of experience which, although different from the kind on which scientific judgments are based, is experience none the less'. This experience is of two kinds. The first kind was a 'dramatic or pointed religious experience'; the second involved 'the diffuse experiences which form the subject of subsequent metaphysical reflection', such as 'the experience of cause which prompts us to postulate the uncaused, the experience of order which prompts us to postulate an ordering agent, and so on' (Soskice 1985: 150).

A parallel debate exists about anthropomorphism in relation to animals (Mitchell, Thompson and Miles 1997). Unlike with God, animal behaviour is directly observable; unlike God, animals have physical bodies. But the vocabulary with which animal behaviour is described or analyzed, in particular the attribution of cognitive processes, emotions, plans, and intentions, inevitably draws in part on concepts that are applied to humans (see discussion in Andrews 2011). As Fisher (1996: 3) suggests, anxieties about anthropomorphism relate directly to Christianity's suspicion of primitive literalism, as well as to non-modern explanations of natural phenomena; yet, '[e]ven if humans are in a different category than other animals, it doesn't follow that to compare them with other animals is a category mistake' (1996: 4). The wider question is whether linguistic norms reflect, or should reflect, real or factual boundaries between classes of entity.

Conclusion

Hume's insistence that what was at stake in philosophy was not a mere 'dispute of words' is telling. The form of intellectual reflexivity involved in investigating the self made distinguishing between definitional questions and ontological inquiry a problematic undertaking to say the least. Nonetheless the distinction between linguistic disputes and real philosophical issues is a repeated theme (Hume [1777] 1912: 155): 'Nothing is more usual than for philosophers to encroach upon the province of grammarians; and to engage in disputes of words, while they imagine that they are handling controversies of the deepest importance and concern'. A question that was 'merely verbal', Hume argued, 'cannot possibly be of any importance' ([1777] 1912: 157). Harris takes Hume to task (2009b: 46): 'What makes Hume such an unreliable guide to knowledge is that he just does not see the language problem at all', assuming language to be a transparent medium. Philosophers, like lawyers, have tended to rely on a conceptual division of labour so that the analysis of philosophical problems can draw on a prior description of a stable ordinary language, this being the province of grammarians, lexicographers, and linguists (Harris 1998b, Hutton 2014, 2018).

John Locke's underlying approach to language was psychocentric, in contrast to Bacon's reocentrism (Harris 2009b: 31). For Locke, problems arise in the relation of words to ideas. In the absence of innate ideas, we are left with the realization of thoughts in words ([1690] 1975: 574):

> Because it is unavoidable, in treating of mental Propositions, to make use of words: and then the Instances given of *Mental Propositions*, cease immediately to be barely Mental *and* become *Verbal.*

Rather than the tangle of words and things, we have the confusion of words and ideas.

The cases of both God and of higher animals offer a profound challenge in terms of linguistic usage. A term like *father* is problematic in theology when used of God, and in zoology when used of an animal. Nothing in linguistic theory gets us any closer to an answer to this problem, not least because no amount of analysis, investigation, or semantic analysis offers clarity on ontologically appropriate usage. Compositional models of meaning leave us ultimately in a field of circularity or tautology; universal semantics fails at precisely the moment when concepts become contentious; metaphor theory assumes that it can identify the known, before characterizing the less known or the unknown. Lurking behind all these approaches is the unarticulated tension between real and verbal definition. The impossibility of distinguishing between these two modes reflects the overweening ambition of the Western tradition in relation to bedrock thinking. Stipulative definition is used to make ontological claims, and ontological claims are invoked in support of stipulated definition.

Note

1 learnthesewordsfirst.com/Lesson-3C.html#3-10.

3 Integrationism and systems theory

Introduction to integrationism

Integrationism is anti-foundational, in that it denies that meaning-making is carried out on the basis of independently established values or givens, whether biological, cognitive, or social. Language or languages lack a stable ontology; they do not exist in the abstract, beyond the sign-making practices that constitute them. In this integrationism runs counter to mainstream linguistic theory, for which it is both a methodological and a theoretical assumption that linguistic values are established at the level of system or *langue* (Saussure 1922). Harris has labelled this systems view the *language myth*. The myth is composed of two interrelated ideas, namely that languages are fixed codes, and that communication proceeds on the basis of the shared form-meaning pairings set up by the code. This process of *telementation* (Harris 1981) reflects a sender-receiver model of communication (Harris 1998a: 20ff.). Wolf (1999: 28) explains that communication is not transference, but rather an engagement: 'The point of engagement is that every aspect of the situation (which can be used to further the communication) is engaged. None of it is transcendent; all of it is immanent'.

The founding tenet of integrationism is that the sign is indeterminate, both in form and meaning. Signs are not used but rather *made* in contexts, by what Harris referred to as *language-makers* (Harris 1980). Sign-makers integrate past experience on the basis of the present circumstances against an envisaged or imagined future. The sign integrates in both a *passive* and an *active* sense: '(i) it itself is an integral part of the communicational context, and (ii) it brings aspects of the communicational context together' (Wolf 1999: 27). Communication does not precede on the basis of shared inventories of signs stored in speakers' memories as part of an internalized code: speakers do not send message to each other but integrate their own and others' speech and actions as part of a dynamic and open-ended process of meaning-making (Pablé and Hutton 2015). Sign-makers are engaged in a dynamic and creative process for which there is no advanced plan or map; their creativity is in this sense thrust upon them since they are compelled to draw on, that is, integrate, their previous experience of sign-making and their understandings of the interactants and contexts with which they are confronted, and with their expectations of future consequences

DOI: 10.4324/9781315143132-4

and effects. It follows that to seek to define the form and the meaning of a sign is to attempt to bring definitional order to an uncertain and ill-defined abstraction, one with no identifiable fixed qualities.

Harris argues (1998a: 29) that 'the possibilities and limits of human communication' are governed by three factors: *biomechanical*, *macrosocial*, and *circumstantial*. Biomechanical factors are those that 'relate to the physical and mental capacities of the human being'; the macrosocial concerns 'practices established in the community or some group within the community', for example if one person is speaking a language unknown to a second, then they cannot communicate in that language. Circumstantial factors 'relate to the specifics of particular situations', for example the ability of two individuals to communicate by telephone although separated by thousands of miles. While these properties are shared by other modes of communication, linguistic communication is distinct in a number of ways, in particular through the property of *reflexivity* (Harris 1998a: 30). Whereas one can commentate on a tennis game without playing tennis, one cannot comment on language without engaging in verbal activity: 'Linguistics itself is a linguistic exercise; whereas tennis commentary is not a form of tennis' (Harris 1998a: 25). It should be noted that Harris restricts this model to human communication, but there is no reason in principle why this should not be applied to animal communication. Possible objections to this would be that animals lack macrosocial regularities governing their behaviour, or that such regularities can be attributed to their biomechanical endowment.

Integrationism rejects all understandings of language that see it as grounded in a dedicated faculty or a particular module of mind or brain, and refuse to separate language as a category of human activity from all its other aspects or dimensions (Wolf 1999: 27):

> the sign cannot be conceived as categorically separate from that which is integrated; for [...] the sign integrates, but is also itself integrated into the continuum. It is *part* of the continuum; it is not something formally isolatable from it.

This semiotic stance has led to suggestions that integrationism is a form of humanism, in that it emphasizes the creative possibilities of humanity, the open-ended character of human meaning-making, and the creativity and originality that of necessity accompanies each communicative act (see Pablé 2017). Sartre coined the famous slogan: 'existence precedes essence', which implied that 'If [...] existence truly does precede essence, man is responsible for what he is' (]1945] 2007: 23).

At the centre of integrationism's vision is the creative individual as active agent, as communicator, and as interpreter. Integrationism places great emphasis on communication as a *moral* activity; models of language and communication that exclude its moral dimension are rejected (Harris 1978). Integrationism understands modern linguistics (and much contemporary philosophy of language) as concerned to pin down indefinable and elusive features of language and formalize aspects of communication, treating them in a naturalized fashion, that is, as if they arose outside human agency and control, or as reifications or abstract objects which have real existence and character independently of the users and contexts in which they occur.

Integrationism rejected the distorted vision of communication offered by linguistics, caught between biological determinism and the mechanistic vision of 'the language machine', based most recently on an analogy between the computer and the brain (Harris 1987). Integration might therefore be understood as voluntaristic, with the individual at its centre, struggling against indeterminacy and contingency to create a web of signification within which to live. The humanist individual can be framed as a hero, creating and sustaining meaning in a universe that threatens moment to moment to destroy it since what has been built in one context, the consensus attained albeit briefly between those co-present in a discussion, is vulnerable to being destroyed in the next of an unfolding series of moments, recontextualizations, and contingencies. The semiotic freedom evoked by integrationism comes at the price of ceaseless labour, the self that makes meaning is also the Sisyphus that must endlessly seek the order that has been eroded by the simple passage of time. The self of this narrative might from one point of view be seen as a creative agent in control of their own communicational experience and conduct; from another that control is asserted against the pure contingencies of others' experiences and behaviour, the indifference of fate, and in the absence of secure foundations for thinking, speaking, acting, and interpreting.

As mentioned in the introduction, integrationism presents itself as *lay-oriented*, in that 'everyone is a linguist' (Harris 1998a: 20) or serves as a 'communication analyst' (Pablé and Hutton 2015: 48). This lay-orientation can be understood in a number of ways. It is a corollary to the tenets of integrational semiology, in that *language-makers* are also reflexively aware. Interactants operate not with a predetermined system that eludes their control and insight, but within a complex of unconscious, intuitive, and overt strategies, acting as agentive individuals. They are, as experienced communicators, adapting and integrating past experience and envisaging, planning and imagining future behaviour, as well as possessing latent or explicit opinions about language use, employing strategies, and subscribing to ideologies concerning language in its broadest sense. An additional element of this lay-orientation is the rejection of the notion of professional expertise, in particular the notion that language structure or linguistic behaviour can be objectively described and rigorously characterized from an external point of view (Orman 2016a). For integrationism, there is no position from which to view language as an object; there is no methodology which can be applied to reduce language to data; and there is no class of experts with a monopoly of insight into language superior to the views and opinions of non-specialist language users. Expertise is unevenly and unknowably distributed between the open-ended and ill-defined class of lay speakers, and roles such as parent, teacher, media professional, advertising copy-writer, lawyer, academic, and so on (Pablé and Hutton 2015: 47ff.). More precisely, everyone is a lay speaker, and everyone is an expert in some or many senses. Harris sees integrationism as part of a quest for self-knowledge and its demythologization of linguistics as a step towards society's reclaiming of its 'linguistic inheritance' (Harris 1987: 174). This suggests a therapeutic and empowering goal to integrational theory.

Integrationism lacks a fully articulated theory of the *human*. Integration as a semiological activity might seem at first glance to be the specific property of the human sign-maker, the agentive and reflexive individual who integrates not only at the level of moment-to-moment communication but also operates complex implicit and explicit communicational strategies, and integrates a whole range of *second-order* presumptions, beliefs, and ideologies (Love 1990, Thibault 2011, Cowley 2017: 47). While it is evident that, in some sense, animals integrate (as do plants and other organisms), the issue is whether this integration is qualitatively distinct from human semiological activity, or whether the distinction is merely one of degree. This question mirrors the long-standing debate in linguistic theory as to whether human beings, by virtue of their biological endowment (i.e. the *language faculty*, see Hauser, Chomsky and Fitch 2002, Berwick and Chomsky 2018), are unique among animals in having language, rather than instinct-based signalling systems or the non-reflexive or limitedly reflexive communicational abilities that characterize higher primates. Humanity is 'the language animal' (Taylor 2016), but how special is *homo integrans*?

The exceptionalism of linguistics when set against Darwinian evolution was reflected in F. Max Müller's insistence that 'Man speaks, and no brute has ever uttered a word. Language is our Rubicon, and no brute will dare to cross it'. This was Müller's response to those 'who speak of development, who think they discover the rudiments at least of all human faculties in apes' (Müller 1864: 367). Even Müller conceded, however, that animals 'though they do not use articulate sounds [...], have nevertheless means of their own for communication' (1864: 368). Philosophers in the Western tradition have generally insisted that animals do not have the capacity for language (Heidegger [1959] 1993: 11), a logocentric tradition that defines animals in terms of a lack (Derrida 2008: 27). Harris (1990: 159–160) terms this the *apartheid thesis*. In talking of animal communication the use of 'an anthropomorphic conceptual framework' is unavoidable ([1984] 1990: 172): 'We cannot somehow avoid the risks of anthropomorphism – whatever they may be – by trying to talk about primate signals in a terminology which draws no implicit comparison between animal and human communication'. The human species is defined by reference to language (properly understood), and language is defined by reference to features of human language. Experiments to demonstrate that apes possess human-like language skills constantly face this contested definitional question, given that we have no access to a culture-free and objective understanding of language (Taylor 1997). When dealing with concepts at this fundamental level, the technique of stipulated definition is used to mitigate circularity.

Integrationism versus systems theory

Integrationism posits agency without system; radical systems theory proposes system without agency (Luhmann 1986). In between these extremes is mainstream social science with its diverse array of attempts to relate structure and agency (Giddens 1984). Systems theory is a complex set of intellectual developments beginning in about 1900, with realizations in psychology, psychoanalysis, economics, evolutionary biology, law, political science, symbolic interactionism, and other domains. The essence of systems theory, including modern linguistics, is that the individual self is epiphenomenal to the system, both in terms of control over it and reflexive insight into it. In Saussurean linguistics the speaker shares in a social code or *langue* as a member of speech community. While an agent in terms of utterances (individual acts of *parole*), the speaker has no way of impacting directly on the language system (*langue*). On one level the speaker knows the language perfectly, in that it is transparent to introspection, yet in another sense the speaker has no reflexive understanding of it. The speaker controls when to speak and what to say, within whatever constraints may pertain, but possesses no reflexive insight into the nature of the system itself. For example, the ordinary speaker is wrong in believing that words are primarily names of things (*nomenclaturism*) (Saussure 1922: 97ff.). The special insight of the linguist, standing outside any particular system, provides the basis for the view that meanings of words are internal to those systems in the form of mutually defining values.

Saussurean structuralism is one of the original points of departure for posthumanist systems theory. The synchronic nature of linguistic structure was imagined from the point of view of the language user. For the ordinary speaker, 'unaware of their succession in time', 'linguistic facts' were static: '[the speaker] is dealing with a state' (or, 'confronted by a state', 'presented with a state', in the original: 'il est devant un état') (1922: 27). The linguist needed to adopt this point of view, in order not to mix up different orders of facts. *Langue* does change, but contingently under the stimulus of its environment, that is, the totality of language (*langage*): 'Language in its totality is unknowable, for its lacks homogeneity' (1922: 19–20). The language system is at once closed, in that it is primarily constituted by internal relationships and the mutual definition of elements (self-referentiality), often termed *autopoiesis* (Maturana and Varela 1980), and open, in that it evolves constantly in response to stimuli external to it. Autopoiesis involves 'order developing from disorder' (Deacon 2012: 21). Agency is found at the level of *parole*, but there is no agency in relation to the system itself.

In economic systems, *value* is at least partially determined by facts external to the system, that is, the value of land is related to the income derivable from it, and this value is at least in part traceable through time so that 'its connexion with things inevitably supplies it with a natural basis'; in linguistics, 'these natural connexions have no place' (Saussure 1922: 116). The conclusion is that 'a language is a system of pure values' 1922: 116), that is, its inner relationships and structures are not determined by any outside factors, be they natural or social, individual or collective. If we take this to its logical conclusion, it implies that the linguistic classification of the world, including types of animals and plants, is arbitrary and bears no relation to natural or functional kinds. There is no link or connection *at all* between natural kinds and linguistic categories; the linguistic system is a transcendent, self-sustaining, and self-organizing (autopoietic) system. On the other hand, all the speakers of the language are like-minded to the extent that they share in the system. This offers them the possibility of communicating seamlessly with one another on the basis of a high degree of shared linguistic knowledge. But, for Saussure, speakers' belief that words refer directly to reality is mistaken. It is a folk fiction generated by the system.

Similarly, Chomskyan linguistics is properly understood as a branch of systems theory (Hutton 2010). The fundamental distinctions drawn within the theory (*competence* versus *performance*, *I-language* versus *E-language*) reflect the boundary between a universal, impersonal, naturalistic system and the disordered, experiential world of human societies. I-language is a state of the mind/brain computational system 'that generates structured expressions, each of which can be taken a set of instructions for the interface systems within which the faculty of language is embedded' (Chomsky 2007: 14). On the one hand, the core competence is given in the biology of human nature and strictly defined in those terms. All human beings share this endowment; no animal has it. On the other hand, language-in-use is vague and open-ended, and has no systematic features. The language faculty did not evolve out of communicational needs or in direct response to environmental pressures, but rather is a by-product of a rewiring or *saltation* (Chomsky 2005: 12). As in systems theory models, the environment is disordered. Order as a property of systems is constructed autopoietically in response to, but not as determined by, the environment. In the case of a child acquiring language, the environment as disorder provides a necessary but not sufficient stimulus for the emergence of the full biosystem.

The ultimate model for systems theory is evolutionary theory, in particular as reinterpreted by figures such as Jakob von Uexküll (1864–1944) and Karl Ludwig von Bertalanffy (1901–1972) (see Duncker 2017: 141–2). An organism is closed in the sense that, given its self-regulatory constitution, it is autonomous in relation to the environment (*Umwelt*), yet its interactions with the environment trigger variation and drive evolutionary change. Chomskyan linguistics is an outlier within orthodox evolutionary theory, in that its key postulation, the human language faculty, is inferred from a set of philosophical premises and has no empirical status. It is simply stipulated to be invariant across the human species and to mark the species boundary between human and non-human animals.

Theories of free-market economics apply the notion of autopoiesis to human economic behaviour. Given the complexity of modern social systems, the idea of central economic planning is presented as incoherent since there is no position from which an observer can gather and analyse enough information to steer the direction of change efficiently. For Friedrich von Hayek (1899–1992), as a methodological individualist, the decentralized market is constituted out of the myriad interventions of individuals acting to the best of their knowledge in local contexts, just as common law jurisprudence is the product of countless case-to-case decisions of individual common law judges, each faced with a specific, distinctive fact-pattern. Hayek's term for autopoiesis is *spontaneous order* (Hayek 1945, 1982, Hutton 2009: 21ff.). For Hayek, judge-made law in an ideal common law system operates by means of *immanent criticism* (1982, 1: 118–19):

> a going order which nobody has designed, an order that has formed itself without the knowledge and often against the will of authority, that extends beyond the range of deliberate organization on the part of anybody, and that is not based on the individuals doing anybody's will, but on their expectations becoming mutually adjusted.

Vilaça (2010) argues that there is no necessary correlation between Hayek's notion of complex systems and his normative ideal of systems of liberal content maximizing individual freedom. He prefers Luhmann's model of a functionally differentiated society where the focus is exclusively at the systems level rather than on the interactions between the individual and an emergent order.

Distributed approaches and systems theory

The tension between integrationism and systems theory is reflected in the relationship between integrational theory and various strands of *distributed*, *embedded*, *embodied*, *enactive, extended*, or *ecological* understandings of language (Cowley 2011, Thibault 2011, 2017; Steffensen 2013, 2015), mind or cognition (Bateson [1972] 2000, Menary 2010), agency (Cobley 2016), and self (Wetherell and Maybin 1996, Gilbert and Forney 2013). Certain frameworks within this broad intellectual direction talk in terms of enactive and embodied relationships between an agent and the environment, leading to concepts such as situated cognition, embodied cognition, or, simply, enactivism. McGann (2014: 1321) cites Maurice Merleau-Ponty (1962: 430): 'The world is inseparable from the subject, but from a subject which is nothing but a project of the world, and the subject is inseparable from the world, but from a world which the subject itself projects'.

Taken together, these (far from uniform) approaches reject the Cartesian and neo-Cartesian understanding of the mind as an internal, autonomous representational system, and notions of the self as a bounded entity with a fully discrete consciousness explicable ultimately as an emanation of the brain (Clark 1997, Noë 2009). Mentalistic understandings see meanings as a set of representations in the head (mind/brain) and linguistic systems as modular, compositional, and decontextual. Arguing for a bio-ecological understanding of language, Cowley comments (2014: 61), 'just as we separate mind from body, we divide animals from the environment and scientific from humanistic knowledge'. In a distributed cognitive system, the parts or components 'constitute a self-organizing "super-agent", operating as a single entity' (Duncker 2017: 147).

Hutchins proposed the notion of *socially distributed cognition* as part of a rejection of 'the ideational definition of culture'. He drew an analogy between the division of labour in social organization and the cognitive domain (1995: xiii): 'Depending on their organization, groups must have cognitive properties that are not predictable from a knowledge of the properties of the individuals in the group'. The 'distributed cognition premise' is explained as follows (Hutchins 2008: 2011): 'the human cognitive system is best conceived as a distributed system that transcends the boundaries of the brain and body'. Whilst it is possible to study cognitive processes at the individual level, 'we must be careful when attributing cognitive processes to individuals who are engaged in cultural practices'. This carries the risk of 'attributing to the individual cognitive properties that belong to the larger distributed system'. Cognition is distributed 'not only among individuals, but also among individuals and *artefacts*' (Giere 2002: 640). The status of this collective cognition is unclear, in that distributed cognition can be thought of as a kind of *collective mind* (Weick and Roberts 1993) or *group agency* (Pardo 2015). Giere and Moffatt (2003: 304) argue that the temptation should be resisted 'to ascribe cognitive agency to the larger system, to say it is the system that knows, perhaps even consciously knows'. Cole and Engeström (1997) construct a complex lineage for the notion of distributed cognition, tracing it in psychology from Wilhelm Wundt (1832–1920) to Lev Vygotsky (1896–1934) and Alexander Luria (1902–1977), and within social anthropology, in particular to programmatic statements of Clifford Geertz (1973: 45):

> The 'control mechanism' view of culture begins with the assumption that human thought is basically both social and public – that its natural habitat is the house yard, the marketplace, and the town square. Thinking consists not of 'happenings in the head' (though happenings there and elsewhere are necessary for it to occur) but of traffic in what have been called, by G. H. Mead and others, significant symbols – words for the most part but also gestures, drawings, musical sounds, mechanical devices like clocks.

Within systems theory, the concept of *coupling* is central (Greif 2017). Clark and Chalmers (1998: 7, 8, 9) deploy the term *active externalism*, involving the 'active role of the environment in driving cognitive processes' so that 'the human organism is linked with an external entity in a two-way interaction, creating a *coupled system* that can be seen as a cognitive system in its own right'. This coupled process 'counts equally well as a cognitive process, whether or not it is wholly in the head'. Bateson ([1972] 2000: 325) made the point as follows:

> Suppose I am a blind man, and I use a stick. I go tap, tap, tap. Where do I start? Is my mental system bounded at the hand of the stick? Is it bounded by my skin? Does it start halfway up the stick? Does it start at the tip of the stick?

The notion of *extension* in relation to technology and media was popularized by Marshall McLuhan ([1964] 1994: 46):

> To behold, use or perceive any extension of ourselves in technological form is necessarily to embrace it. To listen to radio or to read the printed page is to accept these extensions of ourselves into our personal system and to undergo the 'closure' or displacement of perception that follows automatically.

In other words, there is no autonomous self that simply *uses* technology and media; rather, the self is imbricated in its extensions: 'Lewis Mumford, in *The City in History* [1961], considers the walled city itself an extension of our skins, as much as housing and clothing' (McLuhan 1994: 47). Following this line of thought, the most significant technological extension is writing and the artificial or external memory which it creates. Alphabetic writing allowed for the invention of 'a world of abstract entities' which are then mistaken for reality and which allow for the development of philosophies in which human beings 'no longer belong in the natural world' (Gray 2002: 56).

Turkle (2004), in a study originally published in 1984, took an ethnographic approach to the emerging culture of personal computer use, speaking of the computer as an 'evocative object' which even for young children raised questions 'about the machine's "life" and "mind" and then, by extension, wondering what was special about their own' (2004: 2). The question of personal identity was approached through the perceptions of the users (2004: 5):

> The remark about programming that inspired my title (thirteen- year-old Deborah saying, 'There is a little piece of your mind and now it's a little piece of the computer's mind...') has profound analogies with a recent comment by a woman who spoke of her personal digital assistant and said: 'When my Palm crashed, it was like a death. It had my life on it... I thought I had lost my mind'.

Some understandings of externalism or the extended self can be read as retaining the idea of an autonomous self or personhood whilst pointing to the way this autonomous self can be extended beyond the traditional Cartesian mind/body; others suggest that the self only emerges socially as a construct or fiction in particular ecologies or cultural contexts and that both the individual self and the concept of self lack a stable core across time and place.

For systems thinking, social organizations are not to be understood as the aggregation of monadic individuals (as in rational choice theory), nor is thinking an isolated activity carried on internally to the self. Rational choice theory is based on the idea that '[t]he elementary unit of social life is the individual human action. To explain social institutions and social change is to show how they arise as the result of the action and interaction of individuals' (Elster 1989: 13). In *How Institutions Think*, the anthropologist Mary Douglas rejected the premises of rational choice theory: 'the individual's most elementary cognitive process depends on social institutions' (1986: 45). But she also rejected the Durkheimian notion of collective mind, denying that institutions can in any meaningful sense have minds. Bruno Latour is critical of this intellectual compromise (1988: 384):

> Since [Douglas] does not want to grant institutions the character of being proper social actors, complete with will, thought, and beliefs, she has to use the worn-out sociology of knowledge arguments that individual thought is 'constrained,' 'influenced,' 'bound' by institutions, as if anything could be gained by any remaining distinction between cognition and society.

Eduardo Kohn's *How Forests Think* (subtitled *Towards an Anthropology Beyond the Human*, 2013), like Douglas's work, echoes the English translation of Lucien Lévy-Bruhl's *La mentalité primitive* (1922), published in 1926 as *How Natives Think*. In this series there is Marshall Sahlins's *How 'Natives' Think. About Captain Cook, For Example* (1995) and Maurice Bloch's *How We Think They Think* (1998) (see Keck 2013). Kohn argues that encounters with other beings require us to recognize that 'seeing, representing, and perhaps knowing, even thinking, are not exclusively human affairs'. Within a Peircean understanding of semiosis there is no autonomous self at the centre of sign-making: 'Signs don't come from the mind. Rather, it is the other way around. What we call mind, or self, is a product of semiosis'. It follows that 'signs are not exclusively human affairs. All living beings sign' (Kohn 2013: 1, 35, 42).

Anthropology's *ontological turn* is reflected in social theory and other social science disciplines (Blaser 2014: 50). A new politics is required, so the argument goes, now that we are confronted with 'heterogeneous assemblages' that 'overflow stable categorizations of human/non-humans, animate/inanimate, nature/culture and so on' (Blaser 2014: 50). The notion of *social construction*, which has been so dominant, albeit contested (see Hacking 1999) in the social sciences and cultural studies, emerges from the point of view of object-oriented ontology as highly anthropocentric. Social constructionism has its ultimate origins in Marx's concept of *commodity fetishism*, where appearance is a complex product of social forces, and reality is hidden behind the veil of ideology: 'the productions of the human brain appear as independent beings endowed with life' (Marx 1889: 43). This has little resonance in thinking about animal cognition. As a framework it can however be used to study and critique views of animals, showing how these are the products of value-laden language and discourse (Stibbe 2001), or how classifications and distinctions are socially and institutionally embedded (Waldau 2013: 215). But this again emphasizes the dominance of human agency and control in how reality is built up.

Certain philosophical positions evoke a form of distributed agency between speakers and language. Martin Heidegger (1889–1976) suggests that language thinks through us, rather than serving as a tool of thought. This implies that language possesses an autonomous power beyond human agency: 'language is not the work of human beings: language speaks. Humans speak only insofar as they co-respond to language' (Heidegger [1927] 1998: 57). Following Luhmann, Teubner, in a paper entitled 'How law thinks' (1989), argued for what he termed a 'constructivist social epistemology'. Although law might appear to be engaged directly with scientific or social questions, it has its own systemic truth requirements and its own reflexive modes of thought.

Notions of *group mind*, *collective mind*, *hive mind* in their various manifestations come in and out of fashion. Materialist and reductionist understandings of human cognition have been sceptical of the notion of individual mind, let alone a collective one, and consequently denied any clear dividing line between humans and animals (Watson 1913: 158):

> The behaviorist, in his efforts to get a unitary scheme of animal response, recognizes no dividing line between man and brute. The behavior of man, with all of its refinement and complexity, forms only a part of the behaviorist's total scheme of investigation.

At the other extreme, organicist notions such as *Volksseele*, *Volksgeist*, *Völkerpsychologie* (see Klautke 2013), *group mind* (McDougall 1920), *race psychology* (Garth 1931) raised objections on grounds of political ideology or unscientific mysticism. Yet dissatisfaction with methodological individualism (Agassi 1960, Hodgson 2007) constantly provokes renewed attempts to reconcile the mental or cognitive with the social and to find a level of analysis that reflects *Gestalt* or holistic thinking. Amatrudo (2012), for example, argues that *interpersonal relatedness* can provide the basis of a theory of corporate personality.

The discipline of linguistics in the Western tradition has treated language and languages primarily as objects of analysis. One can qualify this in various ways, pointing to Wilhelm von Humboldt's dialectic of *energeia* ('activity') and *ergon* ('product') (Humboldt 1836: 41) or Saussure's distinction between *langue* ('linguistic system') and *parole* ('speech') (Saussure 1922). But in these models *process* is nonetheless subordinate to *product*. Within socially oriented systems theory, one key concept is that of *languaging*. This is understood as an embodied activity within a dynamic socio-cognitive ecology, in preference to the reification of the *language system*. The term *languaging* arose out of a rejection of structuralist models as formalistic and static (Becker 1991): 'Languaging and interactivity have de facto priority over language and language systems' (Cowley 2017: 54). The related concept *translanguaging* is associated with bilingual pedagogies (García-Mateus and Palmer 2017) and has been adapted to a general non-reified theory of language ontology (Li 2018). In their denial or marginalization of individual selfhood or subjectivity, these distributed approaches belong to the broad spectrum of systems theory. They are objectivist, that is, grounded in a third-person perspective, and appeal to the norms of naturalistic science (Orman 2016a, 2016b: 161).

Integrationism's critique of systems theory

For Cowley (2004: 587), without the insights of distributed cognition, 'integrational theory remains locked in a critical tradition that illuminates neither semiogenesis nor the many ways in which multimodal activities are orchestrated'. Cobley comments: 'Agency does not occur in a space occupied by just one commentator'. He rejects the 'parapernalia of humanism' on both intellectual and political grounds, arguing that integrationism needs to engage critically with humanism (2017: 282–3). In a discussion of the compatibility or otherwise of distributed cognition with integrationism, Harris (2004: 727) in effect deployed a set of common-sense and ordinary language arguments. *Distributed mind* and *distributed cognition* were terms that he would 'never use in discussing my own mental activities, or anyone else's; and as far as I can see they haven't got much to recommend them'. They were 'obscure and potentially misleading' and conflicted with our 'vulgar concept of mind', that is 'our commonsense lay ways of talking about the mind' (Harris 2004: 728, invoking Hampshire 1971: 20). While Harris falls short of embracing the folk psychology dismissed, for example, by Dennett (1987: 7), his point is that jargon-laden psychological discourse, what he terms academic *cognobabble*, is misleading in ways that the everyday usage is not. Descartes, he argues, would have accepted many of the arguments put forward by the proponents of distributed cognition (Harris 2004: 728):

> But Descartes would not have drawn from these uncontroversial considerations the conclusion that the mind can be outside the head. It is indeed a very odd conclusion to draw. No one, I suggest, would argue that because seeing a certain distant object requires me to be in the right place, looking in the right direction, and perhaps using certain pieces of apparatus such as spectacles or a telescope, we should on these grounds reach the revolutionary conclusion that vision is 'distributed', and that sight can take place outside the head. [...] I have a similar difficulty with the proposition 'The mind is distributed'.

This was a *category-mistake* as expounded by Gilbert Ryle in *The Concept of Mind* (1949) (Harris 2004: 729):

> I am no more convinced that using my pocket calculator is an extended form of thinking than that riding a bicycle is an extended form of walking, or driving a motor car an extended form of riding on horseback. Thinking by proxy makes no more sense than being happy or sad by proxy. The black tie I wear at the funeral isn't doing my grieving for me. Nor is it a bit of grief that somehow escaped from inside me and got distributed.

Harris considers whether claims of *distributedness* should be seen as metaphorical, citing Sutton (2004) to conclude that they are not, given

> the claim that 'in certain circumstances certain 'artefacts and other external structures are literally cognitive' (Sutton, 2004); and that 'in certain circumstances, along with the brain and body interacting with them, they *are* the mind' (italics in [Sutton]). This doesn't sound very metaphorical to me. So is my pocket calculator, given the right circumstances, my mind or part thereof? No, I don't think so.

Harris's suggestion is to replace the notion of distribution with integration, which would mean to speak of an 'integrated' and 'integrating' mind. This is explained as follows (Harris 2004: 738):

> If we speak of an 'integrated mind', the rationale of the term integrated is that we conceive of our mental activities as part and parcel of being a creature with a body as well as a mind, functioning biomechanically, macrosocially and circumstantially in the context of a range of local environments.

Following on from this, Orman (2016b) explores in greater depth the relationship between the distributed cognition approach and integrationism. As Orman notes, to suggest the abandonment of the notion of distribution was to call for 'an improbable act of self-refutation' (2016b: 165). Orman draws attention to the parallel between Bennett and Hacker's (2003) criticisms of Daniel Dennett for 'ascribing psychological attributes to the brain rather than the human being', the so-called *mereological fallacy*, and Harris's ordinary language critique of distributed cognition. Harris appeals in effect to a set of discourse norms against which the language of distributed cognition offends. For integrationists 'it is individual language-makers who determine the meaning of words and expressions, not the language to which they allegedly belong' (Orman 2016b: 146). This would seem to reduce Harris's claim to a statement of personal preference or taste. Orman also notes that Harris failed to distinguish between Clark and Chalmers's (1998) view of 'the individually distributed or extended mind' and idea of the 'socially distributed cognitive system' as proposed by Hutchins (1995), where the focus is on the accomplishment of practical tasks (1995).

Orman points out that the lay-orientation of integrationism, with its focus on 'individual agency, morality and responsibility', finds no echo in the distributed perspective (Orman 2016b: 164). The distributed view is that integrationism's preoccupation with 'private semiological experience' has blocked the most important lines of inquiry. The integrational response would be to ask 'to what extent viewing language naturalistically as socially coordinated whole-body sense-making activity underplays the role of individuals' second-order metacommunicative beliefs and conceptualizations in shaping their interactional behaviour (dynamics vs. symbols)' (Orman 2016b: 162). The question of whether language should be seen as distributed is arguably not an empirical one at all (Joseph 2017). One might say, with Orman (2016b: 165), that language 'is neither distributed or non-distributed', or make the argument that claims for the distributed status of certain entities involve primarily an insistence on a set of interlocking stipulated definitions. Harris in effect denies the possibility of a real definition of mind (Orman 2016b: 154). This follows from the rejection of reocentric surrogationism and the tendency to reduce surface questions of fact and evidence to questions of meaning: 'the issue between creationists and evolutionists could not be settled by appeal to experience, observation or experiment' (Harris 2005: 36–37).

Integrationism is anthropocentric, whereas systems theory challenges anthropocentric understandings of agency, self, cognition, communication, and language. In the Peirce-Sebeok tradition, biosemiotics employs the term *sign* for an open-ended set of communicational processes (Favareau 2010). Sebeok offers in effect a vitalist definition of the sign (2001: 3): 'The phenomenon that distinguishes life forms from inanimate objects is semiosis. This can be defined simply as the instinctive capacity of all living organisms to produce and understand signs'. Pablé (2016) discusses the semiotician Susan Petrilli's discussion of communication within the biosphere. Overall, nonverbal non-human communication predominates over communication grounded in human language (Petrilli 2015: 218):

> Studies in the sphere of biology now reveal that members forming the other two super kingdoms, plants and fungi, also qualify as communicating. Not only: communication is also present in microorganisms. Communication involves cells endowed with an unencapsulated nucleus, that is, prokaryotes and bacteria. And it also involves the more developed cells endowed with an encapsulated nucleus, that is, eukaryotes.

The question is framed as a scientific one concerning the real definition of communication. Biologists need pay no heed to 'what ordinary language allows the word *communication* to mean' (Pablé 2016: 29). Pablé analyzes a *TED* talk by the Princeton molecular biologist Bonnie Bassler in which she describes bacteria as 'talking to each other' in a 'chemical language' made up of 'chemical words'. Bacteria are 'multilingual', with their own 'native language' but also a 'lingua franca'. At the close of her lecture, Bassler concluded: 'I hope that what you've learned is that bacteria can distinguish self from other. By using these two molecules they can say "me" and they can say "you"' (cited in Pablé 2016: 32). One can of course read these turns of phrase as pedagogically inspired metaphors, but they also reflect the biosemiotic understanding that sign-processes are not confined to the world of human-centred experience and that 'the rudiments of the self' are to be found 'at the level of the cell' (Cobley 2017: 277).

Approaches to cognition based on mental representation tend to stress human uniqueness within a broader similarity (Tomasello and Call 1997, Seed and Tomasello 2010: 414). Tomasello and Herrmann argue that human beings have 'unique adaptations for functioning in cultural groups', though is a strong communality (2010: 3): 'Since great apes are so closely related to one another evolutionarily, it is natural that they share many perceptual, behavioral, and cognitive skills'. With the important exception of Saussurean and Chomskyan linguistics, systems theoretical approaches, with their marginalization of human subjectivity, tend to imply a continuum rather than an unambiguous dividing-line between human species and higher animals in relation to behaviour, language, cognition, and core emotions (Panksepp 1998, Panskepp and Biven 2012).[1] This line of thinking can be traced back through the ethology of Eugène Marais (1871–1936), Konrad Lorenz (1903–1989), and Niko Tinbergen (1907–1973) to Darwin (1871, 1872). Ethology is most familiar to linguists in the form of Karl von Frisch's (1886–1982) discovery of the 'waggle dance' of bees, which he presented as analogous to a language (von Frisch 1923). Similarities in gesture produced by bonobos, chimpanzees, and human children provide evidence that gesture was a 'precursor to symbolic communication for both humans and language-enculturated apes' (Gillespie-Lynch et al. 2014: 1228). Within the distributed cognition discussions of primates, communicational interaction is understood to involve directly observable cognitive events and cognition itself is 'co-constructed' (Johnson 2001). Filippi (2015), for example, argues that there is 'evolutionary continuity' between human language and the communicational systems of animals. Cowley and Spurrett, discussing studies of the linguistic and cognitive abilities of bonobos (see Taylor and Shanker 1996), conclude that '[the bonobo] Kanzi's achievements are appropriately understood in terms of distributed cognition' (2003: 290).

This tension between systems theory and humanism can be found to a degree in integrational writings. For example, in discussing the integrational relations between different communicational processes Harris discusses the workings of a factory (1996: 43):

> Just as it makes more sense to analyse how a factory works by examining the relations between production processes rather than by considering the choices open to individual members of the work force, so it makes more sense to analyse communication by examining how one communication process is related to another in respect of biomechanical, macrosocial and circumstantial requirements.

An analysis of this kind would reflect a systems theory understanding, in that what counts are the formal patterns and interrelationships between the parts of the system, rather than the epiphenomenal acts or intentions of individuals who work within the system. Isolated intentional acts do not affect the factory at the level of system. Set against this is Pablé's assertion of the primacy of the self in integrationism (2017: 6): 'the Harrisian starting point is always the self, never the other'. In illustration Pablé cites *Mindboggling* (Harris 2008: 155):

> 'Do *I* have a mind?' First of all, is the question worth asking? Certainly, because refusing to address it would be tantamount to evading any

> responsibility for self-understanding. And should the answer be 'no' in my own case, I will have no reason for supposing that anyone else has a mind either. That would be to take a very gloomy view of humanity.

The phrase 'responsibility for self-understanding' makes no sense outside a broadly humanistic understanding of the self. Since we are always 'in the middle of things' (*in medias res*), Harris argues that we can only fall back on what he terms the *terra firma* personal experience (Harris 1981: 204):

> The language-bound theorist, like the earth-bound Archimedes, has nowhere else to stand but where he does. He has ultimately no leverage to bring to bear on understanding language other than such leverage as can be exerted from the *terra firma* of his own linguistic experience.

This quotation does not propose that individual experience is an ultimate authority, but rather that it represents the domain in which the linguist, in order to take 'a first step' towards securing 'an analytical grasp of that experience', must 'recognise the language myth for what it is' (Harris 1981: 204). There is no better place to begin since all other modes of inquiry presume abstract, context-free systems of categories that reflect the language myth.

Systems theory taken as an intellectual complex is on a continuum between non-humanism and anti-humanism. Duncker (2017: 148) comments that systems approaches tend to be 'fundamentally anti-human' since 'the person is *powerless*, and in the distributed system, the person is *dissolved* and absorbed into the overall structure'. The question then arises: 'Is it possible to envisage a systems approach that does not carry this load of problems?' (Duncker 2017: 148). Integrationism is avowedly humanistic, while at the same time it offers potential grounds for undercutting this position. For example, the humanistic self can be reinterpreted as a second-order fiction or construct. If Harris's view of the primacy of personal experience is correct, that experience must in some sense be transparent to the self (Harris 1981: 204) and belong to an autonomous and reflexive mind. Duncker (2017: 149–150) argues that the integrating self implies an Other, and that this implied relational sociality is the basis of a recognition that linguistic processes 'are unthinkable without their embeddedness in the social matrix', that is, 'a larger complex based on the simple fact that persons have relations to other persons'. This follows given that 'the only viable, integrationally compatible perspective from which to analyse first-order linguistic processes is that of the first person', and this is 'the perspective of the individual agent *from within* the social ensemble'. In this sense, 'each person is the hub of the system'. This model is intended to retain the autonomy of the individual person as sign-maker whilst developing 'a different and philosophically less problematic understanding of the macroscial category' (Duncker 2017: 150).

Conclusion

Saussure's speaker or self is, from the point of view of the system, merely a node or point of conjunction, disconnected from the agentive self that produces utterances. The continuity that the speaking agent experiences between the present and the past is, to the extent that it is mediated by the values of the system, illusory or epiphenomenal, since the system is undergoing constant autopoietic reconfiguration. The sense that words refer to reality is a fiction generated in the speaker by the system. The question remains as to whether the self in integrational theory is primarily integrating or whether it is also integrated in a radical sense, that is, a dynamic construct of contextual sign-making practices. In its radical anti-foundationalism integrationism might seem to imply that the communicating self is integrated into the dynamical flow of interaction, rather than somehow standing outside it and acting in an agentive manner. If meaning is a creation of the here and now, and signs are made in communication rather than being used or applied, then on what basis can we postulate the existence of an autonomous agentive self? The self, it might be argued, is part of this ongoing semiological process, and is created and recreated within it, in the absence of any cross-contextual stable framework of categories. For, within the logic of integrational theory, what makes the self that communicates today the same self that communicates tomorrow? Is this self not a second-order construct? (Hutton 2017a). In the two following chapters the focus shifts to personhood and law, but questions of the self and personhood within integrational theory are reconsidered in the conclusion.

Note

1 These core emptions are: 1. SEEKING (expectancy); 2. FEAR (anxiety); 3. RAGE (anger); 4. LUST (sexuality); 5. CARE (nurturance); 6. PANIC/GRIEF (separation); 7. PLAY (joy).

4 Animals, personhood, and law

Introduction

Law is sustained by a set of entrenched beliefs about not only the kinds of entities that exist but also the interrelationships between them, and their place in a hierarchy of values. Human beings are its ultimate rationale. Whatever the entities, processes, and mechanisms posited by law, these are ultimately proxies for the rights, interests, and duties of human beings. To the Roman jurist Gaius is attributed the phrase ***hominum causa omne ius constitutum***, that 'each law has been established for the sake of mankind' (Fellmeth and Horwitz 2009). This stance is termed ***juridical humanism***, grounded in the notion of dignity as a distinguishing feature of the human being, understood within a metaphysically constituted personhood. In its modern form this personhood is understood as including the principle of equality before the law (see Pietrzykowski 2018). Common law legal systems distinguish between entities that can be owned (property) and entities that can own (persons). Property is divided into personal property and real estate. Personal property (chattels) can be moved, whilst land and the objects permanently attached to it cannot. For Krauss (1984: 499), these categories have a deeper significance beyond their functional role in legal doctrine (Krauss 1984: 499):

> The dominion of God over the universe is divided into two spheres, heaven and earth; one is tangible and the other intangible, or in the language of both canon and common law, corporeal and incorporeal. The dominion of man is divided into its corporeal phase, called property, and its incorporeal phase, called estate (also known as hereditament). Property is further subdivided into chattels personal and chattels real.

Within this theological-cum-legal cosmology, animals belong to personal property (***chattels personal***): 'Such are animals, household-stuff, money, jewels, corn, garments, and every thing else that can properly be put in motion, and transferred from place to place'. These are 'things moveable; which may be annexed to or attendant on the person of the owner, and carried about with him from one part of the world to another' (Blackstone [1765] 1840: 313). Further, law

DOI: 10.4324/9781315143132-5

distinguishes between animals in the wild, that is, *ferae naturae*, and those that are domesticated, that is, animals that are *mansuetae naturae* or *domitae naturae*.

Animals and humans in law

Legal categories have their foundation in God's ordering of the universe. The precise understanding of the place of humans and animals in that order has been contentious, as humans are also subject to law's artificial reason. As expounded by the Scottish jurist James Dalrymple, Viscount of Stair (1619–1695), following the Roman jurist Ulpian (170–223) and the Institutes of Justinian of the sixth century (Birks and McLeod 1987), there is at the most basic level a natural law that encompasses both human and animal nature, given to all living beings (*quod natura omnia animalia docuit*). This is exemplified in 'the conjunction of Male and Female: or Marriage, the Procreation or Education of Children' (Stair 1781: 4). However this 'Original and Primitive Law' was overlaid with the Law of Nations (*jus gentium*) founded 'in the rational Nature of man', which also included man's emotional side: 'and even that which appeareth to be in the Sensitive Nature, is truely founded in the Rational Nature'. This being the case, the law of nations was 'not properly communicable unto the Beasts', these being non-rational, 'who have no Law but their natural Instincts, having only some resemblance to the Law of Nature' (Stair 1681: 4). In relation to obligations among family members, Stair stated that the obligations between parents and children were not based on consent or any legal rule, 'but from the obedience Man oweth to his Maker, who hath Written this Law in the Hearts of Parents and Children'. These duties were absolute and could not be set aside: 'These Obligations are placed in the Common Nature that Man hath with other Animals, and so is given as an evident Instance of the Law of Nature' (Stair 1681: 45–46).

In his *De jure belli ac pacis*, Grotius explicitly rejected the Roman law notion that there was a common natural law shared by animals and humans (Grotius [1625] 2005: I, cap. 11):

> for nothing is properly susceptible of Right and Obligation, but a Being that is capable of forming general Maxims, as Hesiod has well observed, 'Jupiter has ordained that Fishes, wild Beasts, and Birds should devour each other, because Justice doth not take place amongst them: But to Men he has prescribed the Law of Justice, which is the most excellent Thing in the World.

Human beings in their sociality and provision of mutual aid go far beyond animals, being distinctive in their respect for property rights, their rationality, and capacity for speech. However in relation to waging war, there is an analogy to be drawn (Grotius [1625] 2005: I, cap. 2, para. 1.3):

> Among the first Impressions of Nature there is nothing repugnant to War; nay, all Things rather favour it: For both the End of War (being the

> Preservation of Life or Limbs, and either the securing or getting Things useful to Life) is very agreeable to those first Motions of Nature; and to make use of Force, in case of Necessity, is in no wise disagreeable thereunto; since Nature has given to every Animal Strength to defend and help itself.

The classical authors tell us that 'Man is an Animal by Nature fitted for Peace and War', in that 'he is not indeed born with Arms, but with Hands proper to make and to use Arms, so that we see the very Infants defend themselves with their Hands, without being taught'. Not all wars were to be condemned.

The English theologian Nathaniel Culverwell (1691–1651) satirized this shared natural law as an attempt to bring animals within the domain of conventional law (Culverwell [1652] 2001: 41): 'for certainly these men mean to bring beasts, birds and fishes into their Courts, and to have some fees out of them'. They might also expect 'that the Doves should take Licences before they marry'. The idea that the law of nature was common to both human beings and irrational animals, whereas the law of nations was confined to a human sphere and was a distinction built upon an absurd analogy ([1652] 2001: 43):

> What are those Lawes that are observed by a rending and tearing Lion, by a devouring Leviathan? Does the Wolf oppresse the Lamb by a Law? Can birds of prey shew any Commission for their plundering and violence?

If by chance certain animals did show apparent attributes of lawfulness, this was simply a reflection of their natural endowment. Human beings had no such excuse for misconduct ([1652] 2001: 44):

> Let grant that the several multitudes, all the species of these irrational creatures were all without spot and blemish in respect of their sensitive conversation, can any therefore fancy that they dresse themselves by the glasse of a Law? Is it not rather a faithfulnesse to their own natural inclinations? which yet may very justly condemne some of the sons of men, who though they have the Candle of the Lord, and the Lamp of his Law, yet they degenerate more then these inferiour beings, which have only some general dictates of Nature.

For Culverwell, 'the Law of Nature is built upon Reason' ([1652] 2001: 47).

Culverwell's contemporary, Sir Robert Filmer (1588–1653), an influential proponent of the divine right of kings, diagnosed a deep intellectual confusion in the understanding of natural law, the law of nations, and civil legal systems (1679: 34):

> The Civil Law in one Text allows a threefold Division of Law, into Ius Naturae, Ius Gentium, and Ius Civile. But in another Text of the same Law, we find only a twofold Division, into Ius Civile, and Ius Gentium. This latter Division the Law takes from Gaius [Roman jurist 130–180], the former

> from Ulpian [Roman jurist c. 170–223)], who will have Ius Naturale to be that which Nature hath taught all Creatures, quod Natura omnia animalia Docuit.

Filmer traced this confusion back to assumptions about the primitive equality of mankind when all things were held in common. For Filmer, it was the 'natural and private Dominion of Adam' which was 'the fountain of all Government and Propriety', including 'the Power of Kings' (1679: 58–59). This grounded human society and inequality in the primal family relationships, implying a complete severance of human institutions from animal society.

Thomas Hobbes offers essentially a subtractive definition of the animal: animals are creatures that lack reason and language (Menely 2015: 51). Language underpins the social and legal order that sets humans apart from animals (Hobbes [1651] 1909: 24) such that 'man leaveth all community with beasts at the faculty of imposing names' (Hobbes 1684: 59):

> But the most noble and profitable invention of all other was that of SPEECH consisting of *Names* or *Appellations*, and their Connexion; whereby men register their Thoughts, recall them when they are past; and also declare them one to another for mutuall utility and conversation; without which there had been amongst men neither Commonwealth, nor Society, nor Contract, nor Peace, no more than amongst Lyons, Bears, and Wolves. The first author of Speech was *God* himself, that instructed Adam how to name such creatures as he presented to his sight [...].

In Genesis, animals were merely the objects of naming. This Adamic language was however lost at Babel, giving rise to the 'diversity of Tongues' ([1651] 1909: 24). In contrast to the original God-given distinction, the opposition of human to animal operates symbolically within the transformative power of law, marking the boundary between the commonwealth and the state of nature beyond. For Hobbes 'the difference between humanized animals (subjects) and animalized humans (outlaws) secures the political order'; the commonwealth is a 'circumscribed space in which peace and justice prevail', yet it remains 'haunted by liminal figures' (Menely 2015: 49).

In Hobbes's model, language is what makes human society possible, but it is also an unstable and unreliable instrument: for each *use* of language there is a corresponding *misuse* ([1651] 1909: 25):

> First, when men register their thoughts wrong, by the inconstancy of the signification of their words; by which they register for their conceptions, that which they never conceived; and so deceive themselves. Secondly, when they use words metaphorically; that is, in other sense than that they are ordained for; and thereby deceive others. Thirdly, when by words they declare that to be their will, which is not. Fourthly, when they use them to grieve one another [...].

This last use of language is analogized to the use by animals of the weapons with which they have been naturally endowed: 'for seeing nature hath armed living creatures, some with teeth, some with horns, and some with hands, to grieve an enemy, it is but an abuse of Speech, to grieve him with the tongue' ([1651] 1909: 25). Yet this use of the tongue may be justified in cases where authority is exercised over 'one whom wee are obliged to govern; and then it is not to grieve, but to correct and amend' ([1651] 1909: 25). Brute force and violence are kept outside the commonwealth, yet it is also necessarily admitted within it; similarly, savage or aggressive speech is not fully excluded from the commonwealth; it is misused by some, but required for the exercise of authority.

Law mirrors the natural order, at the same time as it asserts its autonomy from it and over it, through its status as an artificial institution. Nature is both within and outside the law just as Hobbes's commonwealth keeps the wolf from the door whilst enthroning the beast as sovereign (Menely 2015: 48):

> Symbolically, the sovereign is akin to the wild beast, embodying a possibility of violence in excess of law. Yet the sovereign must also identify and kill the beast, thereby producing the order of law and the distinction between just and unjust violence.

It is only if we 'presume the prior categorical identity of the human as a rational animal – that speech (*logos*), which in itself never fully transcends the passions and the voice, can be understood (tautologically) as the source of human exceptionality' (Menely 2015: 25).

Personhood in law

Personhood indicates status or membership in a category, as did, historically, the term which it has in part replaced, *personality* ('the quality of being a person and not a thing', Williams 1983: 232). Personhood is not a well-defined or articulated status in law, though discussion of it constitutes a vast and complex legal literature (Naffine 2003: 347): 'The law of persons is not a discrete field of study in the common law world, but is scattered throughout the different branches of law'. Personhood is a fundamental legal concept (Fagundes 2001: 1746): 'although no coherent body of doctrine or jurisprudential theory exists regarding this legal metaphor, a set of rhetorical practices has developed around it'. It is open to question whether there is a coherent law of personhood at all (Berg 2007: 371). Personhood is rooted in jurisdiction, yet it is not equivalent to citizenship. Bilchitz (2009: 42) notes that personhood

> is generally taken to refer to a being or entity capable of having legal rights or duties: however, it is unclear whether such a being or entity must be capable of having both legal rights and duties or whether such a being or entity must be capable of having either legal rights or duties?

For Smith (1928: 283) to be a legal person 'is to be the subject of rights and duties,' and 'to confer legal rights or to impose legal duties, therefore, is to confer legal personality'. This reflects legal historian Maitland's formulation: 'Like the man, the corporation is [...] a right-and-duty-bearing unit' (1911: 307). But a person held in a migrant detention centre may well have rights and duties, but only those rights and the identity granted by the institution in which they find themselves, through domestic law or in international treaty. Such a person would seem to lack legal personhood in this fuller sense (Saunders 2017), given their status as an *extraneous person* (Dayan 2011) or the effective 'erasure' of legal personhood (Castañeda 2010: 256).

Naffine (2009) divides models of legal personhood into two camps: the *legalists* versus the *metaphysical realists*. The legalists regard personhood as an artificial legal device or a basic unit of analysis, and taking this to its logical conclusion, argue that 'we should sever the philosophical or metaphysical concepts of the person from the legal concept' and abandon terms such as *person* altogether (Naffine 2009: 178, Nekam 1938). The realists are divided into three basic positions, ranging from more restrictive to less: *rationalist*, *religionist*, and *naturalist*. Each of these bases personhood on possession of a basic attribute, respectively: *mind*, *soul*, and *sentience* (2009: 324). For the legalists, there is no *a priori* restriction on what can count as a legal person. In this spirit, Dyschkant argues for a 'conceptual divorce between legal person and human' (2015: 2108). Naffine's categories have direct parallels in non-legal understandings of the person, seen as rational, ensouled, or a naturalistic being (higher animal). The legalist position corresponds to a systems theory model of self as fiction.

Constitutions and human rights instruments frequently employ the category *person*. The preamble to the Universal Declaration on Human Rights (1948), promulgated by the United Nations, speaks in terms of 'faith in fundamental human rights, in the dignity and worth of the human person and in the equal rights of men and women'. Article 5, s. 1 of the European Convention on Human Rights (1953) states, 'Everyone has the right to liberty and security of person. No one shall be deprived of his liberty save in the following cases and in accordance with a procedure prescribed by law'. The preamble to both the International Covenant on Civil and Political Rights (1976) and the International Covenant on Economic, Social and Cultural Rights (1976) proclaims that the rights enumerated 'derive from the inherent dignity of the human person'. *Person* is used both as a synonym for human being and as a status which is normatively to be attached to human beings by operation of law: 'a concept like that of human rights is only conceivable and viable through the lexicon of personhood' (Esposito 2012: 4). Personhood is bound to the notion of embodied living human being, yet there is no consensus as to when it begins or when it ends. The American Convention on Human Rights (1969) includes a Right to Juridical Personality (Article 3): 'Every person has the right to recognition as a person before the law'.[1] Article 4(1) includes the foetus within its scope of protection: 'Every person has the right to have his life respected. This right shall be protected by law and, in general, from the moment of conception. No one shall be arbitrarily deprived of his life'. The human corpse has a special status that reflects its continuing link to personhood within social memory (Ariss 2004) and its liminal position in relation to the social order (see Quigley 1996). One's legal personhood may operate after the self has died, in the form of an estate or a trust.

Historically or actually, the following forms of human person have been either privileged, marginalized, or disputed categories of human being before the law in the sense that they lack the full ingredients of legal personhood: monarch (*corporation sole*); bishop (*corporation sole*); aristocrat; woman; child; foetus; embryo; human genetic material; conjoined twins; prisoner; individual with severe cognitive impairment; member of a stigmatized class, caste, race, or ethnic group; indigenous inhabitant; individual labelled as seriously mentally ill; migrant, refugee, and non-citizen; and slave. In a modern common law system a full legal person has rights to life, liberty, and property; to vote; to education; to form contracts, to marry, and to sue; to enjoy the protection of law and the civil authorities; to bring legal action (standing); to choose one's place of residence; to privacy, and so on. Such rights interact with status, namely citizenship or residency rights, and with the autonomy of self, 'self-sovereignty' or bodily integrity. In modern states, full legal personhood comes with duties and liabilities, for example, requirements to register (birth, death, marriage), the obligation to obey the law and to be subject to lawful punishment (criminal and civil liability), and the requirement to pay taxes. Rights and duties coexist: the right of a child to attend school is also generally a legal obligation.

Categories of non-human that have been, or potentially might be, incorporated within legal personality include: corporation (town, university, monastery, company); river; temple, idol, sacred statute; association, group, partnership; ship; machine (robot, computer, artificial intelligence (AI) system); chimera; cyborg; animal; alien (e.g. a being from another planet). Legal personhood is now debated in particular in relation to systems that use AI, including automatic trading systems and autonomous vehicles. The European Parliament's legal affairs committee has urged that robots be granted the status of *electronic persons* in order that any legal liabilities that arise may be clarified ([EU] 2015, Chopra and White 2011).[2]

The case law on *person* is fragmented and rarely addresses the full significance of the category *person* (Rivard 1992: 1431): 'Rather than developing an underlying theory of personhood, the Supreme Court follows a pragmatic, result-oriented approach'. Legal judgements only reluctantly undertake *de novo* investigations into basic concepts, nor do they critically examine law's own foundations, unless it is unavoidable. In general, law does not require nor provide context-free definitions of bedrock categories, such as *human being*, *God*, *nature, man*, *woman*, *self*, *person*, *citizen*, *privacy*, *animal*: 'The US Constitution does not define "person" in so many words' (*Roe v. Wade*, 410 U.S. 113 (1973), at section IX. The definition of *death* may vary across jurisdictions so that in the United States a person may be legally dead in one state and alive in another

(Price 2013). When statutes provide definitions, for example, clarifying the definition of animal in a law against cruelty to animals,[3] these operate so as to demarcate a specified sub-meaning from the ordinary or everyday meaning, rather than addressing deep philosophical or definitional questions. The US courts treat ambiguities in the scope of the statutory term *person* as a policy question. In *Potomac Engineers v. Walser,* 127 F. Supp.41 (1954) the court held that only a natural person, and not a corporation, could register as a professional engineer. In *U.S. v. Brownfield,* 30 F.Supp.2d 1177 (C.D.Cal. 2001), an agency of the federal government was determined not to be a person, within the context of a statute criminalizing threatening communications addressed to any *person.* The Supreme Court in *Mohamad v. Palestinian Authority*, 566 U.S. 449 (2012) decided that the term *individual*, when used in the Torture Victim Protection Act of 1991, 'encompasses only natural persons', and therefore 'the Act does not impose liability against organizations' (at 449). In a case of identity theft (*U.S. v. Maciel-Alcala,* 2010 WL 1133434 (2010), the fact that the stolen identity belonged to a deceased person did not affect the relevant meaning of *person.* In *Rowland v. California Men's Colony* (91–1188), 506 U.S. 194 (1993), the Supreme Court held that an association of prisoners was not a *person* in the relevant sense and could not initiate legal proceedings *in forma pauperis*, even though the association was not permitted to hold any assets. Among the arguments was the assertion that (at 203, per Justice Souter) 'Artificial entities may be insolvent, but they are not well spoken of as "poor." So eccentric a description is not lightly to be imputed to Congress'.

Historically, slaves are persons in the sense of being human beings, but may or may not be understood as legal persons in a particular legal context. In *Jarman v. Patterson, 23 Ky.* (7 T.B. Mon.) 644 (1828), the Kentucky Court of Appeals offered this summation (at 644):

> However deeply it may be regretted, and whether it be politic or impolitic, a slave by our code, is not treated as a person, but (*negotium*), a thing, as he stood in the civil code of the Roman Empire. In other respects, slaves are regarded by our laws, as in Rome, not as persons, but as things.

By contrast, in *U.S. v. Amy*, 24 F. Cas. 792 (1859), the Circuit Court of Virginia upheld the conviction of a slave, named only as Amy, for the federal offence of stealing a letter. It had been argued for the slave-owner that as a slave was merely a *natural person*, and not 'a legal or civil person', and therefore property (at 797). A slave was a chattel without legal capacity 'under the absolute dominion of the state governments, and known only to the federal government 'as property, and to be protected as such' (at 805). Slaves had 'the twofold character of property and persons', yet it was 'the legal incident of no kind of property whatever to have the capacity to forfeit or affect the title of its owner by any action of its own' (at 806). The District Attorney for the United States countered that, while slaves were property, 'it is equally true that they are recognised in all modern communities where slavery exists as persons also'. He added, 'I cannot prove more plainly that the prisoner is a person, a natural person, at least, than to ask your honors to look at her. There she is. She is without doubt a human being' (at 795). The court agreed, paradoxically defining personhood in terms of Amy's humanity, in proceedings in which she had no status as an independent party.

Corporate personhood

Non-human legal persons such as sovereign states and corporations are characterized using epithets such as *fictive*, *artificial*, *juridical*, and *juristic*. In French usage, *une personne morale* is one that enjoys *personnalité juridique* (Michoud 1906); in German the term is *juristische Person*. *Persona ficta* can be read in multiple ways, depending on what is being declared as non-fictional and the policy reasons behind the designation. Incorporation provides legal form (unity, autonomy, and continuity) to what would otherwise be discrete or disparate actions, transactions, and actors. In Corinthians (I, 1: 12), St. Paul writes, 'For as the body is one, and hath many members, and all the members of that one body, being many, are one body: so also is Christ'. The Church is understood as the mystical body of Christ in communion with the collectivity of believers. The Greek term is *soma*, generally translated as 'body'. The status of the analogy has triggered theological controversy, as to whether this *soma* is a physical body or a metaphor (Lee 2006). It has been argued that, in theologically significant contexts, *soma* refers to the human person taken as a whole; or alternatively, that *soma* refers to the whole person by metonymy or synecdoche. Others insist that the primary meaning is physical body (see Gundry 1976, Ziesler 1983). If *soma* is read as 'person', then we can talk of the bodily, that is, corporate, personality of the Church as the body of Christ. In theological terms, the Church is not a fictional corporation nor an artificial being. Koessler (1949) traces the notion of *persona ficta* to the writings of Innocent IV, Pope between 1243 and 1254. One view is that the Pope wanted to be able to excommunicate guilty members of an ecclesiastical institution, even if the institution itself, lacking a body and a soul, could not be excommunicated (Dewey 1926: 665–6, Rodriguez 1962). The Church was asserting that it created and sustained bodies above the level of individual (Vinogradoff 1924: 600–601). Bauman, however, insists that the Church's approach amounted merely to 'moderate nominalism' (Bauman 1983: 607, fn. 45).

The doctrine of corporate personhood is historically and logically prior to the explicit notion of the natural person. It is in contemplating the fictional or artificial that one becomes aware of the status of its complementary term, the *natural person*. With the rise of empirical science, the term *natural* opened up the possibility of secular, naturalistic accounts of the person, subjecting explanations based on the soul to sceptical intellectual pressure. This triggered a search for the grounding of the person in terms of human psychology, identity, and selfhood. Personification became the framework for understanding the nature of the corporation. Given the existence of fictional persons, law requires a default term for a real person, namely *natural person* or *person in being*. If we interrogate corporate or state personality, we are at the same time inquiring into human personhood. Machen (1911) argues for clarity in usage (1911: 257): 'That which is artificial is real, and not imaginary; an artificial lake is not an imaginary lake, nor is an artificial waterfall a fictitious waterfall'. An entity which is created by the state cannot be seen as purely fictitious, nor can a fictitious entity be composed of natural persons.

A corporation is an organization that has been granted legal recognition of its identity or *personhood*, independently of the individuals that constitute it. For many purposes it is treated as a single entity. It can make contracts, sue and be sued, commit certain crimes, own property, incur debts, and grant credit. As persons, corporations have both rights and duties. Historically, incorporation was a privilege granted by Royal Charter or private act of parliament to religious, educational, trading and other institutions, and to political entities such as towns and colonies. Only the monarch could authorize this: 'none but the King can make a corporation' (Viner 1792: 259). Corporations generally provide limited liability for their members, whose private assets and persons are protected in legal actions against the company for debt, bankruptcy, and most criminal and civil actions. In traditional corporation law, 'one corporation cannot make another' (Shepheard 1659: 112, Viner 1792: 260), but in the modern law of corporations (company law), the members of the company may themselves be other (subsidiary) companies.

The creation of persons by law has been a constant source of disquiet: 'Why do lawyers and judges assume thus to clothe inanimate objects and abstractions with the qualities of human beings?' (Smith 1928: 285). Underlying this anxiety there are a number of concerns, some theological, others economic and/or political. Theologically, there is the question of law's right to create and sustain artificial beings, seemingly usurping God's prerogative as the source of ontology, that is, as the creator of everything that exists. The King is in some sense God's agent or delegate, and the fount of sovereignty on earth as a reflection of God's dominion over all creation, but whether this includes the power to create corporate beings is jurisprudentially and theologically questionable. Corporations in their artificiality required a set of explicit and exhaustive rules to govern their conduct since they had no natural law to fall back on. One answer from Sir Roger Manwood (1525–1592) was that the corporation was a 'body aggregate' rather than a monadic being (cited in Merewether and Stephens 1835: 1521):

> as touching corporations, they were invisible, immortal, and that they had no soul, and therefore no subpoena lieth against them, because they have no conscience nor soul. A corporation is a body aggregate; none can create souls but God; but the king creates them, and therefore they have no souls – they cannot speak nor appear in person, but by attorney.

One of the most famous remarks on the corporation is that attributed to Edward, First Baron Thurlow (1731–1806): 'Did you ever expect a corporation to have a conscience, when it has no soul to damn, no body to kick? By God, it ought to have both' (see Coffee 1981, Clarkson 1996).

The first major text on company law or the law of corporations was produced by the Scottish jurist, Stewart Kyd (1793–4). One can understand the evolving legal discussion as part of the struggle to domesticate the corporation within the increasingly secular ontology of law. The legal evolution is also haunted first by theological doubt about the status of these soulless immortal beings and subsequently by moral and political concerns about the accountability of corporations, their conscience or lack of it, and their place within sociolegal orders. The corporate form has been the prime vehicle of globalizing capitalism, with Joint-Stock Companies playing a central role in early modern exploration and the privatized colonialism of the Dutch and British East Indian Companies. The nineteenth century saw the rise of the company as the dominant unit of economic activity and the creation of an accompanying set of legal norms which stabilized its place within the ontology of law. This was a contested and uneven process, with 'metaphysical perplexity' about the nature of the corporate agency and its actions (Stout 2017: 22). While philosophically or ontologically the corporation was a pure creature of law, a highly circumscribed being, 'a mere creature of the law, invisible, intangible, and incorporeal', nonetheless it accrued many of the rights and privileges of natural persons: 'we find that corporations have been included within terms of description appropriated to real persons' (per Chief Justice Marshall, *Bank of the United States v. Deveaux*, 9 U.S. 61 (1809), at 88). In *Trustees of Dartmouth College v. Woodward,* 17 U.S. (4 Wheat.) 518, 636 (1819), Chief Justice Marshall spoke of 'a perpetual succession of individuals [...] capable of acting for the promotion of the particular object like one immortal being' (at 636).

The Equal Protection Clause of the Fourteenth Amendment to the US Constitution (1868) reads in part as follows:

> No State shall make or enforce any law which shall abridge the privileges or immunities of citizens of the United States; nor shall any State deprive any person of life, liberty, or property, without due process of law; nor deny to any person within its jurisdiction the equal protection of the laws.

A headnote in *Santa Clara County v. Southern Pacific Railroad Company*, 118 U.S. 394 (1886), though not part of the decision itself, has been of historical significance:

> The court does not wish to hear argument on the question whether the provision in the Fourteenth Amendment to the Constitution, which forbids a State to deny to any person within its jurisdiction the equal protection of the laws, applies to these corporations. We are all of the opinion that it does (per Chief Justice Waite).

In *Pembina Consolidated Silver Mining Co. v. Pennsylvania*, 125 U.S. 181 (1888), the Supreme Court held that, while a private corporation was not a citizen of an individual state, it was a *person* under the US Constitution (at 189):

> Such corporations are merely associations of individuals united for a special purpose and permitted to do business under a particular name and have a succession of members without dissolution. As said by Chief Justice Marshall: 'The great object of a corporation is to bestow the character and properties of individuality on a collective and changing body of men.' *Providence Bank v. Billings*, 4 Pet. 514, 29 U. S. 562.

A law that was enacted to protect former slaves became, for its critics, a freedom charter for corporations.

Through the nineteenth century the company form became increasingly accessible, as the barriers to the creation of companies were lowered. The Companies Act 1862 (25 & 26 Vict. c.89) stipulated that:

> Any seven or more persons associated for any lawful purpose may, by subscribing their names to a memorandum of association, and otherwise complying with the requisitions of this Act in respect of registration, form an incorporated company, with or without limited liability.

This was a long way from a Royal Charter. The decision in *Salomon v. Salomon & Co Ltd* [1896] UKHL 1 made clear that this was a purely formalistic requirement and did not necessitate an investigation into the underlying intentions, power structures, or family relationships. The company, even one that derived from a small family firm, was a fully and autonomous independent entity, and the presumption was to be strongly against looking behind the form to investigate the operational substance, the so-called 'piercing the corporate veil'. This was not primarily an ontological autonomy, but rather a declaration that the company was not the sum of its constituent parts and that it had interests which were quite distinct from those of its members or directors individually and collectively. It was the Court of Appeal that derided Aaron Salomon's company as a meretricious fiction, not the House of Lords (Hutton 2012).

In modernity, the vagueness of the division *res/persona* lent personhood 'an untold generative power as fuzziness at its borders enabled person to serve virtually all ends' (Selkala and Rajavuori 2017: 1026). The company became an auto-generating entity, which could reproduce without limit across jurisdictions through subsidiaries, shells structures, and complex forms of overlapping membership. The corporate form has undergone a process of normalization or naturalization (Stone 1972: 452):

> We have become so accustomed to the idea of a corporation having 'its' own rights, and being a 'person' and 'citizen' for so many statutory and constitutional purposes, that we forget how jarring the notion was to early jurists.

One can draw an analogy between the corporate entity and the Freudian self. Rather than having a single centre or gravitational point, the Freudian self is made up of distinct drives, instincts, and motivations. The behaviour of the individual cannot be traced directly to a single unitary consciousness but rather emerges out of the conflicts, repressions, and interactions of different constituent parts. The individual person, like the company, lacks complete insight into what drives and motivates them. Freud's position has been summed up by Watson (2014: 2) as follows: 'We neither are nor contain anything that remains identical over time. Even at one moment of time we are not one thing. Rather we are a multiplicity of interacting systems and processes'. As the idea of a special human self with a unique soul-like personality loses its plausibility, the analogies between human and non-human entities, both seen as the product of autopoiesis, gain in plausibility.

Yet corporate citizenship remains contentious, at both the policy level (e.g. in relation to tax avoidance and evasion) and the level of legal theory. Critics of corporate personhood promote the slogan that 'corporations are not people' and see the Supreme Court's decision in *Citizens United v. Federal Election Commission* 558 U.S. 310 (2010) as drawing on a flawed analogy between the individual citizen and the corporation in relation to free speech rights under the First Amendment (Clements 2014). At the heart of the case was the issue of whether corporations are entitled to free speech rights, specifically in relation to the democratic process and electioneering. A film funded by a corporation attacking Hillary Clinton, at that time seeking nomination for President, was to be shown on cable TV. The Supreme Court ruled that the film was an 'electioneering communication' within the meaning of the Bipartisan Campaign reform Act (BCRA) of 2002, but held by a majority that s. 203 of the BCRA violated the First Amendment with its guarantee of free speech rights to citizens of the United States. Justice Kennedy wrote that (at 17)

> The right of citizens to inquire, to hear, to speak, and to use information to reach consensus is a precondition to enlightened self-government and a necessary means to protect it.

The fact that a corporation was funding political statements, with 'the appearance of influence or access' would not 'cause the electorate to lose faith in our democracy'. This was 'an independent expenditure' and 'political speech presented to the electorate that is not coordinated with a candidate'. Further, 'that a corporation, or any other speaker, is willing to spend money to try to persuade voters presupposes that the people have the ultimate influence over elected officials' (at 44). In dissent, Justice Stevens rejected this reasoning (at 32):

> In the context of election to public office, the distinction between corporate and human speakers is significant. Although they make enormous contributions to our society, corporations are not actually members of it. They cannot vote or run for office.

The distinction was important, in that '[a]lthough they make enormous contributions to our society, corporations are not actually members of it. They cannot vote or run for office' (at 32). There were sound policy reasons for distinguishing individual from corporate speech, and the bedrock legal order also did not envisage corporations as citizens (at 37):

> Unlike our colleagues, [the framers of the Constitution] had little trouble distinguishing corporations from human beings, and when they constitutionalized the right to free speech in the First Amendment, it was the free speech of individual Americans that they had in mind.

Justice Scalia argued that no evidence had been 'that the First Amendment's unqualified text was originally understood to exclude such associational speech from its protection' (at 5). He adopted an aggregationalist position, seeing corporate speech as an ensemble of individual voices (at 7):

> Surely the dissent does not believe that speech by the Republican Party or the Democratic Party can be censored because it is not the speech of 'an individual American'. It is the speech of many individual Americans, who have associated in a common cause, giving the leadership of the party the right to speak on their behalf. The association of individuals in a business corporation is no different – or at least it cannot be denied the right to speak on the simplistic ground that it is not 'an individual American'.

Justice Scalia here adopted a 'the whole is the sum of its parts' argument, finding the individual citizenship of the corporation in its aggregation of the voices of the individuals that make it up.

One underlying political question that shifts with historical period and jurisdiction is the recognition and regulation of economic, religious, and social entitles that fall between the individual and the state. For Maitland (1911: 311), the French Revolution, with its hostility to corporations, represented modern absolutism: 'the absolute State faced the absolute individual'. The French legal theorist Raymond Saleilles (1855–1912) argued that, while talking up the rights of the individual, the revolutionary state had proceeded to remove the most basic right of all, that of free association (1922: 14). For Saleilles, it was collective rights that were primary, and individual rights flowed from, and were protected by, the group (Saleilles 1922: 13). By contrast the English radical William Hazlitt (1778–1830) condemned corporate bodies and established institutions as 'more corrupt and profligate than individuals' ([1822] 1925: 194). Mobs were 'almost always right in their feelings' based on 'the natural sense of justice recognized by all men in common': 'the only class of persons to whom the above courtly and corrupt motives is not applicable is that body of individuals which usually goes by the name of the *People*!' ([1822] 1925: 2140–5).

An individualist understanding of the self may correlate, as in the case of Scalia, with an aggregationalist understanding of the corporate person. Individualistic models of the person may be emphasized by stressing the fictive nature of the corporation, as in Friedrich Carl von Savigny's notion of *fingirte Person* ('artificial' or 'fictional' person) (1840: 240, 241). Similarly, autopoietic notions of the individual self would correlate with an autopoietic concept of the corporation: 'If [...] a systems theory approach is chosen, the very distinction between individualism and collectivism becomes questionable' (Teubner 1988: 132). Rejecting any individualistic understanding, Jung claimed 'the self is like a crowd' (1988: 102). The philosopher Derek Parfit remarks (1984: 275) 'I claim that a person is not like a Cartesian Ego, a being whose existence must be all-or-nothing. A person is like a nation'. Amatrudo likewise argues that 'individuals have the same ontological status as associations', finding a parallel between individual and collective: 'Collectives, of course, are not a free-floating consciousness. They should be broken down into individually conscious parts. But on the other hand, a more thoroughgoing ontological reductionism uncovers that individuals are in turn like miniature associations' (2008: 63). Walt Whitman (1819–1892) comes to mind here: 'Do I contradict myself? Very well then, I contradict myself. I am large – I contain multitudes' (1902: 77).

The state as person

According to Skinner (1999: 2), Thomas Hobbes (1588–1679) 'was the first major philosopher to organize a theory of government around the person of the state'. At the outset of *Leviathan*, Hobbes draws an analogy between God's act of creating nature, and humanity's ability to bring a being into existence ([1651] 1909: 8): 'NATURE (the Art whereby God hath made and governes the World) is by the *Art* of man, as in many other things, so in this also imitated, that it can make an Artificial Animal'. Life is 'but a motion of Limbs', and therefore analogous with automata or 'Engines that move themselves by springs and wheels as doth a watch'. The human body after all had a heart rather than springs, nerves rather than strings, joints rather than wheels, so it was in principle analogous to a machine:

> *Art* goes yet further, imitating that Rationall and most excellent worke of Nature, *Man*. For by Art is created that great LEVIATHAN called a COMMONWEALTH, or STATE, (in Latin, CIVITAS) which is but an Artificall Man; though of greater stature and defence than the Naturall; for whose protection and defence it was intended; and in which the *Sovereignty* is an Artificiall *Soul*, as giving life and motion to the whole body [...].

Hobbes parallels the functions and offices of state and the human body: 'Lastly, the *Pacts* and *Covenants*, by which the parts of this Body Politique were at first made, set together, and united, resemble the Fiat, or the *Let us make man*, pronounced by God in the Creation'. In suggesting that living beings and machines were analogous, Hobbes negated any straightforward opposition between the natural and the artificial. The notion of the sovereign as the *soul* complicates the imagery further since a watch does not have or require a soul, but the artificial body of state, according to this metaphor, does. The state must act, whereas the watch is merely a passive instrument.

Leviathan is centrally concerned with understanding the contrast between life without civil order (the *state of nature*) and the polity under the social contract ([1651] 1909: 66):

> The Greatest of humane Powers, is that which is compounded of the Powers of most men, united by consent, in one person, Naturall, or Civill, that has the use of all their Powers depending on his will; such as is the Power of a Common-wealth[.]

Central to Hobbes's account of personhood is the notion of representation, both as a semiotic and a political category (Pitkin 1967: 14–38). Hobbes defines *person* as follows ([1651] 1909: 123):

> A PERSON is he whose words or actions are considered, either as his own, or as representing the words or actions of another man, or of any other thing to whom they are attributed, whether Truly or by Fiction.

This stipulative definition sets up the ensuing discussion of representation and personhood. A natural person speaks and acts on their own behalf; an artificial person speaks on behalf of another ([1651] 1909: 12):

> When they are considered as his owne, then is he called a *Naturall Person*: And when they are considered as representing the words and actions of an other, then is he a *Feigned* or *Artificiall* person.

Hobbes then talks about the etymology of *person*, in terms of the theatrical metaphor ([1651] 1909: 123):

> The word Person is latine: insteed whereof the Greeks have πρόσωπον [prosopon], which signifies the Face, as *Persona* in latine signifies the *disguise*, or *outward appearance* of a man, counterfeited on the Stage; and sometimes more particularly that part of it, which disguiseth the face, as a Mask or Visard: And from the Stage, hath been translated to any Representer of speech and action, as well as in Tribunalls, as Theatres. So that a *Person*, is the same that an *Actor* is, both on the Stage and in common Conversation; and to *Personate*, is to *Act*, or *Represent* himselfe, or an other; and he that acteth another, is said to beare his Person, or act in his name[.]

Hobbes makes reference to Cicero's statement that in the tribunal he may have three roles: '*Unus sustineo tres Personas*; *Mei, Adversarii, & Judicis*, I beare three Persons; my own, my Adversaries, and the Judges'. The authentic owner of the words and actions is the *author*; the representative is an *actor* ([1651] 1909: 123):

> Of Persons Artificiall, some have their words and actions *Owned* by those whom they represent. And then the Person is the Actor; and he that owneth

> his words and actions, is the AUTHOR: In which case the Actor acteth by Authority. [...] So that by Authority, is alwayes under stood a Right of doing any act: and *done by Authority*, done by Commission, or Licence from him whose right it is.

The actor (agent) can bind the owner (principal/author), so long as the agent acts within the authority granted. Such relationships can also subsist between inanimate things so that almost anything can be 'represented by Fiction', once a society of laws has been established ([1651] 1909: 125):

> Inanimate things, as a Church, an Hospital, a Bridge, may be personated by a Rector, Animate. Master, or Overseer. But things Inanimate, cannot be Authors, nor therefore give Authority to their Actors: Yet the Actors may have Authority to procure their maintenance, given them by those that are Owners, or Governours of those things. And therefore, such things cannot be Personated, before there be some state of Civill Government.

Similarly, 'Children, Fooles, and Mad-men that have no use of Reason, may be Personated by Guardians, or Curators'. But only within a functioning legal order: 'this again has no place but in a State Civill, because before such estate, there is no Dominion of Persons'. The same caveat applies to idols and the like ([1651] 1909: 125):

> An Idol, or meer Figment of the brain, may be Personated; as were the Gods of the Heathen; which by Gods such Officers as the State appointed, were Personated, and held Possessions, and other Goods, and Rights, which men from time to time dedicated, and consecrated unto them. But Idols cannot be Authors: for an Idol is nothing. The Authority proceeded from the State: and therefore before introduction of Civill Government, the Gods of the Heathen could not be Personated.

The implication seems to be that, absent civil society, an idol cannot be 'personated', but within an established legal order, it is the state not the idol that is the author. Hobbes then plunges dramatically into contentious theological terrain ([1651] 1909: 125–6):

> The true God may be Personated. As he was; first by *Moses*; who governed the Israelites (that were not his but Gods people) not in his own name, with *Hoc dicit Moses*; but in Gods name, with *Hoc dicit Dominus*. Secondly, by the Son of man, his own Son, our Blessed Saviour *Jesus Christ*, that came to reduce the Jewes, and induce all Nations into the Kingdome of his Father; not as of himself, but as sent from his Father. And thirdly, by the Holy Ghost, or Comforter, speaking, and working in the Apostles: which Holy Ghost, was a Comforter that came not of himselfe; but was sent, and proceeded from them both.

It is representation that creates persons. It would seem to follow that the Trinity, understood as three persons, is a creation of human beings ([1651] 1909: 384):

> From whence we may gather the reason why those names *Father*, *Son*, and *Holy Spirit* in the signification of the Godhead, are never used in the Old Testament: For they are Persons, that is, they have their names from Representing; which could not be, till divers men had Represented Gods Person in ruling, or in directing under him.

Representation can create a single person out of a multitude ([1651] 1909: 126):

> A Multitude of men, are made *One* Person, when they are by one man, or one Person, Represented; so that be done with the consent of every one of that Multitude in particular. For it is the *Unity* of the Representer, not the Unity of the Represented, that maketh the Person One. And it is the Representer that beareth the Person, and but one Person: And *Unity*, cannot otherwise be understood in Multitude.

The contract or covenant thereby endows the shapeless multitude with unity. But the multitude is not a single individual, even if it is a single person; each individual is the author of the acts and words of their representative ([1651] 1909: 126):

> And because the Multitude naturally is not One, but A Multitude of *Many*; they cannot be understood for one; but many An Actor may be Many Authors, of every thing their Representative saith, or doth in their name; Every man giving their common Representer, Authority from himselfe in particular; and owning all the actions the Representer doth, in case they give him Authority without stint [...].

The representative may be a single individual or a group. There are then two persons, a person by fiction who is the state, and an artificial person who acts for state and by its authority of the state, the sovereign. Once this covenant is established, each member of the multitude has surrendered their right of self-government ([1651] 1909: 132): 'This is the Generation of that great LEVIATHAN, or rather (to speake more reverently) of that Mortall God, to which wee owe under the Immortall God, our peace and defence'. There is no contract between the sovereign and the covenanters. The sovereign is not their agent; he has absorbed their agency in key respects. The essence of the state is found in this one person, of whose acts each member of society is an author ([1651]) 1909: 132: 'And he that carryeth this Person, is called SOVEREIGN, and said to have *Soveraigne Power*; and every one besides his SUBJECT'. The commonwealth itself, while not immortal, has no limit on its temporal existence, so long as it does not perish 'by internal diseases' ([1651] 1909: 247): 'For by the nature of their Institution, they are designed to live, as long as Man-kind, or as the Lawes of Nature, or as Justice it selfe, which gives them life'. The multitude is not all necessarily of like mind, but as individuals they share equally in the covenant of state and a single action of the state can be attributed to each (Skinner 1999: 5). Hobbes's account of representation is an uneasy mix of law, theatrical metaphor, theology, and semiotics. There is no explanation of what constitutes true as opposed to fictional representation. The underlying problem is that the state represents no one, as the multitude has been absorbed into it. The sovereign represents the person of the state, but the state stands only for itself.[4]

The notion of *moral personhood* (Latin, *persona moralis*) was elaborated by Samuel von Pufendorf (1632–1694) as a critical response to Hobbes's theory of the state as *persona ficta* (see Holland 2017), in order to understand the state as a moral actor. This was influential in the development of theories of state personality (Bartelson 2015). Running parallel with the political state as the dominion of a sovereign under God is the notion of nations as given entities in the natural, post-Babel order, in the genealogies that flowed from the sons of Noah, with the nation understood as linking territory, language, and family tree (Genesis 10: 5): 'By these were the isles of the Gentiles divided in their lands; every one after his tongue, after their families, in their nations'. Modern states operate in the tension between these two extremes. On one understanding, the state is seen as imposing unity onto a diverse multitude of human beings through the exercise of sovereignty (derived from God or through a covenant with the people). This is distinct from a model whereby the people or *Volk*, sharing a common language, history, genealogy, or territory, pre-exists the creation of the state. In the first case, the unity is fictional, in the sense that the creation of the state requires an act of sovereignty or state personification acting on a formless aggregate. In the second, the people as a collectivity pre-exists the foundation of the state. Otto von Gierke (1841–1921) saw the first as derived from Roman law; the second as essentially Germanic. Sovereignty as act of creation suggests the mask of incorporation model of legal personhood, whereas the people-as-*Volk* model parallels the natural person-in-being model.

An organicist understanding of the state, and of the relation of the individual to it, suggests organicist theories of corporate personality, as in Gierke's notion of *social organism* (*sozialier Organismus*) (1902: 13) and *reale Verbandspersönlichkeit* or *Gesamtpersönlichkeit* ('real corporate personality') (Gierke 1889). This organicism represented the promotion of a Germanic or Teutonic essence to German and English law (Geldart 1911: 92–93). Gierke compared the recognition of an existing association (*Verband*) with the recognition as a person given to a natural human being at birth (Gierke 1895: 488). Just as law does not create a human being, so law does not necessarily create an association.

The personhood of women

In *Re Goodell*, 39 Wis. 232 (1876) the issue was whether the term *person*, as used in a statute, included women. The matter arose in relation to whether women could be admitted to practice law in Wisconsin. In finding that women could not be admitted, Ryan CJ appealed to the natural order of things: 'The law of nature destines and qualifies the female sex for the bearing and nurture of the children of our race and for the custody of the homes of the world and their maintenance in love and honor'. For women to join the legal profession of law would be to depart 'from the order of nature': 'Nature has tempered woman as little for the juridical conflicts of the court room, as for the physical conflicts of the battle field'. Counsel for Miss Lavina Goodell had argued that the word *person*, as used in the statute, necessarily included women:

> And when counsel was arguing for this lady that the word, person [...] necessarily includes females, her presence made it impossible to suggest to him as *reductio ad absurdum* of his position, that the same construction of the same word in sec. I, ch. 37, would subject woman to prosecution for the paternity of a bastard, and in secs. 39, 40, ch. 164, to prosecution for rape. Discussions are habitually necessary in courts of justice, which are unfit for female ears.

Clearly, this falls far short of a philosophical analysis of the notion of *person*. It understands the category in relation to its natural order of things, but the issue is read contextually in terms of the appropriate understanding of who a person is for the purpose of the statute.

In *Edwards v. Canada (Attorney General)* [1930] A.C. 124 (Privy Council), the question was whether women were *qualified persons* under the *British North America Acts* such that they could run for a seat in the Senate (see Hamilton 2008: 69ff.). The Privy Council heard an appeal from a decision of the Supreme Court of Canada (Re meaning of the word 'Persons' in s. 24 of British North America Act, [1928] SCR 276). Noting that there was no doubt 'that the word "persons" when standing alone *prima facie* includes women', the court added (at 285–6):

> It connotes human beings – the criminal and the insane equally with the good and the wise citizen, the minor as well as the adult. Hence the propriety of the restriction placed upon it by the immediately preceding word 'qualified' in ss. 24 and 26 and the words 'fit and qualified' in s. 32, which exclude the criminal and the lunatic or imbecile as well as the minor, who is explicitly disqualified by s. 23 (1). Does this requirement of qualification also exclude women?

Rejecting the argument that *persons* was used 'in its more general signification', Anglin CJC countered that it was 'a word of equivocal signification, sometimes synonymous with human beings, sometimes including only men' (at 286). He concluded that the question had to be decided by reference to the legal context and background (at 288):

> For the public offices thereby created women were, by the common law, ineligible and it would be dangerous to assume that by the use of the ambiguous

> term 'persons' the Imperial Parliament meant in 1867 to bring about so vast a constitutional change affecting Canadian women, as would be involved in making them eligible for selection as Privy Councillors.

Duff J noted (at 291) that *persons* ordinarily included 'natural persons of both sexes', but that context and occasion of use might radically affect their meaning: 'the nature of the subject matter and object of the legislation, may require us to ascribe to general words a scope more restricted than their usual import, in order loyally to effectuate the intention of the legislature'. The court drew on the disability of women at Common Law in relation to the holding of public office, as well as on a reading of the intent of the Act in relation to *qualified persons.*

The Privy Council reversed. While the court accepted that, in relation to public office, the word *person* would be traditionally understood as referring exclusively to men, this was a reflection of custom, a relic from the Germanic tribes when public office went together with martial ability for defence: 'Customs are apt to develop into traditions which are stronger than law and remain unchallenged long after the reason for them has disappeared' (at 7). The court saw countries 'within the Britannic system' as 'undergoing a continuous process of evolution' (at 8). Agreeing that a constitutional document should be read in 'a large, liberal and comprehensive spirit', they saw the burden as lying on those who would exclude women: 'to those who ask why the word should include females, the obvious answer is why it should not' (at 10).

Masks and persons in legal theory

To propose personhood for a higher animal may be, in one sense, to seek a modest increment in law's recognition of entities deserving of legal protection, but at another level it proposes a revolution in law's basic ontologies. In the case law to date, the courts have resisted as far as possible any *de novo* investigation of legal personhood (see Chapter 5). By contrast, contemporary legal theory is deeply invested in the interplay between law, personhood, and the mask. As a critical metaphor, *mask* points to the gap between appearance and reality, as in a phrase such as *the mask of power* (Runciman 1997). Bentham in his diatribe against Sir William Blackstone speaks of him turning 'with scorn upon those beneficent legislators, whose care it has been to pluck the mask of Mystery from the face of Jurisprudence' ([1823] 1977: 410). For Noonan (2002: 19–20), law imposes a mask that suppresses authentic humanity:

> By masks [...] I mean ways of classifying individual human beings, so that their humanity is disavowed. [...] By mask I mean the legal construct suppressing the humanity of a participant in the process. Mask is the metaphor I have chosen for such a construct, because the human face is where emotion and affection are visible if not deliberately concealed.

To categorize a person as property 'is a perfect mask' (2002: 20). But who or what is behind the mask? If there is 'no such thing as a plain-old person', then 'it is law that defines the categories of person' (Gordon 2018: 50–51). It follows that law constitutes personhood, rather than concealing it. From a Foucaultian perspective, the *human* is constructed within modernity in order to serve as a site for law, for surveillance and control: 'personhood is not a (biologically) given, stable property of human beings that precedes their interaction with the law'; rather 'the notion of personhood is assigned to selected "bodies" by discursive regimes' (Horsman and Korsten (2016: 277). Behind this is Foucault's project of the denaturalization of the human, whereby both human beings and legal persons are 'artefacts of techniques of governing' (Wishart 2016: 759). The *mask of personhood* is a lie (Gray 2002: 58–9):

> Being a person is not the essence of humanity, only – as the word's history suggests – one of its masks. Persons are only humans who have donned the mask that has been handed down in Europe over the past few generations, and taken it for a face.

The liberal critique of law is that it erases the authentic person behind the mask of personhood; the post-humanist sees that fiction of authentic personhood as brought into being by operation of law.

In contemporary legal discussions of personhood, the visual is placed at the centre. Personhood is the 'law of the *imago*, of lineage, of the succession of the paternal form through each generation, symbolised in the household by the pride of place given to the painted death-mask – the effigy – of the ancestral father'. Further, 'the legal subject itself is in one respect to be understood or recognised as a visual fiction drawn upon the natural person' (Goodrich 1996: 95). It is the power of this visual mode that holds the person together, in that it 'crosses the boundaries of natural and legal personality'. The famous frontispiece to Hobbes's *Leviathan* is 'one of the most profound visual renderings of political theory ever produced' (Bredekamp 2007: 30). *Mask* in these discussions operates a metonymy for representation, both in its semiotic and political senses. Representation can reveal as well as conceal, personify or depersonify, appropriate or negate (Goodrich 1990, Douzinas 1999, Agamben 1998, 2009, Parsley 2010). Underlying these works is a critique of the artificial/natural distinction, as reflected in the pairings of mask/human and of legal person/natural person.

Animal personhood and legal categories

The director of the Nonhuman Rights project, Steven Wise, sees law as intrinsically, though non-systematically, conservative. In the words of Oliver Wendell Holmes, Jr., law is susceptible to 'blind imitation of the past', is largely devoid of ideas of its own, feeding on 'ideas from the outside' like a 'scavenger' (Holmes 1897: 457–9, Wise 1995: 15). It follows that 'the understandings and misunderstandings of science, philosophy, and theology therefore frequently underpin important legal principles' (1995: 15–16). In particular, Wise targets the 'master metaphor' of the Great Chain of Being (Lovejoy [1936] 1964), with its fixed hierarchy of beings and teleological anthropocentrism, which while defunct as a scientific theory of nature, remains 'fixed within the living common law' (Wise 1995: 44). The Darwinian revolution brought an end to the idea that inequality was determined by nature: 'The destruction of the Great Chain of Being kicked open the door to the acceptance of modern ideas of social equality. It also opened the human mind to the idea of the nonhuman mind' (Wise 1995: 43). Yet law as regards the relations between human and non-human animals 'is nearly a living fossil of archaic Greek and Roman notions of science and jurisprudence' (Wise 1996: 182). As a result, the status of non-human animals such as chimpanzees and bonobos is one of 'legal thinghood' (1996: 183), and their claims to bodily integrity and bodily liberty, what Wise terms 'dignity-rights' (Wise 1998), are invisible to law.

Darwinism, Wise argues, has discredited an intellectual order based on the assumption of humanity's 'complete and unrestricted domination of nonhuman animals' (Wise 1998: 795). The 'ancient cosmologies' that lent credence to the restriction of legal personhood to human beings were defunct (Wise 1998: 795) and it followed 'contempt for the dignity-rights of qualified nonhuman animals is contempt for Western law' (Wise 1998: 796). Just as dignity-rights are ascribed to humans who lack full cognition and autonomy through a legal fiction, similar rights should be ascribed to those animals that 'possess a full or realistic capacity for autonomy' (1998: 798). This leads to the application of both the principle of equality and that of proportionality, that legal protections should be granted in proportion to autonomy (1998: 798–9).

The process from the legal thinghood to the legal personhood of qualified non-human animals 'beginning with chimpanzees and bonobos' would, after the necessary 'minor legal revolution', follow from ordinary common law principles (Wise 1998: 799). A legal thing has no right to bring an action (*standing*), and therefore cannot assert a claim to legal personhood. Judicial recognition required that 'qualified nonhuman animals' have an immunity-right, rather than a claim-right, to bodily integrity or bodily liberty. This could then be enforced by an action such as *habeas corpus*, which can be brought by a third party: 'If a writ of *habeas corpus* or similar action is available, they would need no other legal rights to enforce their fundamental negative liberty-rights' (Wise 1998: 815).

Law suffers from 'paradigm blindness' (Wise 1998: 836) and should adapt the 'nonpositivist' natural law tradition that grounds rights in abstract moral values rather than in strict doctrine. These rights are found in international treaties and inhere either explicitly or implicitly in national legal regimes (Wise 1988: 846ff.). The notion that Kantian autonomy is required to benefit from dignity-rights is false since these are granted to 'infants, the persistently vegetative, and many younger children and severely mentally limited who lack the abilities sufficient for rationality, autonomy, self-determination or the capacity to make moral choices' (Wise 1998: 870). In practice 'courts may limit the dignity-rights of those who possess the less-than-normal degree of cognition required for full Kantian autonomy to those rights appropriate to the capacity for autonomy and self-determination that they do possess' (Wise 1998: 874). By analogy, courts should recognize dignity-rights appropriate to the capacity for autonomy and self-determination demonstrated by animals (Wise 1998: 875). Human beings with no capacity for autonomy and self-determination were dealt with using the legal fiction of 'substituted judgment' (Wise 1998: 881).

Courts deny dignity-rights for animals 'in the teeth of empirical evidence that at least some nonhuman animals possess it' (Wise 1998: 882). The use of legal fictions is best justified when there is an alignment with the underlying values and principles of the legal system: 'The attribution of legal personhood to entities that might not strictly be entitled to it, such as incompetent humans, corporations, even a Hindu idol, is one example' (Wise 1998: 882).[5] Membership of a species, which follows a taxonomic classification, does not in and of itself imply dignity-rights. What must be demonstrated empirically is 'self-determination, cognition, and sentience': 'Unless the qualities of its members are known, why should its population be eligible for legal personhood?' (Wise 1998: 84). A number of intelligent hominid species have vanished, but if a member of such a species appeared then the ascription of dignity-rights would be based on qualities rather than taxonomic classification (Wise 1998: 887). Common law equality 'requires, at a minimum, that a classification's means be rationally related to any desired end', and the means and the end must be legitimate (Wise 1998: 896). For this reason, courts have allowed suits by infants for injuries suffered *in utero* (Wise 1998: 896), even though a foetus is in law neither a person nor a property. Companion animals have been recognized as falling in between the categories of person and property (Wise 1998: 898fn.).[6]

Following Gewirth (1978: 121), Wise argues for a proportionality principle in relation to animal dignity-rights, as a matter of equality. Any judge who looks with an open mind at the overarching values embedded in the common law could find the means to depart from 'a narrow line of past decisions' to achieve fidelity to more fundamental values (Dworkin 1986: 291). The recognition of dignity-rights for animals is a restorative project, one which requires renewed respect in Western societies for their own highest abstract principles: 'Just as the domestication of nonhuman animals may have served as the model for the enslavement of human beings, so can the destruction of human slavery model for the destruction of the legal thinghood of nonhuman animals' (Wise 1998: 906, drawing on Jacoby 1994). The minor legal revolution required is the legal personhood of qualified non-human animals, and this can be achieved following 'the normal processes of traditional Western law' (Wise 1998: 914).

Wise seeks to apply Darwinism to the unseating of the Great Chain model, and, by implication, the Christian concept of the soul which underlies the special status of human beings within God's creation. Yet the natural law tradition on which Wise draws for his grounding of dignity-rights is intertwined with the history of Christian theology and thoroughly anthropocentric. The relationship between Darwinism and modern notions of equality and rights is ambivalent at best. In place of the rigidity of the Great Chain model, Darwinism saw the natural world as lacking fixed relationships and ceaselessly dynamic over time and space. A radical consequence of Darwinism is that definitions and distinctions between key terms are not fixed, and the point of view from which one contemplates the natural world is itself open to question. Wise makes use of this lack of fixity to argue that the boundary of the human species should not itself provide the criterion for assigning dignity-rights. These should be assigned in proportion to the capacity for autonomy, self-determination, and consciousness (Wise 2002b). Darwinism frees intellectually from the framework of Christianity and the soul as the key criteria for distinguishing between human beings and non-human animals, but it also undermines arguments that draw on self-consciousness, autonomy, free-will, and rationality. In denying these attributes to human beings in a full sense, Darwinism inevitably denies them to non-human animals. Peter Singer regards questions of self-consciousness and autonomy as secondary in relation to the core principle of 'equal consideration of interests'. This is the principle that we give equal weight in our moral deliberations to the like interests of all those affected by our actions (Singer 1987). Yet, equality is not a concept explicated within or relevant to the biological sciences; it is a political ideal.

As has been frequently noted, the category of *non-human animal* is internally highly diverse, both as a matter of biology and in terms of relationships to the human social order. Legal personhood for animals seems to be envisaged for animals brought into, or born within, the human social order. Personhood in law requires a jurisdiction. Kymlicka and Donaldson (2011, 2014) argue for integrating animals within the *polis* into a rights-based order or a form of *citizenship*, whereas the primary human duty towards wild animals is to leave them alone. Shooster (2017) rejects this distinction, which following Nozick (1974), he characterizes as a model of 'Kantianism for humans, utilitarianism for animals'. Wild animals, he argues, should be given positive rights in law. Discussing the history of natural taxonomies and human/animal classifications, Dunbar (1993: 110) points out that 'chimpanzees, gorillas, and orang-utans turn out to be our closest living relatives', sharing not only anatomical features but also genetic similarities. Further, 'chimpanzees share with us a number of psychological characteristics that have not been found in other species', such as 'the ability to engage in pretend play' and 'to see the world from another individual's point of view'. Where human beings lack these abilities, for example, in cases of autism, we nonetheless treat them as human: 'How much more deserving must be the chimpanzee case for equal treatment!' (Dunbar 1993: 110). This is known as the 'argument from marginal cases', that is, an analogy drawn between marginal human cases and higher animals (see Dombrowski 1997).

Objections to animal personhood are frequently put in terms of a key deficit attributed to higher animals. The counter argument is that 'there is no such defect that is possessed by animals that is not also possessed by some group of human beings' (Simon 2006: 4). There is an analogy to be made, it is claimed, between the legal personhood of children and that of higher animals, especially given that children once were seen as a form of property (Rollin 1981, 2006). In any case, these conventional groupings of natural phenomena are the product of the human imagination (Dunbar 1993: 110):

> The biological reality is that all classifications are artificial. They force a certain order on to the rather chaotic mess of the natural world. [...] The real world consists only of individuals who are more or less closely related to each other by virtue of descent from one or common ancestors.

Various proposals that fall short of advocating legal personhood for animals have been put forward. Bryant (2008) considers a narrowly defined category of *aggrieved person*, not based on similarity to human beings, which would have procedural meaning in terms of standing. One reformist view holds that animals are not persons and lack the capacity for 'normative self-government' (Korsgaard 2013: 32):

> but we need not accept the idea that the world is divided into persons and property, or persons and things. Without reclassifying them as persons, we may still regard all animals as ends in themselves, and, as such, the proper subjects of rights against human mistreatment.

The recent trend for some courts in the United States to recognize the special status of pets within families, as a kind of *quasi-property*, has not disturbed law's fundamental schema (Kobil 2015: 626ff). More radically, the category of *non-personal subject of law* has been proposed, for species of sentient beings possessing the 'capability of having subjective experience', that is, 'a sufficiently developed nervous structure, in particular the formation of the brain' (Pietrzykowski 2017: 62–63, Pietrzykowski 2018). A further proposal is the category of *living property* (Favre 2010). Anestal (2017) argues for *limited legal personhood* for chimpanzees, to allow standing to be granted, and for the purpose of habeas corpus relief. In the case of animals, a more radical strategy is the elimination of property as a category for all sentient animals (Francione 1993, 1995, 2008, Francione and Charlton 2015, Hauser, Cushman and Kamen 2006). Francione rejects arguments that higher cognitive capacities should be required for personhood (Francione 2006). Arguments for animal personhood merely reassign some non-human beings from one category (*res*) to another (*persona*), rather than disrupting this repressive legal schema more radically. The category *subject of legally relevant interests* has been proposed for the foetus (ten Haaf 2017).

Conclusion

Law of necessity draws distinctions between kinds of entity, both as a matter of fundamental legal principle and on an *ad hoc* basis. The case of animals, in particular the potential legal personhood of animals, sits problematically within the deep structures of law and 'the epistemic division into *persona/res/acta*' (Lamalle 2014: 305). One way to understand this division is as an exhaustive listing of legal categories. Law only *sees* person, things, and actions. Each and every entity to which law turns its attention must fall under one of these categories. Within the category of *persona*, human beings have a special status, in that they are seen as ends in themselves, in the Kantian sense that they are not to be treated as means to an end (Korsgaard 2013: 29). Animals, in that they are things (*res*) and therefore actual or potential property, serve those human ends, rather than being ends in their own right.

In some legal contexts, *man* might be understood to include women, or *person* to exclude women, or *person* to include both men and women. This problem of the generic masculine is a theological issue, as in whether man and woman are equal as *imago dei* (Horowitz 1979), a translation question, both between languages (as in the Biblical text) or when translating legal language into ordinary language, and a hermeneutic problem, given the social and conceptual distance between the original text and the society in which it is being interpreted. Law, on its surface, moves between (what is understood as) the categories of ordinary language and the internally oriented categories of law. The linguistic culture of law presupposes that legal language can in principle be distinguished from ordinary language, a legal version of the *discontinuity thesis* with regard to the language of science (Harris 2005: 81). Yet legal language circulates beyond law in highly complex ways. Durant (2018: 64) argues that 'semantic indeterminacy in the general terminology of law may function as a conduit for communication between the legal sphere and the wider public'. Dewey (1926: 656) complained that the legal notion of person had been blurred by 'considerations popular, historical, political, moral, philosophical, metaphysical and, in connection with the latter, theological'. The legal concept of person might be defined simply as 'a right-and-duty-bearing unit', thereby maintaining a separation from its meaning in 'popular speech, or in psychology, or in philosophy, or morals'. He drew an analogy with the use of the word *dry* when referring to wine. This specialist usage had nothing in common with 'the properties of dry solids': 'Why should not the same sort of thing hold of the use of person in law?' (Dewey 1926: 656). Parallel questions are raised in theology. A discontinuity approach would emphasize the historical specificity of the meaning of personhood in relation to the Trinity, and its distinctive quality when compared with modern usage (Holmes 2014). By contrast the notion of a *relational* or *social Trinity* seeks to draw parallels between the 'necessary relationship of mutual holy love' between Father, Son, and Holy Spirit, and the most important concerns of human society and interpersonal relationships: 'The substance of God, "God," has no ontological content, no true being, apart from communion' (Zizioulas 1997: 17).

From an integrational point of view, one might argue, law reflects the pervasiveness of the language myth. Law embodies definitional thinking, and is reliant on the fiction that words and texts have a determinate meaning which pre-exists the process of interpretation, that is, when a text is read against the background of particular fact-pattern. Yet one might also see law as an institutionalized form of lay practice. The linguistic culture of law, from this standpoint, represents on one level the denial of indeterminacy but on a deeper level the recognition of indeterminacy and a set of strategies and techniques for dealing with it.

Notes

1 www.oas.org.
2 There are also many kinds of *unincorporated bodies* that law may recognize or regulate in certain ways, for example business partnerships, trade unions, clubs (Maitland 1911). The family is in this sense unincorporated, though it is partly constituted by law and to a degree regulated.
3 *State v. Stockton,* 5 Ariz. 153 (1958); *Commonwealth v. Turner,* 14 N.E. 130 (Mass. 1887).
4 For more on Hobbes and personhood, see Brito Vieira (2009).
5 *Pramatha Nath Mullick v. Pradyumna Kumar Mullick* (1925) LR 52 Ind App 245.
6 *Morgan v. Kroupa*, 702 A.2d 630, 633 (Vt. 1997) (quoting *Corso v. Crawford Dog & Cat Hosp., Inc.*, 415 N.Y.S.2d 182, 183 (City Civ. Ct. 1979)

5 Litigating animal personhood

Introduction

The litigation discussed in the following addresses primarily issues of non-human animal rights and legal status, in contrast to traditional animal welfare activism in the courts (Mouzourakis 2014). The briefs, judgements, and appeals, in dialogue with law review articles and legal commentary, generate a field of discussion where the most basic categories are scrutinized and particular forms of legal reasoning challenged. In parallel with this is the eye-catching claim that non-human animals may, in some sense, be *persons*.[1] One gloss given for *person* in Johnson's *Dictionary* is 'One that may maintain any plea in a judicial court' (1766).

Standing

The central issue in animal litigation is standing to sue, that is, the right to bring an action (*locus standi*). Cases range from the momentous to the trivial. As an example of the latter, one can point to the case known as 'Blackie the Talking Cat' (*Miles v. City Council of Augusta, Georgia*, 710 F.2d 1542 (11th Cir. 1983)). A couple who received donations on the street on the strength of Blackie producing sentences such as 'I love you' or 'I want my mama' were warned by the authorities that they required a business licence. They sued on a number of grounds, including free speech rights under the First Amendment, but lost in the district court. The Court of Appeals for the Eleventh Circuit affirmed. The Court noted in a footnote (para. 13, fn. 5):

> This Court will not hear a claim that Blackie's right to free speech has been infringed. First, although Blackie arguably possesses a very unusual ability, he cannot be considered a 'person' and is therefore not protected by the Bill of Rights. Second, even if Blackie had such a right, we see no need for appellants to assert his right *jus tertii*. Blackie can clearly speak for himself.

For purposes of the discussion here, the question of standing raises the question of law's anthropocentrism, that is, whether there must be a direct, proximate,

DOI: 10.4324/9781315143132-6

and clearly identifiable human interest in the litigation: the so-called *injury-in-fact*:[2] 'Standing's paradigmatic legal subject [...] is the autonomous individual, standing apart from nature and in control of it' (Purdy 2016: 1626). Only legal entities can be parties to lawsuits, such as natural persons, groups, or associations of persons with a common interest or grievance, a class of plaintiffs (as in 'class action suit', in those jurisdictions that permit this), corporations, political entities such as individual states within a federation, or sovereign states. Some natural persons are *non sui juris*, that is, they lack the capacity to bring or defend legal actions (e.g. children, persons with certain incapacities), and in such cases a parent, trustee, ward or guardian may bring an action. But the rights of third parties to bring actions are strictly limited. In the United States, the basic rule is found in the so-called Case or Controversy Clause of Article III of the Constitution. This restricts the federal courts to hearing only actual cases or controversies, that is, where the two parties have an evident and genuine issue at stake.

The standing of natural entities (bodies of water, wetlands, areas of wilderness, individual animals, or categories of animal) is for animal rights activists the exclusionary barrier preventing access to law's remedies (Stone 1972, Babcock 2016, Blake 2017); for critics, this would open the floodgates to legal chaos (Kobil 2015: 638). Stone (1972: fn.18) speaks of 'the increasingly legal fictiveness of the individual human being'. In arguing for the giving of legal rights 'to forests, oceans, rivers and other so-called "natural objects" in the environment – indeed, to the natural environment as a whole' (1972: 456), Stone offers a concomitant downgrading of what might be termed the myth of personhood (1972: fn. 26):

> Consider, for example, the concept of a 'person' in legal or in everyday speech. Is each person a fixed bundle of relationships, persisting unaltered through time? Do our molecules and cells not change at every moment? Our hypostatizations always have a pragmatic quality to them.

Arguments for the legal personhood of animals are in the first instance arguments for animal standing.

Standing and radical exclusion

In *Cherokee Nation v. State of Georgia* 30 U.S. 1 (1831), the Cherokee, in the form of the Cherokee Nation, sought the intervention of the Supreme Court to prevent further territorial dispossession by the State of Georgia, in violation of previous treaties. The legal status of the Cherokee was unclear, neither a foreign state nor fully integrated into the United States. The court found that the Cherokee lacked standing to bring the case. Chief Justice Marshall expressed his regret: 'If Courts were permitted to indulge their sympathies, a case better calculated to excite them can scarcely be imagined' (at 15). The Cherokee people, 'once numerous, powerful, and truly independent, found by our ancestors in the quiet and uncontrolled possession of an ample domain' had been 'gradually sinking beneath our superior policy, our arts and our arms'. Previous treaties had been successively violated, leaving only a small remnant of territory: 'To preserve this remnant, the present application is made' (at 15). The Cherokee did not fall under any of the constitutional categories to be able to bring suit (at 16). The state of Georgia could 'unquestionably be sued in this Court', but was the Cherokee nation 'a foreign state in the sense in which that term is used in the Constitution?' (at 16). It had the status of a ***domestic dependent nation***: 'Their relation to the United States resembles that of a ward to his guardian' (at 17). The Commerce Clause of the US Constitution, which empowered Congress to 'regulate commerce with foreign nations, and among the several States, and with the Indian tribes' (Art. III, s. 8). Chief Justice Marshall found 'three distinct classes', arguing therefore that the designation *foreign nation* could not be applied to the Indian tribes who had been allocated to a category of their own. He concluded with these words (at 20):

> If it be true that the Cherokee Nation have rights, this is not the tribunal in which those rights are to be asserted. If it be true that wrongs have been inflicted, and that still greater are to be apprehended, this is not the tribunal which can redress the past or prevent the future.

In effect, the Cherokee could sign treaties but had no standing to enforce them. Justice Henry Baldwin stressed that 'mere phraseology' could not make a nation out of the Indians, or out of tribes, foreign states (at 44). In 1791, 'in abandoning their last remnant of political right', the Cherokee had contracted under the title of 'Cherokee Nation'. The treaty was a contract, and consciousness of the reality behind these labels would 'divest words of their magic' (at 46).

In *Dred Scott v. Sandford*, 60 U.S. 393 (1856) the Supreme Court decision determined that a 'free negro of the African race', the descendant of slaves, was 'not a "citizen" within the meaning of the Constitution of the United States'. The case involved an enslaved man, Dred Scott, who had been taken from a state where slavery was legal to one where it was unlawful (the 'Missouri compromise'), and then later returned to a slavery jurisdiction. Dred Scott argued that he and his wife were now free because of their residence in free territories. The Chief Justice, Roger B. Taney, while he went on to rule on the merits, was of the opinion that the case failed for lack of standing and the corollary lack of jurisdiction. Even if it had been the case that Dred Scott was technically emancipated, he had no standing to sue. In the legal order that preceded the founding of the United States, it had been unquestioned that those of African descent were (at 407)

> beings of an inferior order, and altogether unfit to associate with the white race either in social or political relations, and so far inferior that they had no rights which the white man was bound to respect, and that the negro might justly and lawfully be reduced to slavery for his benefit.

The notion that such beings might be owned was held axiomatically, being 'at that time fixed and universal in the civilized portion of the white race' (at 407).

The idea that 'all men are created equal' could not have included members of the 'enslaved African race' (at 410). Whatever changes had taken place in public opinion, the construction of the Constitution needed to respect the 'true meaning and intention when it was formed and adopted' (at 394). A 'liberal construction in their favour' was not possible, given the 'plain language' of the founding legal enactments in relation to notions of *people* and *citizen* (at 426).

Standing and nature

In the United States the question of standing has arisen repeatedly, in relation to litigation on behalf of particular species, ecologically valuable terrain or individual animals (Francione 1995: 65–90).[3] In *Sierra Club v. Morton,* 405 U.S. 727 (1972), the Supreme Court held by a majority that the Sierra Club had no standing to bring an action against proposed development by Disney since it did not allege any injury to itself or its members. In dissent, Justice William O. Douglas argued that the issue would be much simplified if standing could be conferred 'in the name of the inanimate object about to be despoiled, defaced, or invaded by roads and bulldozers and where injury is the subject of public outrage' (at 741–742). Parties to litigation went well beyond natural persons (at 742):

> Inanimate objects are sometimes parties in litigation. A ship has a legal personality, a fiction found useful for maritime purposes. The corporation sole – a creature of ecclesiastical law – is an acceptable adversary and large fortunes ride on its cases. The ordinary corporation is a 'person' for purposes of the adjudicatory processes, whether it represents proprietary, spiritual, aesthetic, or charitable causes.

In his reasoning Douglas embraced the radical idea that natural objects were bundles of multiple non-human and human interests. Just as corporations were persons (at 743):

> So it should be as respects valleys, alpine meadows, rivers, lakes, estuaries, beaches, ridges, groves of trees, swampland, or even air that feels the destructive pressures of modern technology and modern life. The river, for example, is the living symbol of all the life it sustains or nourishes - fish, aquatic insects, water ouzels, otter, fisher, deer, elk, bear, and all other animals, including man, who are dependent on it or who enjoy it for its sight, its sound, or its life. The river as plaintiff speaks for the ecological unit of life that is part of it.

Since the river could not speak for itself, those parties 'who have that intimate relation with the inanimate object about to be injured, polluted, or otherwise despoiled are its legitimate spokesmen' (at 745) should have standing to defend it before the courts (at 752):

> That is why these environmental issues should be tendered by the inanimate object itself. Then there will be assurances that all of the forms of life which

> it represents will stand before the court - the pileated woodpecker as well as the coyote and bear, the lemmings as well as the trout in the streams.

In one sense this raised 'Nature's own rights', including the interests or 'nonintrinsic values of' the natural object (Stone 2010: 159). The evocation of autonomous interests in nature hints at a truly radical non-anthropocentricism, but this collapses into human concerns and values.

The Silver Spring monkeys

The Silver Spring monkeys litigation concerned cruelty to macaques held for research purposes. Legal action was instigated by People for Ethical Treatment of Animals (PETA), International Primate Protective League (IPPL), and the Animal Law Enforcement Association (ALEA) as plaintiffs but also as *next friends* of the monkeys. The director of the laboratory had been convicted of animal cruelty (a decision which was later reversed), but while that prosecution was being appealed, two lawsuits were instigated.[4] These actions were dismissed since the Animal Welfare Act (1966) did not recognize the standing of animal rights organizations. Once the conviction for cruelty had been reversed, the National Institute for Health sought to transfer the animals back to the laboratory. Two lower court decisions found that IPPL and other organizations had no standing, and this was affirmed by the Court of Appeals for the Fourth Circuit in *International Primate Protection League et al. v. Institute for Behavioral Research* 799, F.2d 934 (1986). The Court rejected arguments for standing based on the plaintiffs' status as tax payers and their concern for the use of federal funds, as well as the relationship arising their financial contribution to the welfare of the monkeys during the litigation. The court found too remote their claims for a personal interest in 'the preservation and encouragement of civilized and humane treatment of animals' given that 'their own aesthetic, conservational, and environmental interests are specifically and particularly offended' (section II). As for disruption to personal relationships with the monkeys, these relationships had arisen out of the litigation.

In an amicus brief filed by the American Psychological Association,[5] it was argued that granting standing in such cases would turn the federal courts into continual monitors of Congress: 'Plaintiffs seek to have the Court consider a general grievance as to the proper use of research animals' notwithstanding the fact that Congress has dealt with this matter through legislation (at 9–10). The court agreed:

> To imply a cause of action in these plaintiffs might entail serious consequences. It might open the use of animals in biomedical research to the hazards and vicissitudes of courtroom litigation. It may draw judges into the supervision and regulation of laboratory research. It might unleash a spate of private lawsuits that would impede advances made by medical science in

> the alleviation of human suffering. To risk consequences of this magnitude in the absence of clear direction from the Congress would be ill-advised.

This was a policy argument, offered in addition to the legal rules about standing: 'Not only do plaintiffs fail to allege cognizable injuries; they fail also to prove that the implicated federal statute authorizes their right to seek relief' (section III). Klauber (1992: 501–502) argues that the court used 'value-laden statements that were not based on legal reasoning or analysis, but rather ethical and political opinions'. Not only did the court rule on the merits while denying standing, it went one step further and 'suggested that it was ruling on the basis of the *effect* that a granting of standing would have on the defendant and the defendant's colleagues', that is, the laboratory (Klauber 1992: 502).

After a public outcry, several of the monkeys were transferred by the National Institute of Health to Tulane's Regional Primate Center. When plans for killing three of the monkeys became public, a suit was filed in the Louisiana District Court. A temporary restraining order (TRO) issued was continued once the case was transferred to the district (federal) court. The NIH then sought to show that the TRO was in error since there was no plausible legal argument available to the plaintiffs, given that they lacked standing. In *International Primate Protection League v. Administrators of Tulane Educational Fund* 895, F.2d 1056 (5th Cir. 1990) the Court of Appeals for the Fifth Circuit set out the rules for standing under Article III: namely that the plaintiff must show that 'he personally has suffered some actual or threatened injury as a result of the putatively illegal conduct of the defendant' and, second, that 'a causal connection between the injury and the conduct such that the injury is "likely to be redressed by a favorable decision"'. Further, the Supreme Court had recognized that injuries to 'aesthetic, conservational, and recreational' interests are sufficient, though 'some interests are "too abstract, or otherwise not appropriate, to be considered judicially cognizable"' (para. 13).

In order to argue their case for standing, the plaintiffs had set out three claims for injury. First there had been disruption of 'relationships which were established prior to any previous litigation in related matters and which continued during such litigation'. The court rejected this, even though Alex Pacheco, the original whistle-blower, had known the monkeys prior to the litigation (Pacheco 1985). The fact that these were laboratory animals, rather than wild animals, meant that 'even if the defendants were to comply with the laws putatively violated, the plaintiffs would still lack any right to continue their personal relationships with the monkeys' (para. 17). The second argument was that the plaintiffs' 'longstanding, sincere commitment' to preventing cruelty to animals and 'their aesthetic, conservational and environmental interests would be particularly, severely, and detrimentally affected' (para. 24). This was rejected by the court as essentially too vague. Their commitment to the humane treatment of animals was 'insufficient to distinguish them from other members of the public' (para. 27). The third claim argued that the monkeys had no other means of protection.

This was rejected by the court: 'the mere fact that the monkeys would be left without an advocate in court does not create standing where it otherwise does not exist' (para. 34).[6]

As Klauber points out, the animals in this litigation were not just property, they were government property (Klauber 1992: 514). The interests that someone in the enjoyment of watching wild animals in their natural habitat were by contrast potentially recognized (1992: 514):

> Seals, whales, and other wild animals are protected because they are useful in their natural habitat. The Silver Spring monkeys were not protected because they are useful in the lab. This distinction is arbitrary.

The Palila bird as party to litigation

In *Palila v. Hawaii Dept. of Land and Natural Resources*, 852 F.2d 1106 (9th Cir.1988), a case which concerned the endangered Hawaiian honey-creeper, the Court of Appeals stated that (at 1107):

> As an endangered species under the Endangered Species Act [...] (1982), the bird (*Loxioides bailleui*), a member of the Hawaiian honeycreeper family, also has legal status and wings its way into federal court as a plaintiff in its own right. The Palila (which has earned the right to be capitalized since it is a party to this proceeding) is represented by attorneys for the Sierra Club, Audubon Society, and other environmental parties who obtained an order directing the Hawaii Department of Land and Natural Resources ('Department') to remove mouflon sheep from its critical habitat.

The court found in favour of the plaintiff, upholding an earlier district court decision of the relevant definition of *harm*. The Endangered Species Act (ESA, 1973) defines *person* as follows (s. 3(12)):

> an individual, corporation, partnership, trust, association, or any other private entity; or any officer, employee, agent, department, or instrumentality of the Federal Government, of any State, municipality, or political subdivision of a State, or of any foreign government; any State, municipality, or political subdivision of a State; or any other entity subject to the jurisdiction of the United States.

Thus, an endangered species protected under the ESA could qualify as an 'entity subject to the jurisdiction of the United States' under this definition of *person*, 'with the ability to initiate a lawsuit pursuant to the citizen suit provision' (Wymyslo 2007: 53).

In this and a series of other cases,[7] the animal at issue was granted standing as plaintiff, but never as the sole plaintiff. Subsequent commentary has been divided about the status of the statement in *Palila*, whether it had precedential value though being 'germane to the eventual resolution of the case' or was ultimately merely a colourful aside (Armstrong 2006: 189ff.). In *Hawaiian Crow ('Alala') v. Lujan,* No. 91–00191-DAE (D.Haw. Sept. 13, 1991), the District Court denied that the bird in question had standing to maintain a suit. The ESA provided for 'citizen suits' brought by 'persons'. Parties such as Audubon Societies could bring actions. The comment in *Palila* did not have any relevance to the decision on the merits. The ESA defined a person as 'an individual, corporation, partnership, trust, association, or any other private entity' (16 U.S.C. s. 1532(13)). Rules that provided for suits on behalf of infants or incompetent persons did not apply to animals (F.R.Civ.P. 17(c)) (at 4–6). The Alala was 'clearly neither a "person" as defined in section 1532(13), nor an infant or incompetent person under Rule 17(c)' (at 552).

Kama and the question of individual domicile

The question of standing was central to *Citizens to End Animal Suffering and Exploitation, Inc., et al. v. The New England Aquarium et al.,* 836 F. Supp. 45 (1993), heard before the District Court (Massachusetts). This case concerned a dolphin, Kama, which was to be transferred from a commercial aquarium to the Navy. The statute invoked was the Marine Mammal Protection Act (MMPA, 1978), which set out protections for marine mammals and forbade their *taking*. *To take* was defined as 'to harass, hunt, capture, or kill, or attempt to harass, hunt, capture, or kill any marine mammal' (16 U.S.C. § 1362(12)). This could only be done with a permit from the Department of Commerce. At issue was, first, the standing of the Citizens to End Animal Suffering and Exploitation (CEASE) and the Animal Legal Defense Fund, Inc. (ALDF), to bring the action and, second, whether the transfer constituted a *taking* within the meaning of the statute. The court however restricted its arguments to the question of standing, concluding that Kama, as an animal, could not be a party to the suit: 'The MMPA does not authorize suits brought by animals' (at 49). While Kama the dolphin had a *domicile*, he was not an individual in the sense of being a competent party to a legal action. The *Palila* dictum notwithstanding, an animal as plaintiff party had not survived challenge in the Hawaiian Crow case (at 49):

> If Congress and the President intended to take the extraordinary step of authorizing animals as well as people and legal entities to sue, they could, and should, have said so plainly. Furthermore, as in *Alala*, citizen groups, if they satisfy the standing requirements, could seek to obtain the relief the amended complaint requests for Kama.

The court cited from *Lujan v. Defenders of Wildlife*, 504 U.S. 555 (1992), where the question of standing in relation to wildlife actions had been addressed by the Supreme Court. What was required was 'injury in fact', that is, the 'invasion of a legally-protected interest' which was 'concrete and particularized' and 'actual or imminent', rather than not 'conjectural' or 'hypothetical'. Second, there should be 'a causal connection between the injury and the conduct complained of' and thirdly it should be 'likely' as opposed to merely 'speculative' that a favourable decision would redress the injury. Since the MMPA did not authorize citizen suits in a case such as this, the plaintiff organizations had brought the action under 5 U.S.C. s. 702:

> A person suffering a legal wrong because of agency action, or adversely affected or aggrieved by agency action within the meaning of a relevant statute, is entitled to judicial review thereof.

Following *Lujan*, the court rejected the plaintiffs' arguments that they had suffered harm from the transfer by being unable to visit and study Kama. The court found that this was too remote, and did not refer to Kama in particular but dolphins on display. The argument that the taking of dolphins in the wild would limit the plaintiffs' future opportunities to observe and study was not within the 'outermost limit' identified in *Lujan*. The plaintiffs could not argue harm even of this 'outer limit' kind, and there was no evidence of a causal connection between the Department of Commerce's policies and the harm alleged. As to 'procedural harms' alleged to arise as a result of a lack of administrative transparency on the part of the Department of Commerce, the court again found this too abstract and insufficiently distinctive of the individual plaintiffs. The concept of standing 'based only on informational harm' was 'inconsistent' with the requirement for 'concrete and particularized harm' stressed in *Lujan*. The court granted summary judgement for the defendants, pointing out that the plaintiffs had at their disposal other tools, including the requests under the Freedom of Information Act and participation in the political process (at 59).

Sea mammals in court

One case that became central to academic debates about standing is *Cetacean Community v. Bush*, 249 F. Supp. 2d 1206, a decision of the District Court of Hawaii (2003) and the appeal that followed, *Cetacean Community v. Bush*, 386 F.3d 1169 (9th Cir. 2004). The issue was the Navy's use of 'low frequency active sonar' and its potential impact on sea mammals. The complaint invoked the National Environmental Policy Act (NEPA), the MMPA, and the ESA, and sought a regulatory review. The court reviewed the case law on standing, including whether an animal constituted a *person* under the ESA. The District Court cited this dictum from *Salmon v. Pacific Lumber Co.*, 30 F. Supp. 2d 1231 (N.D. Cal. 1998) (at note 2):

> Without delving into the vagaries of the term 'entity,' the court notes that, to swim its way into federal court in this action, the coho salmon would have to battle a strong current and leap barriers greater than a waterfall or the occasional fallen tree.

The other recourse would be the Administrative Procedure Act (APA), U.S.C. s 702 (2003) which provides that 'A person suffering legal wrong because of agency action, or adversely affected or aggrieved by agency action within the meaning of a relevant statute, is entitled to judicial review thereof'. There was no recourse to plaintiffs as an association (at 1211):

> Plaintiffs individual members, which consists of nonhumans, do not have standing to sue in their own right. Accordingly, Plaintiff is unable to satisfy the first prong of the test for associational standing, and is therefore unable to sue on behalf of its members.

The Court of Appeals emphasized that the statements about standing in *Palila* were 'rhetorical flourishes, not intended to be a statement of the law' (at 1174). The court referred to academic arguments (Sunstein 2000) that Congress could in fact grant standing to animals (at 1176):

> It is obvious that an animal cannot function as a plaintiff in the same manner as a juridically competent human being. But we see no reason why Article III prevents Congress from authorizing a suit in the name of an animal, any more than it prevents suits brought in the name of artificial persons such as corporations, partnerships or trusts, and even ships, or of juridically incompetent persons such as infants, juveniles, and mental incompetents.

However the APA gave standing to a defined set: 'A person suffering legal wrong because of agency action, or adversely affected or aggrieved by agency action within the meaning of a relevant statute, is entitled to judicial review thereof'; and from the ESA's definitions of *species*, *endangered species*, *threatened species*, and *fish and wildlife* it was evident that 'animals are the protected rather than the protectors' (at 1177–1178):

> Animals are not authorized to sue in their own names to protect themselves. There is no hint in the definition of 'person' in §1532(13) that the 'person' authorized to bring suit to protect an endangered or threatened species can be an animal that is itself endangered or threatened.

The Cetaceans fared no better if presented as an association (at 1179):

> The complaint presents no evidence that the Cetaceans comprise a formal association, nor can we read into the term 'association' in the APA a desire by Congress to confer standing on a non-human species as a group, any more than we can read into the term "person" Congressional intent to confer standing on individual animals.

The court cited Black's Law Dictionary's definition of *association* (8th edition, 2004): 'A gathering of people for a common purpose; the persons so joined'.

In October 25, 2011, PETA filed a federal lawsuit on behalf of Tilikum and other orcas held by Sea World in the District Court for Southern California (*Tilikum et al. v. Sea World Parks & Entertainment Inc.*, 842 F. Supp. 2d 1259 (S.D. Cal. 2012)).[8] The suit sought a declaration that orcas, captured in the wild, were held as slaves, and as such their captivity violated the Thirteenth Amendment:

> Neither slavery nor involuntary servitude, except as a punishment for crime whereof the party shall have been duly convicted, shall exist within the United States, or any place subject to their jurisdiction.

In the lawsuit, PETA acted as *next friends* for the orcas: 'Plaintiffs cannot bring this action to seek relief for themselves due to inaccessibility and incapacity' (para. 5). PETA asserted that the orcas in the wild 'engage in many complex social, communicative, and cognitive behaviors, including learning-based cooperative hunting strategies and cultural variation among pods and generational transmission of unique cultural traits' (para. 11); their social groups were complex 'with dynamic social roles in intricate networks, many with distinctive cultural attributes in vocal, social, feeding, and play behavior' (para. 12); they teach their young, have problem-solving abilities, and a rich linguistic culture with 'dozens of community, clan, and pod-specific call types' (para. 16):

> Complex and stable over time, dialects are composed of specific numbers and types of discrete, repetitive calls. Calves likely learn their dialects through contact with their mothers and other pod members, maintaining group identity and cohesion. Orcas' transmission of dialects and other learned behaviors from generation to generation is a form of culture. The complex and stable vocal and behavioral cultures of orcas appear to have no parallel outside humans.

Their food culture was social and contained elements of ritual (para. 17); their brains demonstrated high level of development 'in the areas related to emotional processing (such as feelings of empathy, guilt, embarrassment, and pain), social cognition (judgment, social knowledge, and consciousness of visceral feelings), theory of mind (self-awareness and self-recognition), and communication' (para. 18).

In captivity, these 'cultural traditions' were suppressed, and the orcas were deprived of 'the ability to make conscious choices and of the environmental enrichment required to stimulate Plaintiffs mentally and physically for their well-being' (para. 19). Confinement harmed the orcas both physically and mentally, disrupting their social and familial relationships (para. 46):

> Deprived of liberty, forced to live in grotesquely unnatural conditions and perform tricks, manipulated to give his sperm, and prevented from satisfying his basic drives and from engaging in virtually all natural behaviors,

> Tilikum has been subjected to extreme physiological and mental stress and suffering while, at the same time, Defendants and their predecessors have reaped millions of dollars in profits from Tilikum's slavery and involuntary servitude.

The complaint presented the Thirteenth Amendment as prohibiting 'the conditions of slavery and involuntary servitude without regard to the identity of the victim and without reference to "persons"' (para. 104). Although the Amendment had been enacted to end 'African slavery', it was not limited to this: 'it embodied a principle that can be (and over the years has been) defined and expanded by common law to address morally unjust conditions of bondage and forced service existing anywhere in the United States' (para. 105). *Weems v. U.S.*, 217 U.S. 349 (1910) was cited to the effect that 'a constitutional principle, to be vital, must be capable of wider application than the mischief which gave it birth' (at 373–374).

Judge Jeffrey Miller determined that the 'plain language' of the Thirteenth Amendment 'is that it applies to persons, and not to non-persons such as orcas' (at 3). This was shown by the background to its enactment. In 1864, *slavery* was defined as 'The condition of a slave; the state of entire subjection of one person to the will of another' in Webster's *A Dictionary of the English Language*. In the *Slaughter-House Cases*, 83 U.S. 36 (1873), the court had rejected an analogy between an economic monopoly and slavery (at 69): 'As only persons are subject to criminal convictions, the Amendment was designed to apply to persons' (at 4).

The Supreme Court had characterized the Thirteenth Amendment as 'this grand yet simple declaration of personal freedom of all the human race' (at 69, cited para. 4). President Lincoln, in his Emancipation Proclamation of January 1, 1863, had spoken of 'persons held as slaves' (cited at 4). The conclusion 'based upon the plain language of the Thirteenth Amendment, its historical context, and judicial interpretations, was that the Thirteenth Amendment does not afford Plaintiffs any relief as non-humans' (at 4). There was therefore no 'subject matter jurisdiction' under Rule 12(b)(1). Arguing that PETA 'in the main' accepted that the Thirteenth Amendment applied to persons, the judge examined arguments about the extension of the provision from persons to non-persons, just as other provisions had taken on new meanings and provided new forms of protection. However the Thirteenth Amendment was directed at a single issue: 'The Amendment's language and meaning is clear, concise, and not subject to the vagaries of conceptual interpretation' (at 5). The judge ruled that the lawsuit failed for lack of standing, in that the plaintiffs as non-humans could not bring an action: 'Next Friends cite no statute authorizing Plaintiffs to bring a private right of action. Instead, Next Friends contend that they have constitutional standing under the Thirteenth Amendment' (at fn. 1).

Outside the court the argument was waged in the law journals and the media. Flannery (2012: 61) described the attempt to expand the scope of the Thirteenth Amendment as an 'insult' to its original purpose. PETA's attorney Jeffrey Kerr was quoted as saying that 'slavery doesn't depend upon the species of the slave, any more than it depends upon the race, gender or ethnicity of the slave'. SeaWorld was showing the same kind of prejudice that had been used to justify slavery: 'Because [orcas] can suffer from the prohibitive conduct of being enslaved, the 13th Amendment protection against that conduct should be extended to them' (Zelman 2012).

The Nonhuman Rights Project: dignity rights

The Nonhuman Rights Project (NhRP), directed by Steven Wise, has been involved in three cases representing non-human clients, namely the primates Tommy, Kiko, and Hercules and Leo.[9] The NhRP has sought to make use of the prerogative writ of habeas corpus, a common law remedy first given statutory form in the Habeas Corpus Act 1679, but never before used to seek the freedom from detention of a non-human individual. The writ requires that the prisoner be produced before a judge and their detention justified with reference to a positive legal rule. One key element of the writ for animal cases is that a third party can seek it on behalf of the detained person.

On December 2, 2013, the NhRP filed a petition for a common law writ of habeas corpus.[10] The venue was the New York State Supreme Court, Fulton County. The writ sought 'to extend existing New York common law for the purpose of establishing the legal personhood of Petitioner' and to obtain release from 'illegal detention' (at 1). It noted that the New York courts had in the past issued such writs for slaves, who were not at that time legal persons.[11] Neither statute nor common law in New York restricted personhood to *homo sapiens* and had 'already conferred legal personhood status on non-human domestic animals who are the beneficiaries of trusts', as well as on corporations (at 1). Accompanying affidavits set out the qualities of chimpanzees, summarized as follows:

> Chimpanzees possess such complex cognitive abilities as autonomy, self-determination, self-consciousness, awareness of the past, anticipation of the future and the ability to make choices; display complex emotions such as empathy; and construct diverse cultures.

These qualities, which include the ability to use language, were sufficient 'to establish common law personhood and the consequential right to bodily liberty' (at 2). A court judgement from Brazil was appended, with English translation: *In favor of Suica, a Chimpanzee*, No. 833085-3/2005.[12] In that case the Salvador zoo was holding a chimpanzee, Suica, in what were alleged to be unhealthy and cramped conditions. The judge, Edmundo Lucio da Cruz, had not dismissed the habeas corpus claim. He had noted the arguments grounded in the close evolutionary history of human beings and primates in favour of recognizing legal personality for this purpose and sought more information from the Environmental Department. However the chimpanzee was reported to have died, rendering the matter moot: 'The topic will not die with this writ, it will certainly continue to remain controversial. Thus, can a primate be compared to a human being? Can an animal be released from its cage, by means of a Habeas Corpus?'

NhRP also submitted a Memorandum of Law, written by Elizabeth Stein and Steven Wise, setting out the legal and biological background and relevant principles and case law applicable to the writ.[13] The question before the court was 'not whether Tommy is a human being – he is not – but whether, like a human being, he is a "legal person" under the law of New York' (at 1). The term *legal person* was not a synonym for *human being*, rather it designated 'Western law's most fundamental category by identifying those entities capable of possessing a legal right'. As a category, it determined 'who counts, who lives, who dies, who is enslaved, and who is free' (at 1–2). Tommy was already legally recognized as the beneficiary of a trust created by NhRP, and in this sense was a legal person; 'The NhRP now demands that this Court recognize Tommy's additional common law right to the bodily liberty protected by the common law writ of habeas corpus' (at 2). Tommy's classification as a 'legal thing' represented a discriminatory denial of equality and justified his enslavement, using a single trait of being a chimpanzee to deny every right, 'even the capacity to have a legal right' (at 3). One section addressed the issue of standing, and drew on slavery and other cases where third parties as 'next friends' had succeeded in applying for a writ (at 38–39).

In a hearing held on December 3, 2013, Justice Joseph Sise rejected the petition.[14] The plaintiffs argued for the open-endedness of the category of legal person, including not just corporations, partnerships, and ships but Sikh holy books and Hindu idols, and referenced a New Zealand treaty with the Maori 'in which a river was held to be a legal person' (at 11).[15] As for habeas corpus, two slavery cases were offered as precedents, namely *Somerset v. Stewart* (1772) 98 ER 499 and *Lemmon v. People*, 20 N.Y. 562 (1860), which ruled that a slave who had entered New York state temporarily were free. The analogy between human beings who were slaves in the 1800s and chimpanzees in the present was rejected by the court. Wise was careful to clarify, 'We're not comparing chimps to blacks. We are not at all'. Rather the argument from a wide spectrum of cases was about the appropriateness of recognition of legal personhood in a given case (at 11). The judge sought clarification that the petition was based on distinguishing chimpanzees from other animals, in terms of cognitive ability. Wise stressed the affidavits and the question of 'autonomy, self-determination, and self-agency' (at 18), drawing on the argument that *human being* and *person* were not mutually defining categories. While impressed by the arguments, the judge refused to recognize a chimpanzee 'as a human or as a person' for the purpose of the writ (at 26).

NhRP then filed an appeal, which was argued on October 8, 2014. Justice Karen Peters questioned whether the trust created for Tommy established his personhood: 'it's really a legislative construct to allow for the support of animals correct?' (Transcript 15:57). Wise clarified that the point was 'there are many different kinds of legal person' and the argument at hand was restricted to the matter of the writ (Transcript 16:53). Wise also insisted that this was not a welfare issue, but rather was concerned with the legality of the detention (Transcript 21.47). Justice Peters questioned the analogy with slavery, to which Wise responded there was no direct comparison between Tommy and human slaves, rather the issue was autonomy and self-determination (Transcript 25.54 et seq.). Judge Michael Lynch cited Blacks' Law Dictionary, which defined *person* beginning with the statement (Transcript 28:17) 'In general usage, a human being. That is, a natural person', asking whether there had been any cases of applying habeas corpus to non-humans. Wise responded that this was 'a novel case', but reiterated that the concept of *legal person* was a legal not a biological one (Transcript 29:04).

The court, in ruling against the petition,[16] declined to 'enlarge the common-law definition of "person" in order to afford legal rights to an animal', noting that the writ had never been used on behalf of a non-human. The judgement laid stress on the social contract model of rights and the relation between rights and responsibilities (at 4). On this point, the court cited the work of Richard Cupp (2009, 2013). The court also revisited Black's Law Dictionary, emphasizing that it referred to entities as having 'rights and duties'. Further, it stated, 'Persons are the substances of which rights and duties are the attributes. It is only in this respect that persons possess juridical significance, and this is the exclusive point of view from which personality receives legal recognition' (7th edition, 1999). Case law emphasized 'the correlative rights and duties that attach to legal personhood' (at 5). The determination that an entity or an association was a legal person arose 'not from the humanity of the subject but from the ascription of rights and duties to the subject'.[17] Thus, associations involving human beings, 'such as corporations and municipal entities, may be considered legal persons, because they too bear legal duties in exchange for their legal rights'. It was clear, therefore, that this framework could not be applied to chimpanzees since the could not 'bear any legal duties' or 'be held legally accountable for their actions' (at 6).

The conventional rejoinder to this position, known as the argument from marginal cases, is that certain humans are less able or unable to accept such social duties and responsibilities. The court addressed this in a footnote (at 5, fn. 3):

> To be sure, some humans are less able to bear legal duties or responsibilities than others. These differences do not alter our analysis, as it is undeniable that, collectively, human beings possess the unique ability to bear legal responsibility.

This takes the argument to the generic level of species-competence rather than individual-level capacity.

A motion to appeal was denied, and NhRP sought leave directly from the Court of Appeals. Both the constitutional scholar Professor Lawrence Tribe and The Center for Constitutional Rights submitted briefs in support.[18] Professor Tribe argued that the lower courts had misunderstood the purpose of the writ, which was 'to allow courts of competent jurisdiction to consider arguments challenging restraint or confinement as contrary to law' (at 1). Further, Tribe attacked the assumption that habeas corpus only applied to human persons, noting that as it turned on an entity's 'present capacity to bear "both rights and duties"', this would exclude 'third-trimester fetuses, children, and comatose adults (among other entities whose rights as persons the law protects' (at 1–2). He suggested that the court had confused the question of habeas corpus jurisdiction (whether it had the authority to entertain a petition) with that of the relief (the substantive rights and the remedies, if any, available) (at 2). The observation that no chimpanzee had ever been granted relief by a New York court foreclosed the argument that Tommy's detention was contrary to law; law treated slaves as 'mere things', but yet the writ had been available to them (at 4):

> Holding that Tommy and others like him are not welcome in habeas courts is akin to holding that slaves, infants, or comatose individuals cannot invoke the writ of habeas corpus to test the legality of their detention [...].

The distinction between jurisdiction and relief had been elaborated by the Supreme Court in a series of decisions relating to detainees held at Guantanamo Bay (*Rasul v. Bush*, 542 U.S. 466 (2004), *Boumediene v. Bush*, 552 U.S. 723 (2008)).

Tribe challenged the 'reciprocity barrier' to habeas jurisdiction, that is, the equation of legal personhood with capacity to bear rights and duties. Tribe drew on the work of Visa Kurki ([2015] 2017) and Matthew Kramer (2010) in rejecting the presumption that legal personhood is reflected in right-holding and duty bearing. Kurki discusses two approaches to rights, within the structural analysis of legal relations set out by Wesley Newcomb Hohfeld (1916). These are termed the *interest theory* and the *will theory*. According to the interest theory, 'rights may properly be attributed to entities that have interests and whose interests are furthered by duties in a certain manner'. These interests reflect the existence of a correlative duty. Animals held such interest-theory rights, as the court had itself conceded in referring to animal protection laws. In a footnote Tribe rejected the argument that animal welfare laws 'protect the interests of natural persons in preventing harm to animals' (Berg 2007: 404), attributing this to a will theory of rights. Under the will theory, 'an entity holds a right if it has "competence or authorization" to waive/enforce some legal duty'. Thus the class of rights-holders is limited to 'rational beings with mental faculties that correspond to adult human beings of sound minds' (at 9, cited from Kurki [2015] 2017: 11). This implied that certain legal persons, for example, infant children or comatose adults, would be excluded from this class. Tribe's conclusion was that will-theory rights are 'not *necessary* conditions for legal personhood, nor are they *sufficient*' (at 9). During the chattel-slavery period, slaves had the right to appeal against criminal convictions, demonstrating that they possessed will-theory rights without legal personhood.

Tribe challenged the notion that animals could not be endowed with rights, given that they were incapable of complying with legal obligations. He cited Kramer (2001: 42): 'To bear an obligation is simply to be placed under it'.

Comprehension was a separate matter. It was possible, albeit controversial, to envisage animals as bearing duties. These were not pure questions of law and courts needed to hear evidence or look at factual information (at 11). The question of personhood was not merely a question of formal definition but one of 'the social meaning and symbolism of law' (a phrase drawn from Fagundes 2001: 1760), reflecting social values and notions of relative worth. The Court of Appeals had allowed these profound questions to 'paralyze its analysis' (at 13) and should recognize that Tommy was 'an autonomous being' (at 14). In conclusion, Tribe urged the court to look at the issue from the point of view of evolving moral standards, in the tradition of the common law ability to reject 'the prejudices and presumptions of the past' (at 16).

The Court of Appeals denied the motion, and NhRP filed a further habeas petition on December 4, 2015, with a revised and expanded Memorandum,[19] drawing on further affidavits elaborating the cognitive, emotional, and social qualities of chimpanzees, and their similarities to humans, and making assertions concerning their self-awareness, memory, linguistic abilities, imagination and humour, understanding of other consciousness ('theory of mind'), empathy, awareness of death, toolmaking and other cultural attributes, and imitation and emulation of others. This revised document included extensive materials designed to meet the arguments of the court about the requirements for legal personhood (at 24ff), including descriptions of duties and responsibilities which are rule-like and lawful, contractual, cooperative (e.g. hunting) and sharing (including for group defence), responsibility for planning, including a division of labour, as well as kinship-based duties as father, mother, or sibling which also allows for adoption, and have moral content, both within chimpanzee society and in chimpanzee/human societies. The petition was denied by New York County Supreme Court Justice Barbara Jaffe (December 23, 2015).

The NhRP then filed an appeal with the New York Supreme Court, Appellate Division, but in the First Judicial Department.[20] The brief took issue with the Third Department's ruling, rejecting the view that the capacity for bearing duties and responsibilities had to be established at the species level (at 50). The court had improperly taken judicial notice 'that chimpanzees lack the capacity to bear duties and responsibilities' (at 59). If group-level capacity was the criterion, then chimpanzees could meet this (at 60). The court scheduled oral argument, and a flurry of briefs followed. One brief by Professor Justin Marceau and Samuel Wiseman[21] highlighted the question of innocence: 'Nonhuman animals are unquestionably innocent' (at 3). The writ had been used historically 'to bring about social change that would seem unlikely based on controlling legal principles at the time, including within the realms of family law, slavery and detainees being held in Guantanamo Bay' (at 3), and its use in Tommy's case was consistent with this, given his cognitive capacity. They pointed out that laws governing animal behaviour often function in similar ways to criminal statutes, allowing defences to allegations of dangerousness akin to those in human cases, such as self-defence or provocation (at 13–14).

An oppositional brief was filed by Professor Richard Cupp, based on published article.[22] For Cupp, the court's argument concerned legal accountability, not general moral or social accountability, citing this line from the judgement: 'Needless to say, unlike human beings, chimpanzees cannot bear any legal duties, submit to societal responsibilities or be held legally accountable for their actions' (cited at 4–5). Ants work together 'for the greater good of the colony'; animals typically live in family or social units. The question was one of threshold, that is, not whether chimpanzees possess anything that could be characterized as a sense of responsibility, but rather whether they possess a *sufficient* level of moral agency to be justly held legally accountable as well as to possess legal rights under our human legal system (at 5, emphasis in original). In cases where an adult chimpanzee killed a baby chimp, or attacked a woman in an 'unprovoked', 'brutal and lengthy' fashion, there was no suggestion of criminal charges being brought. The notion that the NhRP project was unique in that its clients were 'always innocent' showed that the system did not view them as having moral agency. To the suggestion that his 'philosophical contractualism' arbitrarily excluded every non-human animal, this was asserted to be the philosophical mainstream in the western tradition (at 7). Arguments for rights rightly focussed on human beings: 'While there may be no case law prior to *Lavery* expressly rejecting habeas corpus for animals because no reported lawsuits had previously made such a radical assertion, courts have readily rejected analogous claims' (at 10). The philosopher Carl Cohen had argued that animals could not be the bearers of rights 'because the concept of right is *essentially human*; it is rooted in the human moral world and has force and applicability only within that world' (Cohen 2001: 30l). The 'social compact' or 'moral community' was 'the bedrock of our social structure'. The relationship between rights and duties was not such that every right corresponded to a specific duty, but rather it was a foundational norm 'that persons in our community of humans and human proxies be subjected to responsibilities along with holding rights, regardless of whether a specific right or limitation requires or does not require a specific duty to go along with it' (at 12). It was true that incapacity did not negate bodily liberty, this was 'because bodily liberty is an immunity right that does not require capacity' (at 12). The NhRP's analysis used Hohfeld's conceptual schema but failed to address his foundational assumption: 'since the purpose of the law is to regulate the conduct of human beings, all jural relations must, in order to be clear and direct in their meaning, be predicated of such human beings' (Hohfeld 1916: 701, cited at 12 fn.).

Personhood as granted to corporations was 'created by humans as a proxy for the rights and duties of their human stakeholders' and these were vehicles for 'addressing *human* interests and obligations' (at 13). The so-called 'argument from marginal cases', as discussed in Cupp (2013), was that if a human being who was 'bereft of sentience' was entitled to personhood, then a being such as a chimpanzee, with its much greater autonomy and cognitive capacity, must likewise be entitled to personhood. However 'most of us do not want to think of any humans as being "marginal"' and it was the 'pervasive view' that '*all* humans have distinctive and intrinsic human dignity regardless of their capabilities may have cultural, religious, or even instinctual foundations' (at 14, emphasis in original). Personhood reflected the community of human beings and was 'anchored in the human moral world' (at 16). For Cupp, there was also the danger that linking personhood to capacity might harm the interests of vulnerable humans, something which even Laurence Tribe, otherwise supportive, recognized (Tribe 2001: 7, cited at 19).

Wise's response to this had been that grounds other than autonomy for legal rights might exist, but the entitlement could not be restricted just to human beings (Wise 2002a). For Cupp, if the criterion was capacity for suffering, then all animals capable of suffering would have dignity rights, but this would exclude the comatose infant; if suffering was not the criterion for dignity rights, then it was unclear whether animals that were not capable of suffering would also be included (at 20). Personhood should not be linked to individual cognitive ability (at 21). The granting of personhood to chimpanzees would open the floodgates to complex and expensive litigation.

In a reply to this brief (which the court refused to accept), Stein and Wise argued that Cupp was in a line of debunked responses triggered by Peter Singer's *Animal Liberation* (1975), offering support to the use of animals in medical research (Hoff 1980, Cohen 1986). To Cupp's assertion that chimpanzees lacked sufficient moral agency, Stein and Wise argued that there was no such principle in US or New York law. The issue should be properly argued in court so that a judge 'might rule on the vital issue of the nature of a chimpanzee's cognition' (at 7). The humanistic principle and human moral community evoked by Cupp merely embodied 'the very prejudice and inequality that the NhRP seeks to remedy' (at 8). The rationale of an unchangeable norm had been used to justify slavery and racial segregation (at 9), as in West *Chester & P.R. Co. v. Miles*, 55 Pa. 209, 213 (1867), where the judgement spoke of 'natural boundaries' created by God between the races, and in *Loving v. Virginia*, 388 U.S. 1 (1967), a case on interracial marriage in which the trial court stated (at 3) that God had created the races and placed them on separate continents: 'The fact that he separated the races shows that he did not intend for the races to mix'. Similarly, courts had resisted same-sex marriage and homosexuality on the grounds that the limitation was natural, grounded in Western civilization and Judeo-Christian ethics (at 10). In *Lawrence v. Texas*, 539 U.S. 558 (2003) the Supreme Court had overruled *Bowers v. Hardwick*, 478 U.S. 186 (1986), stating that their obligation was 'to define the liberty of all, not to mandate our own moral code' (at 571). The time was right to invoke 'the broad, flexible, and ancient common law writ of habeas corpus': 'Tommy's thinghood derives from the common law. It is now time to bring this extraordinary being within the protection of the common law' (at 11).

Stein and Wise disputed Cupp's version of social contract theory, arguing that it was the state that takes on a duty to protect citizens. Rights cases invoke a breach of state's responsibilities, not correlations of rights and responsibilities: 'this surely is at the core of the Lockean "social contract" idea' (*Roberts v. Louisiana*, 431 U.S. 633 (1977), at 646). In any case, the social contract was a myth without direct legal relevance, as the Supreme Court had recognized in *FPC v. Natural Gas Pipeline Co.,* 315 U.S. 575 (1942), at 605: 'As a practical concept, from which practical conclusions can be drawn, it is valueless'.[23] Finally, they returned to the point that the determination of personhood was not a matter of biology but rather of public policy and moral principle, as stated by *Byrn v. New York City Health & Hosps. Corp.*, 286 N.E.2d 887 (1972). The court there had declared that it was not the case 'that the legal order necessarily corresponds to the natural order' (at 888).

Subsequently, Stein wrote to the Judicial Department drawing its attention to a series of legal issues.[24] The first was the decision in *Mohd. Salim v. State of Uttarakhand & Others*, (PIL) 126/2014, in which the High Court of Uttarakhand held that a person for purposes of law was 'any entity (not necessarily a human being) to which rights or duties may be attributed' (at 1). For Stein, the 'or' was important since there was no assertion of a necessary correlation between rights and duties. In the judgement itself (not quoted in the letter), the court had declared that:

> the Rivers Ganga and Yamuna, all their tributaries, streams, every natural water flowing with flow continuously or intermittently of these rivers, are declared as juristic/legal persons/living entities having the status of a legal person with all corresponding rights, duties and liabilities of a living person in order to preserve and conserve river Ganga and Yamuna.

Stein then pointed to a law review paper (Ewasiuk 2017). The core of the argument was as follows (2017: 75):

> Modern social contract theory provides a rationale for why certain natural rights of natural persons cannot be compromised by the governments to which we consent; it does not argue that governments cannot grant additional rights or create other forms of legal personhood when, otherwise, the natural rights of natural persons are preserved. In sum, to the extent that social contract theory makes ontological assumptions about human beings and animals, these assumptions do not prohibit extending the writ of habeas to animals.

The letter then turned to the question of definition. In *Lavery*, the court cited Black's Law Dictionary (7th edition), to the effect that the legal meaning of *person* involved 'a subject of legal rights and duties' (at 2). The supporting sources cited by Black's were *Salmond on Jurisprudence* (Fitzgerald 1966) and Gray's *The Nature and Sources of the Law* (1909). In every edition of *Salmond* it was stated quite clearly that 'a person is any being whom the law regards as capable of legal rights or duties'. Gray stated that 'One who has rights but not duties, or has duties but no rights, is [...] a person' (1909: 97). The quotation continues:

> An instance which would commonly be given of the former is the King of England; of the latter, a slave. Whether in truth the King of England has no legal duties, or a slave no legal rights, may not be entirely clear. I will not stop to discuss the question. But if there is any one who has rights though no duties, or duties though no rights, he is, I take it, a person in the eye of the Law.

The editor of Black's, Bryan Garner, had accepted the point and agreed to make a change in the next edition. Further motions in relation to the case were denied. On June 8, 2017, the First Judicial Department ruled that the NhRP could not seek second writs on behalf of Tommy and also of Kiko.[25] Kiko had been previously a TV performer and was now held by Carmen and Christie Presti in Niagara Falls, New York. The NhRP then published an annotated version of this *Lavery* decision, taking issue with the legal reasoning.[26]

The other major habeas corpus case pursued by the NhRP concerned Hercules and Leo, laboratory chimpanzees leased in 2009 by New Iberia Research Center (NIRC) at the University of Louisiana, Lafayette to Stony Brook University's Department of Anatomical Sciences, though later returned to Louisiana. One departure in that case was that Judge Barbara Jaffe, on April 20, 2015, issued an order to show cause,[27] that is, an instruction to the State University of New York to show why an order should not be granted giving relief, in the form of 'a determination that Hercules and Leo are being unlawfully detained, and ordering their immediate release and transfer' (at 2). The order was marked as 'ORDER TO SHOW CAUSE & WRIT OF HABEAS CORPUS' (at 1). The NhRP saw this as a legal victory: 'Justice Barbara Jaffe issues Hercules and Leo a writ of habeas corpus – which we and the media interpret as a tacit recognition of their personhood – and an "order to show cause."'[28] However the order was subsequently amended, with the phrase 'writ of habeas corpus' struck out.[29]

In a memorandum,[30] the respondents (SUNY) described the use of habeas corpus as 'a radical attempt to blur the legal boundaries that exist between humans and animals' (at 2). Chimpanzees had already been determined by courts not to be legal persons and a 'transfer of the chimpanzee to a sanctuary is a change in conditions not cognizable in a habeas proceeding'. Further, the petitioner lacked standing (at 3). The decision in *Lavery* was a binding precedent, and the reasoning there was persuasive legally and in terms of policy (at 14ff).

On May 27, 2015, the case of *Nonhuman Rights Project, Inc., on behalf of Hercules and Leo v. SUNY* was heard before Judge Barbara Jaffe.[31] In addition to legal argument as to the appropriate venue and whether previous decisions were binding on the court, the argument was put by counsel Christopher Coulston on behalf of SUNY that (at 7):

> Here we are in the world of analogy. The whole case is proceeding based on analogy. Petitioner wants to use Article 70 [habeas corpus] as analogy,

> and they want it for their own purposes. And when it doesn't serve their purposes, they want it to be read literally.

Wise stressed the distinctiveness of the writ of habeas corpus. The previous decisions were not binding because there was no settled law. The *Byrn* case showed that in the State of New York personhood was not a biological question but bestowed as a matter of policy (at 21). The finding in the Presti/Kiko case that habeas corpus was restricted to release rather than transfer had narrowed the writ, which had been used in the case of child slaves to transfer them into the custody of a second party (at 23).

The court also heard arguments as to standing, with SUNY arguing that the NhRP had no relationship or acquaintance with the chimpanzees (at 27–28). Wise quoted CPLR 7002(a): 'A person restrained of his liberty within the state or "one acting on his behalf" may bring a suit'. Wise made reference to slavery cases such as *Lemmon v. People*, 20 N.Y. 562 (1860), where there had been no prior relationship to the detained individual. Moving to the central issue of personhood (at 31ff), the writ was free-standing but regulated by the Civil Practice Law and Rules, Article 70. This used the word *person*, but this had not been defined by the legislature. In any case the term *person* referred to the common law (at 32–33):

> Now we argue that both as a matter of liberty and as a matter of equality, Hercules and Leo are indeed legal persons. So the liberty argument is a non-comparative argument, so we're talking about what kind of qualities Hercules and Leo might have that might qualify them for personhood as opposed to our equality argument which is a comparative argument, which we're then going to be comparing Hercules and Leo to someone else who does have personhood and arguing that they indeed should have them too.

The argument was limited to the writ. It was not the contention that just because personhood was recognized in one area, it carried over into all areas (at 33). This was the point made by the court in *Byrn*: 'We're saying we're not asking that Hercules and Leo be seen as persons for any reason other than the common-law writ of habeas corpus'. However Wise also pressed the point that Hercules and Leo were recognized as persons within the Pet Trust Statute of New York: 'not an honorary beneficiary but a real beneficiary, the only one who could do that would be a "person"' (at 33–34). Wise also cited *Rivers v. Katz*, 495 N.E.2d 337, a case which upheld the right of patients in a psychiatric institution to refuse antipsychotic medication, unless there were exigent circumstances, and *In the Matter of John Storar*, 52 N.Y.2d 363 (1981), which concerned the right to discontinue treatment for a person in a vegetative state. Those cases had shown that the 'truly supreme common-law value in the State of New York is the Proceedings protection of autonomy' (at 34–35). Wise then summarized the affidavits in terms of the free-will and self-consciousness of chimpanzees (at 35–36): 'They plan for what their life is going to be like'. They had language or 'language-like abilities', had mathematical abilities and possessed 'symbolic culture'. They were being treated worse than the worst criminal. The writ was there to protect autonomy as a principle, not just human beings (at 38).

The argument for equality drew again on slavery and the interplay between constitutional rights and the common law. In *Romer v. Evans*, 517 U.S. 620 (1996), a case that concerned the Equal Protection Clause and sexual minorities, Justice Kennedy had argued to the effect that 'to choose a single characteristic and then make that on the basis of that characteristic you are no longer essentially protected by law' is a violation of equality values (at 40). Questioned by the judge about the social contract argument, Wise called it a 'mythical thing'. In any case, 'the common-law has always reached entities, and in law itself, has reached entities that are not part of the social contract' (at 41). The slaves who were granted protection of law were not part of any social contract, as in the *Somerset* case. In Guantanamo litigation, the cases had been brought on behalf of 'people whom the government says are not only part of our social contract but are trying to destroy our social contract' (at 41). Wise argued that autonomy and self-determination were values upheld by New York State law (at 42):

> So much so that if someone goes into a hospital in New York and they want to turn down medication or life saving surgery, the courts will not interfere because the courts say we value that person's autonomy and self-determination more than the state interest in their life.

This autonomy was not widespread among animals, but science had shown that it applied to 'four species of great apes, chimpanzees, orangutans and guerrillas, perhaps elephants, and perhaps some cetaceans like orcas or dolphins' (at 44).

In response, Coulston pointed to *Byrn* as having determined that legal personhood was not a justiciable matter for courts. *Lavery* and *Byrn* were consistent. *Lavery* was based on biological fact that 'correlative rights and duties just don't simply make sense with respect to chimpanzees' (at 46). It had been conceded that chimpanzees could not be released into society. The non-human exceptions to personhood all related in one way or another to a human interest, and that was true both of corporations and the New Zealand river which was 'of religious significance' to a defined group of people (at 47). The order sought was for a transfer, where in their new environment the chimpanzees would not have the kind of bodily autonomy which the writ was normally intended to provide (at 48–49).

Coulston insisted on the fundamental difference of chimpanzees and their inability to become members of society. To extend the writ beyond human beings would be to open the floodgates (at 52). On the slippery slope argument, Wise stressed that the line was drawn at autonomy, and there were to be no writs on behalf of ants (at 52). The fact that no animal had been granted a writ before was not persuasive. The slave cases such as *Somerset* had no precedents.

In the Standing Bear lawsuit, it had been argued that a Native American was not a person within the law, but the writ had nonetheless been granted for the first time (*U.S. ex rel. Standing Bear v. Crook*, 25 F. Cas. 695 (1879)). There were no correlated duties to immunity from slavery. What was being argued was that unless one was able to partake in the social contract, one could be enslaved (at 56). *Byrn* talked about the 'rights and privileges' of a person, not 'rights and duties' (at 56). The court in *Byrn* had cited from Paton's *Textbook of Jurisprudence* (1964: 353–354, at 890):

> In ancient systems not all human beings were granted legal personality. The case of the slave is too well known to need stressing. A monk who enters a monastery is regarded in some systems as being 'civilly dead' and his property is distributed just as if death had in fact taken place. In modern times it is normal to grant legal personality to all living within the territory of the State.

Paton had pointed out that legal personality had been 'granted to entities other than human beings' (at 57). Gray's *The Nature and Sources of Law* (1909) had also been cited in *Byrn*, on the policy questions surrounding legal personality. Wise in the transcript cites from Gray as follows: 'There is no difficulty in giving legal rights to a certain natural being and making him or her a legal person'. However Gray (1909: 39) refers to 'a supernatural being'.[32] Wise then quotes Gray as follows: 'There may be systems of law in which animals have legal rights. Animals may conceivably be legal persons' (at 57).[33]

Judge Jaffe issued a judgement on September 29, 2015,[34] in which she made clear that the original order to show cause did not imply a determination that Hercules and Leo were persons. The judge reviewed the arguments and the previously unsuccessful litigation. She accepted that the NhRP had standing to bring the action (at 11), concluded that the venue was appropriate (at 16) and that the matter was not definitively settled in law (*res judicata*) (at 20). On the central issue of personhood, the judge noted that the word *person* was not defined in CPLR article 70 nor in the common law of habeas corpus (at 21). While there was no precedent for including chimpanzees or other non-human animals within the writ, this did not end the matter as had been argued in *Lavery*.[35] Legal personhood was not synonymous with being human; autonomy and self-determination were not prerequisites for granting rights; in any case what was being sought was not 'human rights for chimpanzees', but rather the contention was that (at 21–22):

> the law can and should employ the legal fiction that chimpanzees are legal persons solely for endowing the writ the right of habeas corpus, as the law accepts in other contexts the 'legal fiction' that nonhuman entities, such as corporations, may be deemed legal persons, with the rights incident thereto.

The petitioner argued that the question was one of policy rather than biology. While the underlying policy for 'a supposedly mandatory recognition of chimpanzees as legal persons' had not been clearly articulated, the petitioner argued they were 'demonstrably autonomous, self-aware, and self-determining, and otherwise very much like humans' so that 'justice demands' that they be given 'the fundamental rights of liberty and equality afforded to all humans' (at 22). The judge observed that the notion of legal personhood had evolved significantly in the United States, with originally only white, male, property-owning citizens given the 'full panoply of legal rights', pointing to an academic article by Matambanadzo (2012) and citing from *Obergefell v. Hodges* S. ct. 2584 (2015) (at 18):

> If rights were defined by who exercised them in the past, then received practices could serve as their own continued justification and new groups could not invoke rights once denied.

The past mistreatment of 'slaves, women, indigenous people or others' as property did not serve as a 'legal predicate or appropriate analogy for extending to nonhumans the status of legal personhood' (at 23). The question that remained to be debated by legal theorists and courts was 'the proper allocation of rights under the law'. In effect 'who counts under our law' (at 23). For now, 'persons have rights, duties and obligations; things do not' (at 23, citing from Berg 2007: 403). The basic situation was as follows:

> Animals, including chimpanzees and other highly intelligent mammals, are considered property under the law. They are accorded no legal rights beyond being guaranteed the right to be free from physical abuse and other mistreatment [...] and the right to humane living conditions.

Companion animals were now increasingly being treated as a 'special category of property' (cited from *Feger v. Warwick Animal Shelter,* 2008 NY Slip Op 10122 [59 AD3d 68], at 71) and seen as family members, as, for example, in *Corso v. Crawford Dog and Cat Hospital, Inc.*, 415 N.Y.S.2d (182 N.Y.City Civ.Ct., 1979), where the plaintiff was awarded damages for emotional suffering beyond the market value of the deceased dog. Some commentators were now speaking of animals as 'quasi-persons, being recognized as holding some rights and protections but not others' (Matambanadzo 2012: 61, cited at 25). Ohlin (2005: 222) had characterized arguments for animal rights as based on analogy with human beings but stated that 'this argument only works if the shared characteristics are relevant to the ascription of rights – otherwise the analogy loses its force'.[36]

In *Lavery* the Third Department had applied the social contract argument, as well as the definition of *person* from Black's Law Dictionary. The question that arose was whether the court was bound by *Lavery.* The judge concluded that it was, and also noted that any fundamental change in the law was best made by the legislature or by the Court of Appeals (at 31). Concluding, the judge noted (at 32):

> Efforts to extend legal rights to chimpanzees are [...] understandable; some day they may even succeed. Courts, however, are slow to embrace change, and occasionally seem reluctant to engage in broader, more inclusive interpretations of the law, if only to the modest extent of affording them greater consideration.

Based on cases such as *Lawrence v. Texas,* 539 U.S. 558 (2003), which struck down sodomy laws, and *Obergefell v. Hodges*, U.S. S. ct. 2584 (2015), recognizing same-sex marriage, it seemed that the pace of legal change 'may now be accelerating' (at 32).

Judge Jaffe by implication accepted the argument that progressive legal change involved the gradual extension of personhood rights to stigmatized groups, and that chimpanzees were such a group. Her judgement accepted that questions of personhood were matters of policy rather than reflecting biological categories. In a footnote, she also rejected the 'floodgates of litigation' argument as a ground for denying a cause of action', and found authority for the proposition that the writ of habeas corpus could be used to transfer someone from one institution to another, rather than solely for release from detention (at 32, fn. 2). Taken together with Judge Jaffe's recognition of standing for the NhRP, this constituted a highly sympathetic judgement, and this was emphasized on the NhRP's website.[37]

The monkey selfie case and authorship

At issue in the *monkey selfie* case was the question of whether a non-human animal could own the copyright to a photograph. In intellectual property law, an author must be a natural person, though ownership of copyright can be assigned to corporations. The model of individual human agency which underlies the legal attribution of authorship was the target of sustained sceptical attack in artistic modernism and in twentieth century literary criticism, under the slogan 'the death of the author' (Barthes 1977, Foucault 1980), part of the discourse of the 'death of the subject' (Heartfield 2002). The post-humanist denial of selfhood and agency is ironic, given the ego-fuelled academic self-promotion that has characterized the various branches of post-structuralist and postmodern theory and the cult of personality that surrounds its key proponents. Barthes's 'death of the author' would have been better expressed as 'the empowerment of the critic'.

Literary theorists have long been open to the possibility that a computer programme might be an author or co-author (Koch 1996, Milde 1969). Corporate authorship might in future be understood in terms of distributed cognition or extended mind in action (Kuykendall 2010: 632). Debate has arisen however in relation to post-humanist selves, potentially socially recognized beings such as cyborgs, robots, and AI systems, and whether at some point they might be legal persons (Willick 1983, Solum 1992, Teubner 2006, Hubbard 2011). A further question was whether *machine speech* might benefit from protection under the First Amendment (Benjamin 2013, Wu 2013). Where texts are held to be of divine origin this may prevent a community of believers from obtaining the protection of copyright (Cotter 2003). This problem arises in relation to ***automatic writing*** and forms of speech dictated by spiritual forces through a purely passive human vessel (*Cummins v. Bond* [1927] 1 Ch. 167, Lee 1926).

In 2011 a six-year-old crested black macaque, Naruto, resident in a national park on the island of Sulawesi, Indonesia, used a camera belonging to the wildlife photographer David Slater to take multiple self-portraits. These photographs became known as the *monkey selfies*. Two pictures in particular caught the public imagination, one showing Naruto grinning at the camera, and another 'full-body' selfie. These became popular on the web and were subsequently uploaded to Wikimedia Commons with the explanation: 'This file is in the public domain, because as the work of a non-human animal, it has no human author in whom copyright is vested'. This sentence is also used currently in relation to a painting by a chimpanzee named Congo.[38] Slater threatened legal action for breach of copyright. The counterclaim consisted of the argument that there was no copyright in the image at all, as the creator was not a legal person, or, alternatively, that Naruto himself, as the creator of the image, was the copyright owner.

In 2015 PETA filed a lawsuit as *next friends* of Naruto, claiming that the macaque's copyright had been violated by David Slater, Blurb Inc., and Wildlife Personalities Ltd. In their complaint,[39] PETA asserted that Naruto was 'free and autonomous' and had taken a number of photographs. The photographs 'resulted from a series of purposeful and voluntary actions' which resulted in 'original works of authorship not by Slater, but by Naruto' (para. 2). Given this, 'Naruto has the right to own and benefit from the copyright in the Monkey Selfies in the same manner and to the same extent as any other author' (para. 5). Slater himself had talked of the need for the recognition that animals such as macaques have 'personality' and 'rights to dignity and property' and that they were 'intelligent – artistic – complex' (para. 6). Profits from the image were to be used 'solely for the benefit of Naruto, his family and his community, including the preservation of their habitat' (para. 7). It was argued that macaques had 'stereoscopic color vision with depth perception and are vision dominant', as well as 'grasping hands and thumbs' (paras. 26 and 27). 'Naruto's use of his hands in any activity results from his intentional, purposeful, and concentrated action, not mere happenstance or accident' (para. 27). Given the extent of tourism, Naruto had become 'accustomed to observing and recognizing his own image in some or all of these reflective surfaces' and was very familiar with cameras (para. 29). Slater had not assisted Naruto, and the macaque had (para. 33)

> authored the Monkey Selfies by his independent, autonomous actions in examining and manipulating Slater's unattended camera and purposely pushing the shutter release multiple times, understanding the cause-and-effect relationship between pressing the shutter release, the noise of the shutter, and the change to his reflection in the camera lens.

Slater's book had conceded this point: 'Sulawesi crested black macaque smiles at itself whilst pressing the shutter button on a camera' (cited, para.

34a) and 'A Sulawesi crested black macaque pulls one of several funny faces during its own photo shoot, seemingly aware of its own reflection in the lens' (cited para.34b). Slater had spoken of 'fun and artistic experiment', and attributed 'self-awareness' and an understanding of self-representation to Naruto (paras. 34b, c, e).

US District Judge William Orrick dismissed the claim.[40] He noted that the US Copyright Act (1976) defined neither *works of authorship* nor *author* (at 4). The judge followed the Cetacean Community[41] decision in asserting that an explicit legislative statement would be required to extend standing to animals (at 4). The Copyright Act did not offer any such suggestion and courts had repeatedly referred to *persons* when interpreting it. The US Copyright Office had set out guidelines for interpreting the Copyright Act, to which courts owed deference. Authorship in copyright works was specifically restricted to works created by a human being fixed in a tangible medium of expression. Policy dictated that works produced by 'nature, animals, or plants', including 'a photograph taken by a monkey' (at 6), could not be registered. The judge therefore concluded that Naruto was not an author within the meaning of the Act. It was up to Congress to decide if recognition could be given to animal art (at 6).

PETA filed an appeal to the Ninth Circuit Court of Appeals in San Francisco,[42] arguing that the law protected the originality of the work, not the humanity of the author. The purpose of the law was to promote creative outputs and the Copyright Act 'was intended to be broadly applied and to gradually expand to include new forms of expression unknown at the time it was enacted' (at 5). PETA pointed to complex controversies over computer authorship using artificial intelligence. The term *author* had not been defined in the Act, and it came directly from the US Constitution.[43] Case law had determined that the author of a photograph was the individual who physically took the picture, that is, the one 'who effectively is as near as he can be the cause of the picture which is produced'.[44] While the statutory requirements for standing under the Act did not expressly include animals, there was no express definition at all. The statutes at issue in *Cetacean* involved a waiver of US sovereign immunity and were therefore narrowly construed, unlike the Copyright Act. In employment relationships, rights of authorship were vested directly in the corporate owner.[45] It was possible to have copyright protection for anonymous works, that is, works for which 'no natural person is identified as author' (17 U.S.C. s. 101). Just as *writings* had been extended to include *photographs*, so the Act's notion of authorship could be extended to include animals (at 16). To deny animals this right would create a gap in copyright protection, contrary to the aim of protecting all original works (at 17). Profit-seeking was not required for copyright protection: copyright even obtained in secret documents (at 18):

> Moreover, it is irrelevant that Naruto cannot exploit his copyright without the assistance of humans. Human children – and even certain incapacitated adults – cannot reproduce or sell copyrighted works without the assistance of others. But they are still 'authors' under the Copyright Act.

This was an issue of first impression, but there was no legal bar to extending authorship to animals.[46] It was settled law that copyright applied to every photograph, given the minimal level required to demonstrate originality (at 22ff). The Compendium on which the court had relied was not definitive. While it was stated there that 'for a work to be copyrightable, it must owe its origin to a human being',[47] in *Urantia Foundation v. Maaherra*, 114 F.3d 955, at 958 (9th Cir. 1997) the court cited the following: 'The copyright laws, of course, do not expressly require "human" authorship, and considerable controversy has arisen in recent years over the copyrightability of computer-generated works'.[48] Since originality was the chief criterion, and the photographs were undoubtedly original, the Compendium's conclusion was 'inconsistent with the plain language of the Copyright Act, the breadth with which it is interpreted, and the constitutional purposes for which it was enacted' (at 26).

In a hostile decision, the Court of Appeals upheld the District Court ruling, noting that next friend status was defined narrowly by statute and PETA did not qualify (per Circuit Judge Bea, at 4–18). There was no explicit authorization for animal standing under the copyright legislation. However, following *Cetacean Community*, 386 F.3d at 1171, there remained standing under Article III of the Constitution. The lack of a next friend was therefore not fatal to a hearing on the merits, with the aim of analyzing whether the incompetent party's (Naruto) interests were properly represented. However *Cetacean Community* had laid down the principle that the court could not go beyond the positive terms of the statute, and therefore there was no standing for Naruto. Circuit Judge Smith went further (at 19–41), denying that the court had jurisdiction. Animal-next-friend standing was open to abuse (at 28–29):

> We have no idea whether animals or objects wish to own copyrights or open bank accounts to hold their royalties from sales of pictures. To some extent, as humans, we have a general understanding of the similar interests of other humans. In the habeas corpus context, we presume other humans desire liberty. Similarly, in actions on behalf of infants, for example, we presume the infant would want to retain ownership of the property she inherited. But the interests of animals? We are really asking what *another* species desires. Do animals want to own property, such as copyrights? Are animals willing to assume the duties associated with the rights PETA seems to be advancing on their behalf?

Judge Smith concluded that the case should have been dismissed for lack of jurisdiction, rather than be considered on its merits.

Conclusion

Case law operates on the social surface as far as possible, creating a 'museum of precedent' (Goodrich 1990: 273) in order to avoid a confrontation with its own foundations. The litigation analyzed earlier is trapped between two competing different visions of law, that is, law as a mundane mode of social adjustment and law as a mode for the investigation, recognition, creation, and dissolution of deep ontologies. Courts when faced with fundamental arguments about modes of being typically cling to the first view, and deflect any more substantial powers of redefinition onto the legislature. Litigation on behalf of animal personhood takes the form of seeking in the textual body of law statements or principles that can be analogized or transformed into ontological arguments, relating either directly to legal ontology and the kinds of entities that law recognizes or to natural ontology, that is, arguments that chimpanzees are autonomous and creative creatures, akin to human beings.

The project of promoting animal personhood is caught on the horns of a dilemma. This reflects the tension between law as grounded in natural categories and law as artificial reasoning. On the one side are arguments for the human-like nature of higher primates and cetaceans, and their autonomy, free-will, agency, and other traits analogous to human ones: the 'similarity argument' (Bryant 2007). The category of the human being must remain at the centre since the appeal is to the anthropocentrism of law on behalf of the higher animal as human-by-analogy. On the other, there is the analogy with the corporation, as an artificial creature of law. Being human or human-like is not a prerequisite for legal personhood. Personhood for animals in this sense reflects anti-anthropocentric thinking. This would dethrone the human from its position as the sole *telos* of law.

On the definitional level, integrationism would recognize that the word *person*, whether understood as a natural kind or an artificial category of law, has no intrinsic boundary. There is no rule of language that restricts how particular linguistic categories are applied. At the ideological level, integrationism is arguably anthropocentric, but it does not follow that it takes any particular view of arguments for or against animal personhood. Rather it points to the limitations of our capacity to think through fundamental or bedrock issues to reasoned conclusions. Law, like the study of language, is always *in medias res*, buffeted about by the contingencies of socio-political and cultural forces and attempting to carve out a coherent narrative underlying its decision-making whilst being subject to pressures of which it is only partially aware.

Notes

1 For overviews of the litigation, see Fitzgerald (2015), Davison-Vecchione and Pambos (2017) and the critique in Cupp (2018).
2 *Data Processing Svc. Orgs. v. Camp,* 397 U.S. 150 (1970).
3 This discussion focuses on the United States – for discussion of the Canadian case *Reece v. Edmonton (City)*, 2011 ABCA 238, see Totten (2015).
4 *Humane Society v. Block,* Civil Action, Civil Action No. 81-2691 and *Fund For Animals v. Malone,* Civil Action No. 81-2977.
5 Available at: www.apa.org/about/offices/ogc/amicus/primate.pdf.
6 The decision was reversed by the Supreme Court, as the petitioners had standing to contest the removal of the case (*International Primate Protection League v. Administrators of Tulane Educational Fund,* 500 U.S. 72 (1991)). It was remanded to the

District Court to be further remanded to Louisana state court – see *In re the Administrators of Tulane Educational Fund*, 954 F.2d 266 (1992).

7 *Mt. Graham Red Squirrel v. Yeutter*, 930 F.2d 703 (9th Cir.1991); *Northern Spotted Owl v. Lujan*, 758 F.Supp. 621 (W.D.Wash.1991); *Northern Spotted Owl v. Hodel*, 716 F.Supp. 479 (W.D.Wash.1988).

8 The complaint can be found at: seaworldparks.com.

9 See www.nonhumanrightsproject.org.

10 Supreme Court of New York County of Fulton, *In the Matter of a Proceeding under Article 70 of the CPLR for a Writ of Habeas Corpus, The Nonhuman Rights Project on behalf of Tommy v. Patrick C. Lavery, individually and as an officer of Circle L trailer Sales Inc. and Circle L trailer Sales Inc.*, available at www.nonhumanrights.org/client-tommy/.

11 New York State allows multiple filings of habeas corpus writs, which made the venue particularly attractive.

12 The text is also available at: www.animallaw.info/case/suica-habeas-corpus.

13 Available at www.nonhumanrights.org/client-tommy.

14 Available at www.nonhumanrights.org/client-tommy/.

15 The river in question is the Whanganui on the North Island, now recognized by statute as having legal personality (Rogers 2017).

16 (*The People of the State of New York ex rel. The Nonhuman Rights Project, Inc., on Behalf of Tommy, v Patrick C. Lavery, Individually and as an Officer of Circle L Trailer Sales, Inc., et al.*, 124 AD3d at 149 (2014))

17 Cited from *Amadio v. Levin*, 509 Pa 199, at 225.

18 www.nonhumanrights.org/content/uploads/Tribe-Amicus-Curiae-Letter-Brief-FINAL.pdf; www.nonhumanrights.org/content/uploads/letter-brief-of-amicus-curiae-CCR.pdf

19 www.nonhumanrights.org/content/uploads/Tommy-Memo-of-Law-Dec-2-2015.pdf.

20 www.nonhumanrights.org/content/uploads/Tommy-Appellate-Brief-Oct-2016.pdf.

21 www.nonhumanrights.org/content/uploads/2015_162358_The-Nonhuman-Rights-Project-Inc.-v.-Patrick-C.-Lavery_Brief.pdf.

22 www.nonhumanrights.org/content/uploads/CuppAmicus.pdf.

23 The argument in the case actually focused on the notion of *fair value*, which belonged to 'the great juristic myths of history, with the Law of Nature and the Social Contract'.

24 www.nonhumanrights.org/content/uploads/Letter-to-First-Dept-re-Tommy-and-Kiko-3.27.17-FINAL-1.pdf.

25 www.nonhumanrights.org/client-kiko/.

26 *Matter of Nonhuman Rights Project, Inc. v. Lavery*, 2017 NY Slip Op 04574 [152 AD3d 73]; www.nonhumanrights.org/content/uploads/Footnotes-with-annotated-Tommy-Kiko-appellate-court-opinion-FINAL-6-22-17.pdf.

27 iapps.courts.state.ny.us.

28 www.nonhumanrights.org/hercules-leo/.

29 www.nonhumanrights.org/content/uploads/Order-to-Show-Cause-Amended-4-21-15.pdf.

30 www.nonhumanrights.org/content/uploads/Reply-Brief-from-AG-5-22-15.pdf.

31 INDEX NO.152736/15, www.nonhumanrights.org/content/uploads/Transcript-of-5.27.15-Hearing-Hercules-and-Leo.pdf. Evident misspellings have been corrected.

32 The transcript may be in error.

33 Gray states there that (1909: 42) while 'beasts have no legal rights', there are statutes for their protection which are understood primarily as relating to human interests. However it was conceivable there might be a system of law 'in which animals have legal rights, – for instance, cats in ancient Egypt, or white elephants in Siam'. In such cases, 'the wills of human beings must be attributed to animals'.

34 www.nonhumanrights.org/content/uploads/Judge-Jaffes-Decision-7-30-15.pdf.
35 *The People of the State of New York ex rel. The Nonhuman Rights Project, Inc., on Behalf of Tommy, v. Patrick C. Lavery, Individually and as an Officer of Circle L Trailer Sales, Inc., et al.*, 124 AD3d at 149 (2014).
36 This is the full quotation rather than the partial quotation given by the court.
37 www.nonhumanrights.org/hercules-leo.
38 en.wikipedia.org/wiki/File:Chimpanzee_congo_painting.jpg.
39 *Naruto et al v. David John Slater*, US District Court, Northern California, Case No. 15-cv-4324 (2015).
40 Judgement of Judge William H. Orrick, *Naruto et al v. David John Slater*, US District Court, Northern California, Case No. 15-cv-4324 (2016).
41 *Cetacean Community v. Bush*, 249 F. Supp. 2d 1206 (D. Haw. 2003).
42 arstechnica.com/wp-content/uploads/2017/07/narutoopeningbrief9thcircuit.pdf.
43 Article I, Section 8, Clause 8 grants Congress the power: 'To promote the Progress of Science and useful Arts, by securing for limited Times to Authors and Inventors the exclusive Right to their respective Writings and Discoveries'.
44 *Burrow-Giles Lithographic Co. v. Sarony*, 111 U.S. 53 (1883), at 61, citing *Nottage v. Jackson*, 11 Q.B.D. 627 (1883)).
45 *Warren v. Fox Family Worldwide, Inc.*, 328 F.3d 1136, 1145 (9th Cir. 2003).
46 'If rights were defined by who exercised them in the past, then received practices could serve as their own continued justification and new groups could not invoke rights once denied'. *Obergefell v. Hodges*, 135 S.Ct. 2584, at 2602 (2015).
47 Compendium of the US Copyright Office Practices, 2d Edition § 202.02(b) (1984).
48 The quotation comes from Miller (1993) and the *Urantia* case concerned claims that supernatural beings had authored the work (see Rhee 1998).

Conclusion

A personalist perspective

The *person/res/acta* distinction conceals the underlying anthropocentricism of law. *Res* and *acta* are emanations from *persona. Person* is for these reasons the central legal category, in which are crystallized law's definitional and interpretative dilemmas. It cannot be replaced by *right-and-duty-bearing entity*, as law requires its ambivalent status as simultaneously an ordinary English word and a legal term of art.

In *The Mirror and the Lamp* (1953), M. H. Abrams distinguished two metaphors for the mind. The first was the *mirror*: the mind was mimetic, 'a reflector of external objects'. The second was the *lamp*: the mind was 'a radiant projector which makes a contribution to the objects it perceives' (1953: viii). This dichotomy can be adapted to characterize the two orientations of law. When faced with bedrock categories such as *person, man/woman* or *thing*, law may mirror the natural, social or theological order. Alternatively, law defines or illuminates such concepts for its own internal ('artificial') purposes, invoking or constructing a technical legal meaning. *Person* can mirror a natural category ('human being'), a social category ('recognized member of a social order'), a theological category ('being with a body and a soul'), or be defined specifically for law's purposes as a 'right-and-duty bearing entity'. Law's bi-directional orientation is institutionalized to a degree in terms of the *fact/law* distinction (see Allen and Pardo 2003). But it is also obscured by the category of *ordinary language*. Within the interpretative culture of law, ordinary language is a reification of everyday usage (fact) constructed for legal purposes (law) – in that sense it partakes of the fact/law ambiguity. It is the judge who determines the *category* of language (ordinary, technical, or legal) that is at issue in any particular case. Further, the judge can stipulate that a particular ordinary meaning is the relevant one. In *Brutus v. Cozens* [1973] AC 854, a case which hinged on whether a protest during the Wimbledon tennis tournament amounted to *insulting behaviour*, Lord Reid stated that (at 861) 'The meaning of an ordinary word of the English language is not a question of law. The proper construction of a statute is a question of law'. The *factual* determination of linguistic meaning is framed by a prior overall *legal* interpretative inquiry.

For a court, it might be a conclusive argument to say that an individual, registered at birth as male, is not a *woman* according to the ordinary meaning of

DOI: 10.4324/9781315143132-7

the word, drawing on biology, social convention (accessed through intuition or dictionary definitions), or theological anthropology (Hutton 2018). By contrast, the assertion that a chimpanzee is not a *person* has a different status. *Woman* is not a legal term of art, whereas *person* is, albeit ambivalently so. That a corporation is a *persona* is not the result of an investigation into the properties of certain religious, municipal, economic, or political entities. It is not a discovery about reality. The designation of corporate personality as fictional suggests nonetheless an underlying real ontology, a world of extralegal facts (natural, social or theological) on which law can draw if required. If we take the case of the human foetus in its relationship to personhood – frequently seen as 'not a person, but only a potential person' (Luker 1984: 140) – these ambiguities are evident. It is possible to frame the biological case for foetal personhood as a factual argument: 'All the known evidence supports the human foetus as being a true ontological human individual and consequently a human person, in fact if not in law' (Kurjak et al. 2009: 339). *Person* in law neither is, nor is not, a biological concept. For law, understood as an artificial domain, biological facts may or may not be deemed legally relevant. The same ambivalence attends the assertion that 'animals are not things' (Grandin 2006). Is *thing* an ordinary language category (reflecting a natural or social fact) or does it reflect the legal category, *res*? *Res*, like *persona*, sits on the fact/law borderline and is ontologically promiscuous. From one theological point of view, 'God is *res*, and, in respect of him, all else is *signum*' (Williams 2016: 44).

In law's deep structure, the following model of personhood can be discerned. At one pole can be found fully natural beings, non-human animals. The non-human animal lies by default outside of law, and is only brought into the jurisdiction of law as the object of human processes, such as hunting, or when domesticated or farmed, or held as a pet in the form of property. The habits and drives that govern animal existence are entirely derived from nature (though these may be curbed and tamed to a degree), and the species into which animals fall are part of a God-given taxonomic order. At the other pole is the corporation, which as an artificial being has no existence outside the legal rules that create and sustain it. It has no natural drives or God-given essence; it is a creature of law, not of nature. It is potentially immortal, so long as it is economically and organizationally viable, and the jurisdiction itself continues. It is a fictional person, treated 'as if' it were a person for some purposes (Vaihinger 1922). The human realm sits at the intersection of these two extremes. A human person has both an animal existence and a social mode of being, belongs to nature and to culture, possesses an instinctual body but also a mind or soul. This union is hypostatic, in that human beings are fully animal as well as fully social. Similarly, human language is both a natural endowment and a social institution. Unlike animals, whose existence is extinguished in their life cycle, and unlike humans, whose bodies are mortal but who have an immortal soul, a company is an immortal being with neither soul nor body.

The word *person* at its most banal means 'human being'; yet it also refers to a member of the Trinity. The Jesuit theologian Karl Rahner (1904–1985) came to this blunt conclusion: 'What do we mean by the human person? My reply, stripped to its essentials, is simple: The person is the question to which there is no answer' (2000: 73). Like a subset of their legal counterparts, theologians such as Rahner and Karl Barth (1886–1968) had reservations about the term *person* used as a term of art. Barth sought to replace it with a technical term less implicated in modern philosophical and secular usage, namely: *Seinsweise* ('mode of being') (Letham 2004: 277, Whapham 2010), just as some legal scholars understand personhood as referring to *right-and-duty-bearing entities*. For Barth, the modern term *person* implied a centre of consciousness or a self-sustaining *I*, wrongly suggesting autonomous individuals. The theology of how the *ousia* of Godhead relates to the *hypostases* of the Trinity is the prototypical problem of the attribution of states and actions to a corporate entity as distinct from the individuals that compose it. One of those persons, Christ, is the word (*logos*) made flesh. Christ acts in historical time and suffers as a person on behalf of humanity, whilst being both fully human and fully divine. Boethius's definition of *person*, in seeking to reconcile philosophical categories with the mysteries of the Trinity, could only resort to a stipulated definition, incorporating a fundamental equivocation as to *substance*.

The intense anxieties that surround the notion of corporate personality need to be read against this theological background. The case of the Trinitarian *person* can stand as a metonym for the definitive unknowability of categories in general, and the consequent necessity of stipulation. From an integrational perspective, the attempt to define abstract categories like *personhood* triggers inevitably a set of core-margin problems. These arise in relation to any category, even the most mundane, since definition involves in part a form of contextualization by imagination. Just as I can think of a range of marginal phenomena in relation to *table*, so I can imagine problematic or contentious issues in relation to *person*. If I ask for a real definition of *person*, I can bring to mind a range of marginal cases, both actual and imagined. If I then seek to come up with a verbal definition, I am already constrained by my previous inquiry. As a consequence, stipulated definition is deployed overtly or covertly.

Language is fundamental to law's mediation between the natural/social/theological (extralegal) and the artificial (legal). Its categories move elusively between these domains. It is unclear which should be ontologically or conceptually prior, the naturalistic human being (*homo sapiens*), the social *persona* as mask, or the being created in God's image (*imago dei*) endowed with both a soul and a body. In terms of conventional semantics and abstract conceptual analysis, the word *person* lacks a literal meaning, and as a metaphor the implication of the meaning 'mask' in *persona ficta* lacks a stable point of comparison. Like corporations, individual humans can be understood to wear social masks and are constituted as legal subjects by law.

Its complex place in the Western tradition means that the word *person* is a case of profound *semantic satiation* or *meaning-blindness* at the level of bedrock cultural concepts. The history of thinking about selfhood and personhood stages a constant collapse of real definition into verbal definition, and verbal definition into stipulative definition. In early modernity, philosophers established the self/person divide as a reflection of philosophical individualism and subjectivism on the one hand, and the law and politics of personhood on the other. The secularized, autonomous self of modernity sits, as it were, as the incumbent within the status or office of personhood. *Person* is the social mask for *self*. This dualistic model of self/person, where agency or will was located in the individual, never stabilized since no satisfactory secular framework could be found for characterizing the self, for explaining its relation to the body, and for harmonizing the inner reality of self with the outer mask of personhood. The autonomous secular self encountered its most profound intellectual challenge in post-Darwinian naturalism. In its wake came the radical impersonality of systems theory, and the various strands of post-humanism. In modern polities, the boundary between inner self and social persona, between private and social self, became a politically contentious matter. The Christian concept of *person* retained its power, taking a central role in modern secular humanism as well as in theological responses to secular modernity. Personhood in this humanistic sense is associated with an inalienable and irreducible dignity, with first-person ownership not just of property, rights, and citizenship (legal personhood) but also of a self with memories, feelings, and aspirations.

Integrational semiology is confronted with difficult questions about the status of the individual agentive self that integrates. Does this self itself stand outside the process of integration? Harris (2004) talks of an *integrating mind*; Duncker of an *integrating self* (2017). Viewed from the lay perspective, the denial of the self is the purest academic nonsense, especially when a stipulated distinction is drawn between the reality of *person* and the fiction of *self*. It is arguably as absurd to stipulate that the self exists as to stipulate that it does not: 'Explanations come to an end somewhere' (Wittgenstein [1953] 2009: 6e), as do stipulations. There are two intellectual extremes in play here. For integrationism, there is the self without system; for Luhmann's systems theory, there is system without the self. Set against first-person experiential sense-making is the third-person systems view, where selves are epiphenomenal. Integrationism's agentive self stands on the *terra firma* of personal experience; yet integrationism recognizes that everything about communication is contingent, provisional, and radically contextual. In that sense, the self cannot understand communication in full, from an omniscient third-person perspective. Nonetheless, *qua* language-maker, the individual is able to create or impose understanding on the flow of interaction and offer a reading, narrative, or interpretation of a particular episode or text.

From the first-person perspective, what is created moment-to-moment is spontaneous sense-making, from which a third-person impersonal landscape ('reality') is imagined or projected. The first-person self cannot adopt a truly third-person perspective, but this projected impersonal reality can be understood as the inchoate background against which the individual self operates and both experiences and creates order (or disorder), pattern (or its absence), or regularity (or irregularity). This sense-making is not a solipsistic activity. As Duncker suggests, integration involves centrally an orientation to others. It implies an Other, echoing the humanist *I/you* duality (2017). The 'person in concrete, living, individuality' who is 're-created again and again in the perpetual flux of life' is at the heart of theological personalism (Bonhoeffer 2009: 48). For personalism as a philosophy, 'there are characteristic qualities of human beings that cannot be reduced to the elements of other, nonpersonalist realities' (Smith 2010: 102). Assertions that the self is a fiction make sense from the (imagined) third-person point of view, but are nonsense from the first-person perspective.

A future social order may well condemn the totality of previously existing human civilizations for their infliction of violence upon the diversity of sentient creatures that inhabit the earth (Bernstein 2004). There is nothing intrinsic to the word *person* that prevents it being applied to higher animals. But whether legal personhood for animals is a plausible innovation is open to question. The argument that higher animals are biologically analogous to humans draws on the naturalistic category; the argument that higher animals understand mutual social obligations draws on the social category; the argument that animals have immaterial souls extends theological anthropology (Thurow 2018). To argue that legal personhood is open-ended, in that it includes fictional persons, is to highlight the artificiality of the category. But, within the interpretative culture of law, the gravitational pull of the reified ordinary language category, *person* as 'human being', is extremely powerful.

Integrationism is anthropocentric, but it offers no fixed opinions about personhood in relation to animals or, indeed, the members of the Trinity. Ideological critiques of humanism or personhood point to the multiple exclusions, including genocide, that have been enacted under these categories. But these polemics arguably anthropomorphize the category itself as agent, ignoring the political systems responsible, and the acts of human agents who applied those systems to the domain of political action. The evocation of post-humanism, where there is formal equality between the human, animal, and inorganic realms, reflects a paradoxical cult of the impersonal. The impersonal third-person view is idealized as non-reductionalist: 'Modern humanists are reductionist because they seek to attribute action to a small number of powers, leaving the rest of the world with nothing but simple mute forces' (Latour 1993: 138). To give voice to the impersonal requires belief in the possibility of accessing a non-fictional or authentic third-person reality.

Yet a post-humanist world would be a world drained of affect, compassion, and love. Integrationism, I would argue, should be seen as a form of personalism. It rejects the third-person impersonal perspective. The label of personalism captures the personal, first-person nature of sign-making, as well as its ethical dimension. It is arguably a more accurate label for integrationism than individualism or humanism, and builds on the notion of a *person-centred* approach to human behaviour (Klemmensen 2018). Sign-making is personal, rather than individual or human. In its personal nature lies the assumption that others are also persons and that sign-making must orient itself to them. The third-person perspective is best understood as an imaginary, a projection, or, indeed, a *fiction.* What emerges from accounts of human-animal interaction is that many people have a powerful first-person experience of the co-personhood of animals. Belief in the *personal* suffering of animals offers then the only ethical imperative.

References

Abrams, Meyer (1953) *The Mirror and the Lamp*. Oxford: OUP.

Ackrill, J. L., ed. (2002) *Aristotle: Categories and De Interpretatione*. Oxford: Clarendon.

Adams, Carol (2014) The war on compassion. In Patricia MacCormack, ed., *The Animal Catalyst: Towards Ahuman Theory*. London: Bloomsbury, 15–25.

Adriano, Elvia (2015) The natural person, legal entity or juridical person and juridical personality. *Penn State Journal of Law and International Affairs* 4: 364–391.

Agamben, Giorgio (1998) *Homo Sacer: Sovereign Power and Bare Life*. Stanford: Stanford UP.

Agamben, Giorgio (2009) *Nudità*. Rome: Nottetempo.

Agassi, Joseph (1960) Methodological individualism. *The British Journal of Sociology* 11: 244–270.

Ahearn, Laura (2001) Language and agency. *Annual Review of Anthropology* 30: 109–137.

Allen, Ronald and Michael Pardo (2003) The myth of the law-fact distinction. *Northwestern University LR* 97: 1769–1808.

Alston, William (1989) *Divine Nature and Human Language*. Ithaca: Cornell UP.

Amatrudo, Anthony (2008) The illusory nature of ontological status and its implications for legal, moral and social organisation. *International Journal of Law in Context* 4: 63–77.

Amatrudo, Anthony (2012) An intentional basis for corporate personality. *International Journal of Law in Context* 8: 413–430.

Anderson, Benedict (1983) *Imagined Communities*. London: Verso.

Andrews, Kirtsin (2011) Beyond anthropomorphism: attributing psychological properties to animals. In Tom L. Beauchamp and R.G. Frey, eds., *The Oxford Handbook of Animal Ethics*. Oxford: OUP, 469–495.

Anestal, Davidson (2017) Chimpanzees in court: limited legal personhood recognition for standing to challenge captivity and abuse. *Dartmouth Law Journal* 15: 75–110.

Anscombe, Elizabeth (1975) The first person. In Samuel Guttenplan, ed., *Mind and Language*. Clarendon: Oxford, 45–65.

Arendt, Hannah (1973) *On Revolution*. London: Penguin.

Ariss, Rachel (2004) Bring out your dead: law, human remains and memory. *Canadian Journal of Language and Society* 19: 33–54.

Aristotle (1910) *Historia Animalium*. Oxford: Clarendon Press. Written 350BCE.

Armstrong, Matthew (2006) *Cetacean Community v. Bush*: the false hope of animal rights lingers on. *Hastings West-Northwest Journal of Environmental Law and Policy* 12: 185–204.

Arnauld, Antoine and Nicole, Pierre (1996). *Logic or the Art of Thinking*. Cambridge: CUP. First published, 1662.

Ashworth, William (2008) Natural history and the emblematic worldview. In Marcus Hellyer, ed., *The Scientific Revolution*. Oxford: Blackwell, 132–156.

Atkins-Sayre, Wendy (2010) Articulating identity: people for the ethical treatment of animals and the animal/human divide. *Western Journal of Communication* 74: 309–328.

Augustine (2002) *On the Trinity: Books 8–15*. Cambridge: CUP.

Ayer, Alfred (1946) *Language, Truth and Logic*. London: Victor Gallancz.

Ayres, Lewis (2010) *Augustine and the Trinity*. Cambridge: CUP.

Babcock, Hope (2016) A brook with legal rights: the rights of nature in court. *Ecology Law Quarterly* 43: 1–52.

Bacon, Francis (1733) *Philosophical Works*, vol. 3, Peter Shaw, ed. London: Knapton.

Bacon, Francis (1838) *Works*, vol. 1. London: Ball.

Bacon, Francis (1883) *Essays*. New York: Hurst.

Bacon, Francis (2000) *The New Organon*. Lisa Jardine and Michael Silverthorne, eds. Cambridge: CUP. First published, 1620.

Bahun, Sonya (2013) *Modernism and Melancholia*. Oxford: Oxford University Press.

Baker, Lynne (2007) Naturalism and the first-person perspective. In Georg Gasser, ed., *How Successful is Naturalism?* Frankfurt: Ontos, 203–226.

Bakhurst, David and Christine Sypnowich (1995) Introduction: problems of the social self. In David Bakhurst and Christine Sypnowich, eds., *The Social Self*. London: Sage, 1–17.

Balcombe, Jonathan (2016) *What a Fish Knows*. New York: Farrar.

Balibar, Etienne (2013) *Identity and Difference: John Locke and the Invention of Consciousness*. London: Verso.

Balthasar, Hans Urs von (1986) On the concept of person. *Communio* 13: 18–26.

Barker, Ernest (1934) Translator's introduction. *Natural Law and the Theory of the Society 1500–1800*, by Otto Gierke, vol. 1. Cambridge: CUP, ix–xci.

Baron-Cohen, Simon (2010) Review of Cordelia Fine, *Delusions of Gender*, New York, Norton, 2010. *The Psychologist* 23: 904–905, available at: thepsychologist.bps.org.uk.

Barney, Rachel (2001) *Names and Nature in Plato's Cratylus*. New York: Routledge.

Barney, Stephen, W.J. Lewis, J.A. Beach, and Oliver Berghof, eds. (2006) *The Etymologies of Isidore of Seville*. Cambridge: CUP.

Barresi, John and Raymond Martin (2011) History as prologue: Western theories of the self. In Shaun Gallagher, ed., *The Oxford Handbook of the Self*. Oxford: OUP, 33–56.

Bartelson, Jens (2015) Sovereignty and the personality of the state. In Robert Schuett and Peter Stirk, eds., *The Concept of the State in International Relations*. Edinburgh: Edinburgh UP, 81–107.

Barth, Timotheus (1965) Being univocity, and analogy according to Duns Scotus. In John Ryan and Bernardine Bonansea, eds., *John Duns Scotus 1265–1965*. Washington: The Catholic University of America Press, 210–262.

Barthes, Roland (1977) The death of the author. In Stephen Heath, ed., *Image – Music – Text*. London: Fontana, 142–148.

Bateson, Gregory (1979) *Mind and Nature: A Necessary Unity*. New York: Dutton.

Bateson, Gregory (2000) *Steps to an Ecology of Mind*. Chicago: University of Chicago Press. First published, 1972.

Bateson, Gregory, Don D. Jackson, Jay Haley, and John Weakland (1956) Toward a theory of schizophrenia. *Behavioural Science* 1: 251–254.

Bauman, Harold (1983) *Law and Revolution*. Cambridge: Harvard UP.

Becker, Alton (1991) Language and languaging. *Language and Communication* 11: 33–35.
Belk, Russell (1988) Possessions and the extended self. *Journal of Consumer Research* 15: 139–168.
Benjamin, Stuart (2013) Algorithms and speech. *University of Pennsylvania LR* 161: 1445–1494.
Bennett, Max and Peter Hacker (2003). *Philosophical Foundations of Neuroscience.* Oxford: Blackwell.
Bentham, Jeremy (1977) *A Fragment on Government.* J.H. Burns and H.L.A. Hart, eds. Oxford: Clarendon.
Bentham, Jeremy (1879) *The Principles of Morals and Legislation.* Oxford: Clarendon. Based on the revised 1823 edition.
Benveniste, Émile (1971) *Problems in General Linguistics.* Miami: University of Miami Press.
Berg, Jessica (2007) Of elephants and embryos. *Hastings Law Journal* 59: 369–406.
Berger, Adolf (1953) *Encyclopedic Dictionary of Roman Law.* Philadelphia: American Philosophical Society.
Berger, Peter and Thomas Luckmann (1966) *The Social Construction of Reality.* London: Penguin.
Bernardette, Seth and Michael Davis, eds. (2002) *Aristotle: On Poetics.* South Bend, Indiana: St. Augustine's Press.
Bernstein, Mark (2004) *Without a Tear: Our Tragic Relationship with Animals.* Champaign: University of Illinois Press.
Berryman, Sylvia (2016) Ancient atomism. *The Stanford Encyclopedia of Philosophy,* Edward Zalta, ed., available at: plato.stanford.edu.
Berti, Enrico (2006) The classical notion of person in today's philosophical debate. In E. Malinvaud and M.A. Glendon, eds., *Conceptualization of the Person in Social Sciences.* Vatican City: Pontifical Academy of Social Sciences, 63–77.
Berwick, Robert and Noam Chomsky (2018) *Why Only Us: Language and Evolution.* Cambridge: MIT Press.
Bilchitz, David (2009) Moving beyond arbitrariness: the legal personhood and dignity of non-human animals. *South African Journal on Human Rights* 25: 38–72.
Birks, Peter and Grant McLeod (1987) *Institutes of Justinian.* Ithaca: Cornell UP.
Blackmore, Susan (1999) *The Meme Machine.* Oxford: OUP.
Blackstone, Williams (1840) *Commentaries on the Laws of England: In Four Books: With an Analysis of the Work,* vol. 1. New York: Dean. First published, 1765.
Blake, Emilie (2017) Are water body personhood rights the future of water management in the United States? *Texas Environmental Law Journal* 47: 197–216.
Blaser, Mario (2014) Ontology and indigeneity on the political ontology of heterogeneous assemblages. *Cultural Geographies* 21: 49–58.
Blatti, Stephan and Paul Snowden (2016) Editors' introduction. *Animalism.* Oxford: OUP, 1–27.
Bloch, Maurice (1998) *How We Think They Think: Anthropological Approaches to Cognition, Memory and Literacy.* Boulder: Westview Press.
Bode, Christoph (2008) Discursive constructions of the self in British Romanticism. *Romanticism and Victorianism on the Net* 51, available at: www.erudit.org.
Boethius (1936) *The Theological Tractates and the Consolation of Philosophy.* H.F. Stewart and E.K. Rand, eds. Cambridge: Harvard UP.
Bondi, Damiano (2015) Gaia and the Anthropocene; or, the return of teleology. *Telos* 172: 125–127.

Bonhoeffer, Dietrich (2009) *Sanctorum Communio: A Theoretical Study of the Sociology of the Church*. Minneapolis: Fortress Press.

Bourne, Craig and Emily Caddick Bourne (2018) Personification without impossible content. *The British Journal of Aesthetics* 58: 165–179.

Boyle, Becky (2016) Free Tilly?: Legal personhood for animals and the intersectionality of the civil and animal rights movements. *Indiana Journal of Law and Social Equality* 4: 169–192.

Braaten, Carl (1963) Modern interpretations of Nestorius. *Church History* 32: 251–267.

Bradshaw, David (2009) The *Opuscula sacra*: Boethius and theology. In John Mernborn, ed., *The Cambridge Companion to Boethius*. Cambridge: CUP, 105–127.

Bredekamp, Horst (2007) Thomas Hobbes's visual strategies. In Patricia Springborg, ed., *The Cambridge Companion to Hobbes' Leviathan*. Cambridge: CUP, 29–60.

Brehaut, David (2003) *An Encyclopedist of the Dark Ages; Isidore of Seville*. Digital edition, prepared by David Badke, available at: http://bestiary.ca/etexts/brehaut1912/brehaut1912.htm. First published, 1912.

Brinkmann, Klaus (2005) Consciousness, self-consciousness, and the modern self. *History of the Human Sciences* 18: 27–48.

Brito Vieira, Monica (2009) *The Elements of Representation in Hobbes*. Leiden: Brill.

Broadie, Sarah (2001) Soul and body in Plato and Descartes. *Proceedings of the Aristotelian Society* 101: 295–308.

Brown, Dennis and John Theodore (1989) *The Modernist Self in Twentieth-Century English Literature*. Basingstoke: Palgrave Macmillan.

Brown, Stuart (1998) Soul, body and natural immortality. *The Monist* 81: 573–590.

Bruner, Jerome (1990) *Acts of Meaning*. Cambridge: Harvard UP.

Bryant, Taimie (2007) Similarity or difference as a basis for justice: must animals be like humans to be legally protected from humans. *Law and Contemporary Problems* 70: 207–254.

Bryant, Taimie (2008) Sacrificing the sacrifice of animals: legal personhood for animals, the status of animals as property, and the presumed primacy of humans. *Rutgers LJ* 39: 247–330.

Buber, Martin (1937) *I and Thou*. New York: Scribner.

Buckland, William and Arnold Mcnair (1965) *Roman Law and Common Law*. Cambridge: CUP.

Buffon, Come de (1749–1804) *Histoire naturelle, générale et particulière*. 36 vols. Paris: Imprimerie royale.

Burling, Robbins (1964) Cognition and componential analysis: God's truth or hocus pocus. *American Anthropologist* 66: 20–28.

Calarco, Matthew (2008) *The Question of the Animal: From Heidegger to Derrida*. New York: Columbia UP.

Cameron, Sharon (2007) *Impersonality: Seven Essays*. Chicago: The University of Chicago Press.

Carlson, Marla (2011) Furry cartography: performing species. *Theatre Journal* 63: 191–208.

Carnap, Rudolf (1974). Religious language is meaningless. In M.J. Charlesworth, ed., *The Problem of Religious Language*. New Jersey: Prentice-Hall, 121–131.

Cassirer, Ernst (1946) *The Myth of the State*. New Haven: Yale UP.

Castañeda, Heide (2010) Deportation deferred: 'illegality,' visibility, and recognition. In Nicholas De Genova and Nathalie Peutz, eds., *Deportation Regime*. Durham: Duke UP, 245–261.

Cavalieri, Poala (2001) *The Animal Question: Why Nonhuman Animals Deserve Human Rights.* Oxford: OUP.
Chalmers, Alan (2014) Atomism from the 17th to the 20th century. *The Stanford Encyclopedia of Philosophy*, Edward Zalta, ed., available at: plato.stanford.edu.
Charlton, William (1980) Aristotle's definition of soul. *Phronesis* 25: 170–186.
Chomsky, Noam (2002) *Media Control.* 2nd edition. New York: Open Media.
Chomsky, Noam (2005) Three factors in language design. *Linguistic Inquiry* 36: 1–22.
Chomsky, Noam (2007) Of minds and language. *Biolinguistics* 1: 9–27.
Chopra, Samir and Laurence White (2011) *A Legal Theory for Autonomous Artificial Agents.* Ann Arbor: University of Michigan Press.
Clark, Andy (1997) *Being There: Putting Brain, Body, and World Together Again.* Cambridge: MIT Press.
Clark, Andy and David Chalmers (1998) The extended mind. *Analysis* 58: 7–19.
Clarkson, Carrol (2009) *J. M. Coetzee: Countervoices.* Basingstoke, Hampshire: Palgrave.
Clarkson, C.M.V. (1996) Kicking corporate bodies and damning their souls. *The Modern LR* 59: 557–572.
Clements, Jeffrey (2014) *Corporations Are Not People.* 2nd edition. San Francisco: Berrett-Koehler.
Cobley, Paul (2016) *Cultural Implications of Biosemiotics.* Berlin: Springer.
Cobley, Paul (2017) Discussion: integrationism, anti-humanism and the suprasubjective. In Adrian Pablé, ed., *Critical Humanist Perspectives: The Integrational Turn in Philosophy of Language and Communication.* London: Routledge, 267–284.
Coetzee, John Maxwell (1992) *Doubling the Point: Essays and Interviews.* Cambridge: Harvard UP.
Coffee, John (1981) 'No soul to damn: no body to kick': an unscandalized inquiry into the problem of corporate punishment. *Michigan LR* 79: 386–459.
Cohen, Carl (1986) The case for use of animals in biomedical research. *New England Journal of Medicine* 315: 865–869
Cohen, Carl (2001) In defence of the use of animals. In Carl Cohen and Tom Regan, eds., *The Animal Rights Debate.* New York: Rowman and Littlefield, 3–123.
Cole, Michael and Yrjö Engeström (1997) A cultural-historical approach to distributed cognition. In Gavriel Salomon, ed., *Distributed Cognitions.* Cambridge: CUP, 1–46.
Cooley, Charles (1902) *Human Nature and the Social Order.* New York: Scribner.
Cooper, John (2015) Scripture and philosophy on the unity of body and soul. In Joshua R. Farris and Charles Taliaferro, eds., *The Ashgate Research Companion to Theological Anthropology.* London: Routledge, 27–42.
Cotter, Thomas (2003) Gutenberg's legacy: copyright, censorship, and religious pluralism. *California LR* 91: 323–392.
Cowley, Stephen (2004). Contextualizing bodies: human infants and distributed cognition. *Language Sciences* 26: 565–591.
Cowley, Stephen, ed. (2011) *Distributed Language.* Amsterdam: Benjamins.
Cowley, Stephen (2014) Bio-ecology and language: a necessary unity. *Language Sciences* 41: 60–70.
Cowley, Stephen (2017) Changing the idea of language: Nigel Love's perspective. *Language Sciences* 61: 43–55.
Cowley, Stephen and David Spurrett (2003) Putting apes (body and language) together again. *Language Sciences* 25: 289–318.

Cram, David (1992) Language universals and 17th century universal language schemes. In Joseph L. Subbiondo, ed. *John Wilkins and 17th-century British Linguistics*. Amsterdam: Benjamins, 191–204.
Cram, David and Jaap Maat (2001) *George Dalgarno on Universal Language: 'The Art of Signs' (1661),'The Deaf and Dumb Man's Tutor' (1680), and the Unpublished Papers*. Oxford: OUP.
Cribb, Robert, Helen Gilbert and Helen Tiffin (2014) *Wild Man from Borneo: A Cultural History of the Orangutan*. Hawai'i: University of Hawai'i Press.
Crick, Francis (1995) *The Astonishing Hypothesis*. New York: Touchstone.
Cross, Stephen (2013) *Schopenhauer's Encounter with Indian Thought: Representation and Will and Their Indian Parallels*. Honolulu: University of Hawai'i Press.
Crutzen, Paul (2006) The 'Anthropocene'. In Eckart Ehlers and Thomas Krafft, eds., *Earth System Science in the Anthropocene*. Berlin: Springer, 13–18.
Crystal, David (1965) *Linguistics, Language and Religion*. London: Burns and Oates.
Cuddihy, John (1974) *The Ordeal of Civility*. New York: Basic Books.
Culbertson, Tucker (2009) Animal equality, human dominion and fundamental interdependence. *Journal of Animal Law* 5: 33–48.
Culverwell, Nathaniel (2001) *An Elegant and Learned Discourse of the Light of Nature, with several other Treatises*. Robert Greene and Hugh MacCallum, eds. Indianapolis: Liberty Press. First published, 1652.
Cuneo, Pia, ed. (2017) *Animals and Early Modern Identity*. London: Routledge.
Cupp, Richard (2009) Moving beyond animal rights: a legal/contractualist critique. *San Diego LR* 46: 27–84.
Cupp, Richard (2013) Children, chimps, and rights: arguments from 'marginal' cases. *Arizona State Law Journal* 45: 1–52.
Cupp, Richard (2018) Litigating nonhuman animal legal personhood. *Texas Tech LR* 50: 573–598.
Cuvier, George (1817) *Le Règne Animal*. Paris.
Dahill, Lisa (2012) Con-formation with Jesus: Bonhoeffer, social location and embodiment. In Jens Zimmermann and Brian Gregor, eds., *Being Human, Becoming Human: Dietrich Bonhoeffer and Social Thought*. Cambridge: James Clarke, 176–190.
Dalgarno, George (1661) *Ars Signorum*. London.
Dalrymple, James (1681) *The Institutions of the Law of Scotland* [...]. Edinburgh.
Darwin, Charles (1859) *On the Origins of Species*. London: Murray.
Darwin, Charles (1871) *The Descent of Man and Selection in Relation to Sex*. London: John Murray.
Darwin, Charles (1872) *The Expression of the Emotions in Man and Animals*. London: John Murray.
Davison-Vecchione, Daniel and Kate Pambos (2017) Steven M. Wise and the common law case for animal rights: full steam ahead. *Canadian Journal of Jurisprudence* 30: 287–309.
Dawkins, Richard (2000) *Unweaving the Rainbow*. New York: Houghton.
Dayan, Colin (2011) *The Law is a White God; How Legal Rituals Make and Unmake Persons*. Princeton: Princeton UP.
Deacon, Terence (2012) *Incomplete Nature*. New York: Norton.
Deckha, Maneesha (2013) Initiating a non-anthropocentric jurisprudence: the rule of law and animal vulnerability under a property paradigm. *Alberta LR* 50: 783–814.
Delaney, David (2003) *Law and Nature*. Cambridge: CUP.

DeMott, Banjamin (1958) The sources and development of John Wilkins' philosophical language. *The Journal of English and Germanic Philology* 57: 1–13.
Dennet, Daniel (1987) *The Intentional Stance.* Cambridge: MIT Press.
Dennett, Daniel (1991) *Consciousness Explained.* New York: Little, Brown.
Dennett, Daniel (1992) The self as a center of narrative gravity. In F. Kessel, P. Cole and D. Johnson, eds., *Self and Consciousness.* Hillsdale: Erlbaum, 103–115.
Derrida, Jacques (2008) *The Animal That Therefore I Am*, Marie-Luise Mallet, ed. New York: Fordham UP.
DesCamp, Mary Therese and Eve Sweetser (2005) Metaphors for God: why and how do our choices matter for humans? The application of contemporary cognitive linguistics research to the debate on God and metaphor. *Pastoral Psychology* 53: 207–238.
Descartes, René (1637) *Discours de la méthode.* Leiden.
Descartes, René (1680) *Six Metaphysical Meditations.* London: Benjamin Tooke. Originally published, 1642.
De Waal, Frans (2016) *Are We Smart Enough to Know How Smart Animals Are?* London: Granta.
Dewey, John (1926) The historic background of corporate legal personality. *Yale Law Journal* 35: 655–673.
Dolezal, James (1982) *All That Is in God: Evangelical Theology and the Challenge of Classical Christian Theism.* Grand Rapids: Reformation Heritage Books.
Dombrowski, Daniel (1997) *Babies and Beasts: The Argument from Marginal Cases.* Champaign: University of Illinois Press.
Douglas, Mary (1986) *How Institutions Think.* Syracuse: Syracuse UP.
Douzinas, Costas (1999) Prosopon and antiprosopon: prolegomena for a legal iconology. In Costas Douzinas and Lynda Nead, eds., *Law and the Image.* Chicago: University of Chicago Press, 36–67
Douzinas, Costas and Adam Gearey (2005) *Critical Jurisprudence.* Oxford: Hart.
Dumont, Louis (1992) *Essays on Individualism.* Chicago: University of Chicago Press.
Dunbar, Robin (1993) What's in a classification? In Paola Cavalieri and Peter Singer, eds., *The Great Ape Project.* New York: St. Martin's Griffin, 109–112.
Duncan, Patrick (1942) Immortality of the soul in the Platonic dialogues and Aristotle. *Philosophy* 17: 304–323.
Duncker, Dorthe (2017) The notion of an integrated system. In Adrian Pablé, ed., *Critical Humanist Perspectives: The Integrational Turn in Philosophy of Language and Communication.* London: Routledge, 135–153.
Duncker, Dorthe (2018) Sign making in dialogue. *Language and Dialogue* 8: 139–158.
Dupré, John (1999) Are whales fish? In Douglas Medin and Scott Atran, eds., *Folkbiology.* Cambridge: MIT Press, 461–476.
Dupré, John (2002) *Humans and Other Animals.* Oxford: OUP.
Durant, Alan (2018) Seeing sense: the complexity of key words that tell us what law is. In Janny Leung and Alan Durant, eds., *Meaning and Power in the Language of Law.* Cambridge: CUP, 32–70.
Dutton, Blake (2016) *Augustine and Academic Skepticism.* Ithaca: Cornell UP.
Dworkin, Ronald (1986) *Law's Empire.* Cambridge: Harvard UP.
Dyschkant, Alexis (2015) Legal personhood: how we are getting it wrong. *University of Illinois LR* 5: 2075–2110.
Eiland, Howard (1982) Heidegger's etymological web. *boundary 2*: 39–56.
Elster, Jon (1989) *The Cement of Society.* Cambridge: CUP.

Emery, Clark (1948) John Wilkins' universal language. *Isis* 38: 174–185.
Epley, Nicholas, Adam Waytz, and John T. Cacioppo (2007) On seeing human: a three-factor theory of anthropomorphism. *Psychology Review* 114: 864–886.
Esposito, Roberto (2012) *Politics of Life and Philosophy of the Impersonal.* Cambridge: Polity.
[EU] (2015) Draft Report, with Recommendations to the Commission on Civil Law Rules on Robotics. Committee on Legal Affairs Rapporteur. Brussels: European Parliament. Available at: www.europarl.europa.eu.
Evnine, Simon (2008) *Epistemic Dimensions of Personhood.* Oxford: OUP.
Ewasiuk, Craig (2017) Escape routes: the possibility of habeas corpus protection for animals under modern social contract theory. *The Columbia Human Rights LR* 48: 69–110.
Fagundes, Dave (2001) What we talk about when we talk about persons: the language of a legal fiction. *Harvard LR* 114: 1745–1768.
Farbman, Herschel (2016) Corporate personhood and modernist 'impersonality': Woolf's drama. *Law and Literature* 28: 379–402.
Favareau, Donald, ed. (2010) *Essential Readings in Biosemiotics.* Berlin: Springer.
Favre, David (2010) Living property: a new status for animals within the legal system. *Marquette LR* 93: 1021–1071.
Fellmeth, Aaron and Maurice Horwitz (2009) *Guide to Latin in International Law.* Oxford: OUP.
Ferrari, G.R.F. (2005) *City and Soul in Plato's Republic.* Chicago: University of Chicago Press.
Feser, Edward (2014) God's wounds. April 18, 2014, available at: edwardfeser.blogspot.com.
Fichte, Johann (1808) *Reden an die deutsche Nation.* Berlin: Realschulbuchhandlung.
Filippi, Piera (2015) Before Babel: the evolutionary roots of human language. In Ekaterina Velmezova, Kalevi Kull, and Stephen Cowley, eds., *Biosemiotic Perspectives on Language and Linguistics.* Berlin: Springer, 191–204.
Filmer, Robert, Sir (1679) *The Free-Holders Grand Inquest Touching our Sovereign Lord the King and his Parliament* [...]. London.
Fine, Cordelia (2010) *Delusions of Gender.* New York: Norton.
Fintel, Kai von and Lisa Matthewson (2008) Universals in semantics. *The Linguistic Review* 25:139–201.
Fisher, Andrew (1996) The myth of anthropomorphism. In Marc Bekoff and Dale Jamieson, eds., *Readings in Animal Cognition.* Cambridge: MIT Press, 3–16.
Fitzgerald, Emily (2015) [Ape]ersonhood. *The Review of Litigation* 34: 338–378.
Fitzgerald, Patrick John, ed. (1966) *Salmond on Jurisprudence.* 12th edition. London: Sweet and Maxwell.
Flannery, Sheri (2012) The Thirteenth Amendment won't help free Willy. *The Scholar* 15: 29–62.
Foster, Charles (2016) *Being a Beast: Adventures Across the Species Divide.* New York: Metropolitan Books.
Foucault, Michel (1980) What is an author? In Donald F. Bouchar, ed., *Language, Counter-memory, Practice: Selected Essays and Interviews.* Ithaca: Cornell UP, 113–138.
Foucault, Michel (1989) *The Order of Things.* London: Routledge. First published, 1966.
Francione, Gary (1993) Personhood, property and legal competence. In Paola Cavalieri and Peter Singer, eds., *The Great Ape Project.* New York: St. Martin's Griffin, 248–257.
Francione, Gary (1995) *Animals, Property and the Law.* Philadelphia: Temple UP.

Francione, Gary (2006) Taking sentience seriously. *Journal of Animal Law and Ethics* 1: 1–20.

Francione, Gary (2008) *Animals as Persons.* New York: Columbia UP.

Francione, Gary and Anna Charlton (2015) *Animal Rights: The Abolitionist Approach.* Newark: Exempla Press.

Freud, Sigmund (1904) *Zur Psychopathologie des Alltagslebens.* Berlin: Karger.

Freud, Sigmund (1923) *Das Ich und das Es.* Wien: Internationaler Psycho-analytischer Verlag.

Freud, Sigmund (1930) *Das Unbehagen in der Kultur.* Wien: Internationaler Psychoanalytischer Verlag.

Frisch, Karl von (1923) Über die ‚Sprache' der Bienen. Eine tierpsychologische Untersuchung. *Zoologische Jahrbücher (Physiologie)* 40: 1–186.

Fukuyama, Francis (2018) *Identity. The Demand for Dignity and the Politics of Resentment.* New York: Farrar, Straus and Giroux.

Gaakeer, Jeanne (2016) '*Sua cuique persona*?' A note on the fiction of legal personhood and a reflection on interdisciplinary consequences. *Law and Literature* 28: 287–317.

Gaita, Raimon (2003) *The Philosopher's Dog.* London: Routledge.

García-Mateus, Suzanne and Deborah Palmer (2017) Translanguaging pedagogies for positive identities in two-way dual language bilingual education. *Journal of Language, Identity and Education* 16: 245–255.

Garth, Thomas (1931) *Race Psychology.* New York: Whittlesey.

Geertz, Clifford (1973) *The Interpretation of Cultures.* New York: Basic Books.

Geertz, Clifford (1984) 'From the native's point of view': on the nature of anthropological understanding. In Richard Shweder and Robert LeVine, eds., *Culture Theory: Essays on Mind, Self, and Emotion.* Cambridge: CUP, 123–136.

Geldart, W. M. (1911) Legal personality. *Law Quarterly Review* 27: 90–108.

Gellner, Ernst (2004) *Language and Solitude: Wittgenstein, Malinowski and the Habsburg Dilemma.* Cambridge: CUP.

Gergen, Kenneth (2011) The social construction of self. In Shaun Gallagher, ed., *The Oxford Handbook of the Self.* Oxford: OUP, 633–653.

Gewirth, Alan (1978) *Reason and Morality.* Chicago: The University of Chicago Press.

Giddens, Anthony (1984) *The Constitution of Society.* Cambridge: Polity Press.

Giddens, Anthony (1990) *The Consequences of Modernity.* Cambridge: Polity Press.

Giere, Ronald (2002) Discussion note: distributed cognition in epistemic culture. *Philosophy of Science* 69: 637–644.

Giere, Ronald and Barton Moffatt (2003) Distributed cognition: where the cognitive and the social merge. *Social Studies of Science* 33: 301–310.

Gierke, Otto von (1895) *Deutsches Privatrecht Band 1: Allgemeiner Teil u. Personenrecht.* Leipzig: Duncker & Humblot.

Gierke, Otto von (1889) *Personengemeinschaften und Vermögensinbegriffe in dem Entwurfe eines Bürgerlichen Gesetzbuches für das Deutsche Reich.* Berlin: Guttentag.

Gierke, Otto von (1902) *Das Wesen der menschlicher Verbände.* Berlin: Schade.

Gilbert, Richard and Andrew Forney (2013) The distributed self: virtual worlds and the future of human identity. In Robin Teigland and Dominic Power, eds., *The Immersive Internet.* London: Palgrave, London, 23–36.

Gillespie-Lynch, Kristen, Patricia Greenfield, Heidi Lyn, and Sue Savage-Rumbaugh (2014) Gestural and symbolic development among apes and humans: support for a multimodal theory of language evolution. *Frontiers in Psychology* 5: 1228.

Gleason, Philip (1983) Identifying identity: a semantic history. *The Journal of American History* 69: 910–931.

Goddard, Cliff (2010) The natural semantic metalanguage approach. In Bernd Heine and Heiko Narrog, eds., *The Oxford Handbook of Linguistic Analysis*. Oxford: OUP, 459–484.

Goddard, Cliff (2011) *Semantic Analysis: A Practical Introduction*. Oxford: OUP.

Goddard, Cliff (2017) Minimal English – the science behind it. In Cliff Goddard, ed., *Minimal English for a Global World*. Berlin: Springer, 29–70.

Goddard, Cliff and Anna Wierbiczka (2011) Global English, Minimal English: towards better Intercultural Communication, distributed at Symposium 'Global English, Minimal English', held at Australian National University, Canberra, 2–3 July, 2015, available at: hrc.anu.edu.au.

Godfrey-Smith, Peter (2016) *Other Minds: The Octopus, the Sea, and the Deep Origins of Consciousness*. New York: Farrar.

Godlovitch, Stanley, Rosalind Godlovitch and John Harris, eds. (1971) *Animals, Men and Morals: An Inquiry into the Maltreatment of Non-humans*. London: Gollancz.

Goffman, Erving (1956) *The Presentation of Self in Everyday Life*. New York: Anchor.

Goodenough, Ward (1956) Componential analysis and the study of meaning. *Language* 32: 195–216.

Goodrich, Peter (1990) *Languages of Law from Logics of Memory to Nomadic Masks*. London: Weidenfeld and Nicolson.

Goodrich, Peter (1996) *Law in the Courts of Love: Literature and Other Minor Jurisprudences*. London: Routledge.

Goodrich, Peter (2014) *Legal Emblems and the Art of Law:* Obiter Depicta *as the Vision of Governance*. Cambridge: CUP.

Gordijn, Bert (1999) The troublesome concept of the person. *Theoretical Medicine and Bioethics* 20: 347–359.

Gordon, Gwendolyn (2018) Environmental personhood. *Columbia Journal of Environmental Law* 43: 49–91.

Gorman, Michael (2000) Christ as composite according to Aquinas. *Traditio* 55: 143–157.

Grandin, Temple (2006) Animals are not things. In Marc Hauser, Fiery Cushman and Matthew Kamen, eds., *People, Property, or Pets?* West Lafayette: Purdue UP, 205–211.

Gray, John Chipman (1909) *The Nature and Sources of Law*. New York: Columbia UP.

Gray, John (2002) *Straw Dogs: Thoughts on Humans and Other Animals*. London: Granta.

Grayling, Anthony (2006) *Descartes: The Life and Times of a Genius*. New York: Walker.

Greif, Hajo (2017) What is the extension of the extended mind? *Synthese* 194: 4311–4336.

Griffin, Donald (1976) *The Question of Animal Awareness*. New York: Rockefeller.

Grotius, Hugo (2005) *De jure belli ac pacis Hugo Grotius, The Rights of War and Peace*, vol. 1, based on the 1718 edition Jean Barbeyrac and Richard Tuck, ed. Indianapolis: Liberty Fund, available at: oll.libertyfund.org. First published, 1625.

Grusin, Richard, ed. (2015) *The Nonhuman Turn*. Minneapolis: University of Minnesota Press.

Gundry, Robert (1976) *Sōma in Biblical Theology: Emphasis on Pauline Anthropology*. Cambridge: CUP.

Haaf, Lisette ten (2017) Unborn and future children as new legal subjects: an evaluation of two subject-oriented approaches – the subject of rights and the subject of interests. *German Law Journal* 18: 1091–1119.

Hacking, Ian (1999) *The Social Construction of What?* Cambridge: UP.

Hakala, Walter (2016) *Negotiating Languages: Urdu, Hindi, and the Definition of Modern South Asia*. New York: Columbia UP.

Hamilton, Sheryl (2008) *Impersonations: Troubling the Person in Law and Culture*. Toronto: University of Toronto Press.

Hamilton, Sheryl (2016) 'Human no like smart ape': figuring the ape as legal person in *Rise of the Planet of the Apes*. *Law and Humanities* 10: 300–321.

Hampshire, Stuart (1971) Review of Gilbert Ryle, *The Concept of Mind*, Hutchinson, 1947. In Oscar Wood and George Pitcher, eds., *Ryle: A Collection of Critical Essays*. London: Macmillan, 17–44.

Haraway, Donna (1991) A cyborg manifesto: science, technology, and socialist-feminism in the late twentieth century. In *Simians, Cyborgs and Women: The Reinvention of Nature*. New York: Routledge, 149–181.

Harding, Stephen (2006) *Animate Earth Science, Intuition and Gaia*. Vermont: Chelsea Green Publishing.

Harré, Rom (1998) *The Singular Self*. London: Sage.

Harris, Roy (1978) *Communication and language. Inaugural lecture delivered before the University of Oxford on 24 February, 1978*. Oxford: Clarendon Press.

Harris, Roy (1980) *The Language-Makers*. London, Duckworth.

Harris, Roy (1981) *The Language Myth*. London: Duckworth.

Harris, Roy (1987) *The Language Machine*. London: Duckworth.

Harris, Roy (1990) Must monkeys mean? In Nigel Love, ed., *The Foundations of Linguistic Theory: Selected Writings of Roy Harris*. London: Routledge, 158–179.

Harris, Roy (1996) *Signs, Language and Communication*. London: Routledge.

Harris, Roy (1998a) *Introduction to Integrational Linguistics*. Oxford: Pergamon.

Harris, Roy (1998b) Murray, Moore and the myth. In Roy Harris, ed., *Linguistic Thought in England 1914–1945*. London: Duckworth, 2–26.

Harris, Roy (2004) Integrationism, language, mind and the world. *Language Sciences* 26: 727–739.

Harris, Roy (2005) *The Semantics of Science*. London: Continuum.

Harris, Roy (2008) *Mindboggling*. Luton: Pantaneto Press.

Harris, Roy (2009a) Freedom of speech and philosophy of education. *British Journal of Educational Studies* 57: 111–126.

Harris, Roy (2009b) *After Epistemology*. Sandy, Bedfordshire: Bright Pen.

Harris, Roy (2011) On ultimate questions. *Integrationist Notes and Papers 2009–2011*. Sandy, Bedfordshire: Bright Pen, 91–97.

Harris, Roy and Christopher Hutton (2007) *Definition in Theory and Practice*. London: Continuum.

Harris, Roy and Talbot Taylor (1989) *Landmarks in Linguistic Thought*. London: Routledge.

Harrison, Peter (1992) Descartes on animals. *The Philosophical Quarterly* 42: 219–227.

Hauser, Marc, Fiery Cushman and Matthew Kamen, eds. (2006) *People, Property, or Pets?* West Lafayette: Purdue UP.

Hauser, Marc, Noam Chomsky and Tecumseh Fitch (2002) The faculty of language: what is it, who has it, and how did it evolve? *Science* 298: 1569–1579.

Hayek, Friedrich A. (1945) The use of knowledge in society. *American Economic Review* 35: 519–530.

Hayek, Friedrich A. (1982) *Law, Legislation and Liberty: A New Statement of the Liberal Principles of Justice and Political Economy*. 3 Vols. London: Routledge.

Hazlitt, William (1925) On corporate bodies. In *Table-Talk or Original Essays.* Paris: Galignani, 194–214. First published, 1822.

Heartfield, James (2002) *The 'Death of the Subject' Explained.* Sheffield: Sheffield Hallam UP.

Hegel, Georg (2018) *The Phenomenology of Spirit.* Cambridge: CUP. First published, 1807.

Heidegger, Martin (1993) *Unterwegs zur Sprache.* Pfullingen: Günther Neske. First published, 1959.

Heidegger, Martin (1998) *Pathways*, William McNeill, ed. Cambridge: CUP. First published 1927.

Heijnol, Andreas (2017) Ladders, trees, complexity, and other metaphors in evolutionary thinking. In Anna Tsing, Heather Swanson, Elaine Gan and Nils Bubandt, eds., *Arts of Living on a Damaged Planet.* Minneapolis: University of Minnesota Press, 87–101.

Henry, John (2002) *The Scientific Revolution and the Origins of Modern Science.* 2nd edition. Basingstoke: Palgrave.

Herrmann, Eberhard (2004) *Religion, Reality, and a Good Life.* Tübingen: Mohr Siebeck.

Herzing, Denise and Thomas White (1998) Dolphins and the question of personhood. *Ethics and Animals* 9: 64–84.

Hinman, Lawrence (1982) Nietzsche, metaphor and truth. *Philosophy and Phenomenological Research* 43: 179–199.

Hobbes, Thomas (1684) *Humane Nature or The Fundamental Elements of Policy* [...]. 3rd edition. London.

Hobbes, Thomas (1839) *Concerning Body.* In William Molesworth, ed., *The English Works of Thomas Hobbes of Malmesbury.* London: Bohn. First published, 1655.

Hobbes, Thomas (1909) *Leviathan or The Matter, Forme and Power of a Common Wealth Ecclesiasticall and Civil.* W. Pogson Smith, ed. Oxford: Clarendon. First published, 1651.

Hobbes, Thomas (1999) *The Elements of Law Natural and Politic.* Oxford: OUP. First published, 1640.

Hodgson, Geoffrey (2007) Meanings of methodological individualism. *Journal of Economic Methodology* 14: 211–26.

Hohfeld, Wesley Newcombe (1916) Fundamental legal conceptions as applied in judicial reasoning. *Yale Law Journal* 26: 710–770.

Hoff, Christina (1980) Immoral and moral uses of animals. *New England Journal of Medicine* 302: 115–118.

Hofstadter, Douglas (2007) *I am a Strange Loop.* New York: Perseus.

Holland, Ben (2017) *The Moral Person of the State: Pufendorf, Sovereignty and Composite Polities.* Cambridge: CUP.

Holmes, Oliver Wendell (1897) The path of the law. *Harvard LR* 10: 457–478.

Holmes, Stephen (2014) Classical Trinity: evangelical perspective. In S.N. Gundry, ed., *Two Views of the Doctrine of the Trinity.* Michigan: Zondervan, 25–68.

Horowitz, Maryanne (1979) The image of God in man: is woman included? *The Harvard Theological Review* 72: 175–206.

Horsman, Yasco (2016) Braying, howling, growling for justice: animal personhood in law, literature, and cinema. *Law and Literature* 28: 319–334.

Horsman, Yasco and Frans-Willem Korsten (2016) Introduction: Legal Bodies: *Corpus/Persona/Communitas. Law and Literature* 28: 277–285.

Hubbard, F. Patrick (2011) Do androids dream: personhood and intelligent artifacts. *Temple LR* 83: 405–474.

Humboldt, Wilhelm von (1836) *Über die Verschiedenheit des menschlichen Sprachbaues.* Berlin: Königliche Akademie der Wissenschaften.

Hume, David (1888) *A Treatise of Human Nature.* Oxford: Clarendon: Oxford. Reprint of 1738–40 edition.

Hume, David (1912) *An Enquiry Concerning the Principles of Morals.* Chicago: Open Court. First published, 1777.

Hume, David (2007a) *An Enquiry Concerning Human Understanding*, Peter Millican, ed. Oxford: OUP. Based on the 1777 edition.

Hume, David (2007b) Of the immortality of the soul. In Peter Millican, ed., *David Hume: An Enquiry Concerning Human Understanding.* Oxford: OUP, 146–151.

Hume, David (2007c) *Dialogues Concerning Natural Religion and Other Writings.* Dorothy Coleman, ed. Cambridge: CUP.

Hutchins, Edwin (1995) *Cognition in the Wild.* Cambridge: MIT Press.

Hutchins, Edwin (2008) The role of cultural practices in the emergence of modern human intelligence. *Philosophical Transactions: Biological Sciences* 363 (1499): 2011–2019.

Hutchins, John (1995) Machine translation: a brief history. In E.F.K. Koerner and R.E. Asher, eds., *Concise History of the Language Sciences: From the Sumerians to the Cognitivists.* Amsterdam: Benjamins, 431–445.

Hutton, Christopher (1990) *Abstraction and Instance.* Oxford: Pergamon.

Hutton, Christopher (1995) The critique of primitive belief and modern linguistics. *Journal of Literary Semantics* 24: 81–103.

Hutton, Christopher (2009) *Language, Meaning and the Law.* Edinburgh: Edinburgh UP.

Hutton, Christopher (2010) Universalism and human difference in Chomskyan linguistics. In Douglas Kibbee, ed., *Chomskyan (R)evolutions.* Amsterdam: Benjamins, 337–351.

Hutton, Christopher (2012) 'I crave the law': *Salomon v Salomon*, uncanny personhood and the Jews. In Marco Wan, ed., *Reading the Legal Case: Cross-currents between Law and the Humanities.* London: Routledge, 29–46.

Hutton, Christopher (2014) *Word Meaning and Legal Interpretation.* Basingstoke: Palgrave.

Hutton, Christopher (2017a) The self and the 'monkey selfie': law, integrationism and the nature of the first order/second order distinction. *Language Sciences* 61: 93–103.

Hutton, Christopher (2017b) Bedrock concepts and integrational theory: selves, animals and legal persons. In Adrian Pablé, ed., *Critical Humanist Perspectives: The Integrational Turn in Philosophy of Language and Communication.* London: Routledge, 28–44.

Hutton, Christopher (2018) Hiding in plain sight: the category of ordinary language and the case law domain of transgender marriage. In Janny Leung and Alan Durant, eds., *Meaning and Power in the Language of Law.* Cambridge: CUP, 71–91.

Immler, Manfred (1991) Is semantics universal, or isn't it? On the relation of language, thought and semantic structure. In Dietmar Zaefferer, ed., *Semantic Universals and Universal Semantics.* Berlin: Foris, 37–59.

Ishiguro, Hidé (1980) The primitiveness of the concept of a person. In Zak Van Straaten, ed., *Philosophical Subjects.* Oxford: Clarendon, 62–75.

Jacoby, Karl (1994) Slaves by nature? Domestic animals and human slaves. *Slavery and Abolition: A Journal of Slaver and Post-Slave Studies* 15: 89–99.

James, William (1890) *The Principles of Psychology.* New York: Holt.

Janaway, Christopher (1989) *Self and World in Schopenhauer's Philosophy.* Oxford: Clarendon.

Johnson, C. M. (2001) Distributed primate cognition: a review. *Animal Cognition* 4:167–183.

Johnson, Mark (1987) *The Body in the Mind.* Chicago: Chicago UP.

Johnson, Samuel (1766) *Dictionary of the English Language.* 4th edition. London: Strahan.

Jolley, Nicholas (2000) Malebranche on the soul. In Steven Nadler, ed., *The Cambridge Companion to Malebranche.* Cambridge: CUP, 31–58.

Jones, Peter (2011) Signs of activity: integrating language and practical action. *Language Sciences* 33: 11–19.

Joseph, John (1996) The immediate sources of the 'Sapir-Whorf Hypothesis'. *Historiographia Linguistica* 23: 365–404.

Joseph, John (2000) *Limiting the Arbitrary.* Amsterdam: Benjamins.

Joseph, John (2017) *Language, Mind and Body: A Conceptual History.* Cambridge: CUP.

Jowett, Benjamin (1875) *The Dialogues of Plato*, vol. 2. Revised edition. Oxford: Clarendon.

Jung, Carl (1921) *Psychologische Typen.* Zürich: Rascher.

Jung, Carl (1928) *Two Essays on Analytical Psychology.* London: Baillière.

Jung, Carl (1988) *Nietzsche's Zarathustra: Notes of the Seminar given in 1934–1939*, vol. 1. London: Routledge.

Kagan, Shelly (2012) *Death.* New Haven: Yale UP.

Kammer, Sean (2017) No-analogue future: challenges for the laws of nature in a world without precedent. *Vermont LR* 42: 227–296.

Kamp, Hans and Barbara Partee (1995) Prototype theory and compositionality. *Cognition* 57: 129–191.

Kant, Immanuel (1991) *The Metaphysics of Morals.* Cambridge: CUP. First published, 1797.

Kant, Immanuel (2006) *Anthropology from a Pragmatic point of View.* Cambridge: CUP. First published, 1798.

Katz, Jerrold and Jerry Fodor (1963) The structure of a semantic theory. *Language* 39: 170–210.

Keck, Frédéric (2013) Review of Eduardo Kohn *How Forests Think.* University of California Press, 2013. *Somatosphere*, Spetmere 23, 2013, available at: somatosphere.net.

Keane, Webb (1997) Religious language. *American Review of Anthropology* 26: 47–71.

Kemmerer, Lisa (2006) *In Search of Consistency: Ethics and Animals.* Brill: Leiden.

Kenny, Anthony (2014) Theology, naturally. *The Tablet*, November 13, 2014, available at: www.thetablet.co.uk.

King, Richard (2007) The soul and its instrumental body. A reinterpretation of Aristotle's philosophy of living nature by A. P. Bos. *The Classical Review* 57: 322–323.

Klauber, Bridget (1992) See no evil, hear no evil: the federal courts and the Silver Spring monkeys. *University of Colorado LR* 63: 501–520.

Klautke, Egbert (2013) *The Mind of the Nation.* New York: Berghahn.

Klement, Kevin (2016) Russell's logical atomism. *The Stanford Encyclopedia of Philosophy*, Edward Zalta, ed., available at plato.stanford.edu.

Klemmensen, Charlotte (2018) *Integrating the Participants' Perspective in the Study of Language and Communication Disorders.* Cham: Palgrave.

Kobil, Kelsey (2015) When it comes to standing, two legs are better than four. *Penn State LR* 120: 621–642.

Koch, Lawrence (1996) *Silicon Poetics: The Computer as Author and Artifice.* Unpublished MA thesis, The University of Montana.
Koessler, Maximillian (1949) The person in imagination or the persona ficta of the corporation. *Louisiana Law Review* 9: 435–449.
Kohn, Eduardo (2013) *How Forests Think: Towards an Anthropology Beyond the Human.* Berkeley: University of California Press.
Kondo, Dorinne (1990) *Crafting Selves.* Chicago: University of Chicago Press.
Kooi, van der Cornelis and Gijsbert van den Brink (2017) *Christian Dogmatics.* Grand Rapids: Eerdsmann.
Korsgaard, Christine (2013) Personhood, animals and the law. *Think: Philosophy for Everyone* 34: 26–32.
Kraal, Anders (2014) Neo-positivism, religious language, and the problem of evil in Eberhard Herrmann's philosophy of religion. *Studia Theologica – Nordic Journal of Theology* 68: 41–55.
Kramer, Matthew (2001) Getting rights right. In Matthew Kramer, ed., *Rights, Wrongs and Responsibilities.* Basingstoke: Palgrave, 28–95.
Kramer, Matthew (2010) Refining the interest theory of rights. *American Journal of Jurisprudence* 55: 31–39.
Krauss, E. P. (1984) On the distinction between real and personal property. *Seton Hall LR* 14: 485–519.
Kurki, Visa (2017) Why things can hold rights: reconceptualizing the legal person. In Tomasz Pietrzykowski and Visa Kurki, eds., *Legal Personhood: Animals, Artificial Intelligence and the Unborn.* Berlin: Springer, 69–89.
Kurjak, Asim, Ana Tikvica Leutic, Berivo Miskovic and Frank Chervenak (2009) When does a fetus become a person? *Periodicum Biologorum* 3: 337–340.
Kuykendall, Mae (2010) Producing corporate text: courtrooms, conference rooms and classrooms. *New York Law School LR* 55: 593–637.
Kyd, Stewart (1793–4) *A Treatise on the Law of Corporations.* 2 vols. London.
Kymlicka, Will and Sue Donaldson (2011) *Zoopolis: A Political Theory of Animal Rights.* Oxford: OUP.
Kymlicka, Will and Sue Donaldson (2014) Animals and the frontiers of citizenship. *Oxford Journal of Legal Studies* 34: 201–219.
La Mettrie, Julien Offray de (2003) *Machine Man and other Writing.* Ann Thomson ed. Cambridge: CUP. First published, 1747.
Laing, Ronald (1990) *The Divided Self.* London: Penguin. First published, 1959.
Lakoff, George and Mark Johnson (2003) *Metaphors We Live By.* Chicago: Chicago UP.
Lakoff, George and Mark Turner (1989) *More Than Cool Reason: A Field Guide to Poetic Metaphor.* Chicago: Chicago UP.
Lamalle, Sandy (2014) Multilevel translation analysis of a key legal concept: persona juris and legal pluralism. In Cheng Le, Sin King Kui and Anne Wagner, eds., *The Ashgate Handbook of Legal Translation.* Farnham: Ashgate, 299–312.
Lamb, Jonathan (2011) *The Things Things Say.* Princeton: Princeton UP.
Lamb, Sydney (1965) Kinship terminology and linguistic structure. *American Anthropologist* 67: 37–64.
Lamont, John (2006) The nature of the hypostatic union. *The Heythrop Journal* 47: 16–25.
Lash, Scott (1999) Objects that judge: Latour's parliament of things. *transversal*, June, 1999, available at: eipcp.net/transversal.

Latour, Bruno (1988) Review of Mary Douglas, *How Institutions Think*. Syracuse UP, 1986. *Contemporary Sociology* 3: 383–385.

Latour, Bruno (1993) *We Have Never Been Modern*. Cambridge: Harvard UP.

Latour, Bruno (2017) *Facing Gaia*. Cambridge: Polity.

Lee, Blewett (1926) Copyright of automatic writing. *Virginia LR* 13: 22–26.

Lee, Michelle (2006) *Paul, the Stoics and the Body of Christ*. Cambridge: CUP.

Leibniz, Gottfried Wilhelm (1960) Vorrede zur Allgemeinen Wissenschaft. In *Fragmente zur Logik*. Berlin: Akademie-Verlag, 87–92. First published, 1677.

Lennan, Richard (1998) *An Introduction to Catholic Theology*. New York: Paulist Press.

Letham, Robert (2004) *The Holy Trinity*. Phillipsburg: P&R Publishing.

Lévy-Bruhl, Lucien (1910) *Les fonctions mentales dans les sociétés inférieures*. Paris: Presses universitaires de France.

Lévy-Bruhl, Lucien (1922) *La mentalité primitive*. Paris: Alcan.

Lewis, Clive Staples (1967) *Studies in Words*. Cambridge: CUP.

Li Wei (2018) Translanguaging as a practical theory of language. *Applied Linguistics* 39: 9–30.

Lichtenberg, Christian (1994) *Schriften und Briefe*, vol. 2. Frankfurt: Zweitausendeins.

Lindsay, Wallace, ed. (1911) *Isidori Hispalensis episcopi Etymologiarum*. Oxford: Clarendon.

Linnaeus, Carolus (1735). *Systema naturae*. Leiden: Haak. Tenth edition, 1758.

Locke, John (1975) *An Essay Concerning Human Understanding*. Peter Nidditch, ed. Oxford: Clarendon. First published, 1690–1694.

Locke, John (1980) *Second Treatise on Government*. C. B. Macpherson, ed. Indianapolis: Hackett. First published, 1690.

Love, Nigel (1990) The locus of languages in a redefined linguistics. In Hayley Davis and Talbot Taylor., eds., *On Redefining Linguistics*. London: Routledge, 53–117.

Lovejoy, Arthur (1964) *The Great Chain of Being*. Cambridge: Harvard UP. First published, 1936.

Lovelock, James (1979) *Gaia: A New Look at Life on Earth*. Oxford: OUP.

Lovelock, James (2006) *The Revenge of Gaia*. London: Penguin.

Luhmann, Niklas (1986) The autopoiesis of social systems. In F. Geyer and J. Van d. Zeuwen, eds., *Sociocybernetic Paradoxes*. London: Sage, 172–192.

Luhmann, Niklas (1989) *Ecological Communication*. Chicago: University of Chicago Press.

Luhmann, Niklas (1994) How can the mind participate in communication? In H.J. Gumbrecht and K.L. Pfeiffer, eds., *Materialities of Communication*. Stanford: Stanford UP, 371–87.

Luhmann, Niklas (1996) *Social Systems*. Stanford: Stanford UP.

Luker, Kristin (1984) *Abortion and the Politics of Motherhood*. Berkeley: University of California Press.

Lutz, Catherine (1985) Ethnopsychology compared to what? Explaining behavior and consciousness among the Ifaluk. In G. M. White and J. Kirkpatrick, eds., *Person, Self, and Experience: Exploring Pacific Ethnopsychologies*. Berkeley: University of California Press, 35–79.

MacCormack, Patricia, ed. (2014) *The Animal Catalyst: Towards Ahuman Theory*. London: Bloomsbury.

MacCulloch, Diarmaid (2005) *The Reformation*. London: Penguin.

Machen, Arthur (1911) Corporate personality. *Harvard LR* 24: 253–267.

Magee, John (2002) Boethius. In Jorge Gracia and Timothy Noone, eds., *Companion to Philosophy in the Middle Ages*. Oxford: Blackwell, 217–226.
Maitland, Frederic (1900) Translator's introduction. *Otto Gierke: Political Theories of the Late Middle Ages*. Cambridge: CUP, vii–xlv.
Maitland, Frederic (1911) *The Collected Papers of Frederic William Maitland*. H.A.L. Fisher, ed. Cambridge: CUP, 304–320.
Makoni, Sinfree and Alastair Pennycook, eds. (2006) *Disinventing and Reconstituting Languages*. Clevedon: Multilingual Matters.
Malkiel, Yakov (1993) *Etymology*. Cambridge: CUP.
Marais, Eugène (1937) *The Soul of the White Ant*. London: Methuen.
Marais, Eugène (1969) *The Soul of the Ape*. London: Atheneum.
Marenborn, John (2004) *Boethius*. Oxford: OUP.
Marias, Eugène (1969) *The Soul of the Ape*. New York: Atheneum.
Marshall, Bruce (2004) *Trinity and Truth*. Cambridge: CUP.
Martin, Jack and Mark Bickhard, eds. (2012) *The Psychology of Personhood*. Cambridge: CUP.
Matambanadzo, Saru (2012) Embodying vulnerability: a feminist theory of the person. *Duke Journal of Gender and Policy* 20: 45–83.
Marx, Karl (1889) *Capital*. London: Swan Sonnenschein.
Mathews, Freye (2003) *For Love of Matter A Contemporary Panpsychism*. Albany: SUNY Press.
Maturana, Humberto and Francisco Varela (1980) *Autopoiesis and Cognition: The Realization of the Living*. Dordrecht: Reidel. First published, 1973.
Mauss, Marcel (1985) A category of the human mind: the notion of person; the notion of self. In Michael Carrithers, Steven Collins, and Steven Lukes, eds., *The Category of the Person: Anthropology, Philosophy, History*, Cambridge: CUP, 1–25. First published, 1908.
McDougall, William (1920) *The Group Mind*. Cambridge: CUP.
McFague, Sally (1982) *Metaphorical Theology*. Minneapolis: Fortress Press.
McFague, Sally (1993) *The Body of God*. Minneapolis: Fortress Press.
McGann, Marek (2014) Enacting a social ecology: radically embodied intersubjectivity. *Frontiers in Psychology* 5: 1321.
McGuckin, John (2008) *The Orthodox Church*. Malden: Blackwell.
McLuhan, Marshall (1994) *Understanding Media*. Cambridge: MIT Press. First published, 1964.
Mead, George (1936) *Movements of Thought in the Nineteenth Century*. Chicago: Chicago UP.
Mead, George Herbert (1962) *Mind, Self and Society*. Chicago: The University of Chicago Press. First published, 1934.
Melehy, Hassan (2005) Silencing the animals: Montaigne, Descartes, and the hyperbole of reason. *symplokē* 13: 263–282.
Melehy, Hassan (2006) Montaigne and the question of ethics. *L'Esprit Créateur* 46: 96–107.
Menary, Richard, ed. (2010) *The Extended Mind*. Cambridge: MIT Press.
Menely, Tobias (2015) *The Animal Claim: Sensibility and the Creaturely Voice*. Chicago: University of Chicago Press.
Merewether, Henry and Archibald Stephens (1835) *The History of the Boroughs and Municipal Corporations of the United Kingdom*, vol. 3. London: Stevens.

Merleau-Ponty Maurice (1962) *The Phenomenology of Perception*. London: Routledge and Kegan Paul.

Merrill, Sarah (1998) *Defining Personhood: Towards the Ethics of Quality in Clinical Care*. Amsterdam: Rodopi.

Metzinger, Thomas (2003) *Being No One: The Self-Model Theory of Subjectivity*. Cambridge: MIT Press.

Michoud, Léon (1906) *La théorie de la personalité morale et son aplication au droit français*. Paris: Librairie Générale de Droit.

Midgley, Mary (1995) *Man and Beast; The Roots of Human Nature*. London: Routledge. First published, 1979.

Midgley, Mary (2011) *The Myths We Live by*. London: Routledge.

Milde, Karl (1969) Can a computer be an 'author, or an 'inventor'? *Journal of the Patent Office* 51: 378–405.

Mill, John Stuart (1843) *System of Logic: Ratiocinative and Inductive*, vol I. London: Parker.

Miller (1993). Copyright protection for computer programs, databases, and computer-generated works: is anything new since CONTU?', *Harvard LR* 106: 977–1073.

Mitchell, Robert, Nicholas Thompson and H. Lyn Miles, eds. (1997) *Anthropomorphism, Anecdotes, and Animals*. Albany: SUNY Press.

Moore, Jason, ed. (2016) *Anthropocene or Capitalocene?* Oakland: PM Press.

Moran, Dermot (2017) The personal self in the phenomenological tradition. In Rafael Winkler, ed., *Identity and Difference: Contemporary Debates on the Self*. Cham: Springer Nature, 3–35.

Morton, Timothy (2007) *Ecology without Nature*. Cambridge: Harvard UP.

Morton, Timothy (2017) *Humankind: Solidarity with Nonhuman People*. New York: Verso.

Morell, Virginia (2013) *Animal Wise: The Thoughts and Emotions of Our Fellow Creatures*. New York: Crown.

Morris, Clarence (1964) The rights and duties of beasts and trees: a law teacher's essay for landscape architects. *Journal of Legal Education* 17: 185–192.

Mounier, Emmanuel (1952) *Personalism*. London: Routledge & Kegan Paul.

Mouzourakis, Brittany (2014) Tilikum's splash: lessons learned from animal rights-based litigation strategies. *Journal of Animal and Natural Resource Law* 10: 223–251.

Müller, Friedrich Max (1864) *Lectures on the Science of Language, Delivered at the Royal Institution of Great Britain in April, May, and June, 1861*. London: Longman.

Mumford, Lewis (1961) *The City in History*. New York: Harcourt.

Murphy, Nancey (1997) Human nature: historical, scientific and religious issues. In Warren Brown, Nancey Murphy and H. Newton Malony, eds., *Whatever Happened to the Soul?* Minneapolis: Fortress Press, 1–30.

Naess, Arne (1973) The shallow and the deep, long-range ecology movement: a summary. *Inquiry* 16: 95–100.

Naffine, Ngaire (2003) Who are law's persons? *The Modern LR* 66: 346–367.

Naffine, Ngaire (2009) *Law's Meaning of Life: Philosophy, Religion, Darwin and the Legal Person*. Oxford: Hart.

Naffine, Ngaire (2011) Review essay: liberating the legal person. *Canadian Journal of Law and Society* 26: 193–203.

Nagel, Thomas (1974). What is it like to be a bat? *The Philosophical Review* 83: 435–450.

Nekam, Alexander (1938) *The Personality Conception of the Legal Entity*. Cambridge: Harvard UP.

Nemeth, Elisabeth and Friedrich Stadler, eds. (1996) *Encyclopedia and Utopia: The Life and Work of Otto Neurath (1882–1945)*. Berlin: Springer.

Neurath, Otto (1921) *Anti-Spengler*. München: Callwey Verlagsbuchhandlung.

Neurath, Otto (1936) *International Picture Language; the First Rules of Isotype*. London: Kegan Paul.

Neurath, Otto (1937) *Basic by Isotype*. London: Kegan Paul.

Nibert, David (2013) *Animal Oppression and Human Violence*. New York: Columbia UP.

Nietzsche, Friedrich (1954) On truth and lie in an extra-moral sense. In Walter Kaufman, ed., *The Portable Nietzsche*. London: Penguin, 46–7. Written in 1873.

Nietzsche, Friedrich (2013) *On the Genealogy of Morals*. Robert Holub, ed. London: Penguin. First published, 1887.

Noë, Alva (2009) *Out of Our Heads*. New York: Hill and Wang.

Nolan, Daniel (2015) Personification and impossible fictions. *British Journal of Aesthetics* 55: 57–69.

Noonan, John (2002) *Persons and Masks of the Law*. Berkeley: University of California Press.

Nozick, Robert (1974) *Anarchy, State, and Utopia*. New York: Basic Books.

Nussbaum, Martha (2006) *Frontiers of Justice: Disability, Nationality, Species Membership*. Cambridge: Harvard UP.

O'Callaghan, Paul (2016) *Children of God in the World*. Washington, DC: Catholic University of America Press.

Ogden, Charles (1932) *Bentham's Theory of Fictions*. London: Kegan Paul.

Ogden, Charles and Ivor Richards (1923) *The Meaning of Meaning*. London: Kegan Paul.

Ohlin, Jens (2005) Is the concept of the person necessary for human rights? *Columbia LR* 105: 209–249. New York: Harcourt.

Olshewsky, Thomas (1976) On the relations of soul to body in Plato and Aristotle. *Journal of the History of Philosophy* 14: 391–404.

Olson, Eric (2007) *What are We? A Study in Personal Ontology*. Oxford: OUP.

Orman, Jon (2016a) Scientism in the language sciences. *Language and Communication* 48: 28–40.

Orman, Jon (2016b) Distributing mind, cognition and language: exploring the (un)common ground with integrational linguistics. *Language and Cognition* 8:142–166.

Orwell, George (1969) Politics and the English language. In W.F. Bolton and D. Crystal, eds., *The English Language*. Cambridge: CUP, 217–228. First published, 1946.

Otter, Monika (2010) Vuldus adest (*the face helps*): performance, expressivity and interiority. In Mary Carruthers, ed., *Rhetoric Beyond*. Cambridge: CUP, 151–172.

Pablé, Adrian (2011) Why the semantics of 'good' and 'bad' isn't good enough: popular science and the 'language crux'. *Language Sciences* 33: 551–558.

Pablé, Adrian (2012a) Excommunicated on the grounds of Harrisy. Roy Harris, linguistics and freedom of speech. *Geolinguistics* 37: 1–12.

Pablé, Adrian (2012b) Logophilia, logophobia and the *terra mota* of persona linguistic experience. *Language and Communication* 32: 257–264.

Pablé, Adrian (2016) Global semiotics vs. human semiology. Understanding communication in the twenty-first century. *Chinese Semiotic Studies* 12: 25–43.

Pablé, Adrian (2017) Introduction: humanism, existentialism and integrational semiology. In Adrian Pablé, ed., *Critical Humanist Perspectives: The Integrational Turn in Philosophy of Language and Communication*. London: Routledge, 3–9.

Pablé, Adrian and Christopher Hutton (2015) *Signs, Meaning and Experience*. Berlin: de Gruyter.

Pacheco, Alex with Anna Francione (1985) The Silver Spring monkeys. In Peter Singer, ed., *In Defense of Animals*, New York: Basil Blackwell, 135–147.

Panksepp, Jaak (1998) *Affective Neuroscience: The Foundations of Human and Animal Emotions*. New York: OUP.

Panksepp, Jaak and Lucy Biven (2012) *The Archaeology of Mind*. New York: Norton.

Pardo, Michael (2015) Group agency and legal proof; or, why the jury is an 'it'. *William and Mary LR* 56: 1793–1858.

Parfit, Derek (1984) *Reasons and Persons*. Oxford: Clarendon.

Park, Robert Ezra (1950) *Race and Culture: Essays in the Sociology of Contemporary Man*. New York: Free Press.

Parsley, Connal (2010) The mask and Agamben: the transitional juridical technics of legal relation. *Law Text Culture* 14: 12–39.

Parsons, James (1767) *Remains of Japhet*. London.

Paton, George (1964) *A Textbook of Jurisprudence*. Oxford: OUP. First published, 1940.

Paulhan, Jean (1953) *Alain, ou la preuve par l'étymologie*. Paris: Éditions de Minuit.

Pennycook, Alistair (2018) *Posthumanist Applied Linguistics*. London: Routledge.

Petrilli, Susan (2015) Language, communication, and speech: human signs in global semiosis. *Semiotica* 204: 173–237.

Pietrzykowski, Tomasz (2017) The idea of nonpersonal subjects of law. In Tomasz Pietrzykowski and Visa Kurki, eds., *Legal Personhood: Animals, Artificial Intelligence and the Unborn*. Berlin: Springer, 49–68.

Pietrzykowski, Tomasz (2018) *Personhood Beyond Humanism*. Berlin: Springer.

Pippin, Robert (2010) *Hegel on Self-Consciousness*. Princeton: Princeton UP.

Pitkin, Hanna (1967) *The Concept of Representation*. Berkeley: University of California Press.

Pollack, Sheldon (2009) Future philology? The fate of a soft science in a hard world. *Critical Inquiry* 35: 931–961.

Porter, James (2000) *Nietzsche and the Philology of the Future*. Stanford: Stanford UP.

Poser, Hans (2016) *Leibniz' Philosophie: Über die Einheit von Metaphysik und Wissenschaft*. Hamburg: Meiner Verlag.

Posner, Richard (2000) Animal rights. *Yale Law Journal* 110: 527–541.

Price, Jeanne Frazier (2013) Wagging, not barking: statutory definitions. *Cleveland State LR* 60: 999–1055.

Price, Richard and Michael Gaddis, eds. (2005) *The Acts of the Council of Chalcedon*. Vol 1. Liverpool: Liverpool UP.

Purdy, Jedediah (2016) Coming into the Anthropocene. *Harvard LR* 29: 1619–1650.

Quigley, Christine (1996) *The Corpse: A History*. Jefferson: McFarland.

Radin, Margaret (1992) Property and personhood. *Stanford LR* 34: 957–1015.

Radin, Max (1925) Fundamental Concepts of the Roman Law. *California LR* 13: 207–228.

Rahner, Karl (2000) *Content of Faith*. New York: Crossroad.

Ramshaw, Gail (1995) *God Beyond Gender*. Minneapolis: Fortress.

Ratamäki, Outi (2014) Animal perceptions in animal transport regulations in the EU and Finland. *Relations Beyond Anthropocentrism* 2: 79–96.

Regan, Tom (2001) The case for animal rights. In Carl Cohen and Tom Regan, eds, *The Animal Rights Debate*. New York: Rowman and Littlefield, 127–222.

Regan, Tom and Peter Singer, eds. (1976) *Animal Rights and Human Obligations*. Englewood Cliffs: Prentice-Hall.

Remes, Paulina and Sihvola, eds. (2008) *Ancient Philosophy of the Self*. Berlin: Springer.

Rhee, Christina (1998) *Urantia Foundation v. Maaherra. Berkeley Technology Law Journal* 13: 69–81.

Rivard, Michael (1992) Toward a general theory of constitutional personhood: a theory of constitutional personhood for transgenic humanoid species. *UCLA LR* 39: 1425–1510.

Rodriguez, Michael (1962) Innocent IV and the element of fiction in juristic personalities. *The Jurist* 22: 287–318.

Rogers, Christopher (2017) A new approach to protecting ecosystems: the Te Awa Tupua (Whanganui River Claims Settlement) Act 2017. *Environmental LR* 19: 266–279.

Rollin, Bernard (1981) *Animal Rights and Human Morality.* Buffalo: Prometheus.

Rollin, Bernard (2006) Animal ethics and legal status. In Marc Hauser, Fiery Cushman and Matthew Kamen, eds., *People, Property, or Pets?* West Lafayette: Purdue UP, 33–45.

Rose, Nikolas (1998) *Inventing Our Selves: Psychology, Power, and Personhood.* Cambridge: CUP.

Rull, Valentí (2017) The 'Anthropocene': neglects, misconceptions, and possible futures. *EMBO Reports* 18: 1056–1060.

Runciman, David (1997) *Political Hypocrisy: The Mask of Power, from Hobbes to Orwell and Beyond.* Princeton: Princeton UP.

Russell, Betrand (1918) The philosophy of logical atomism. *The Monist* 29: 190–222.

Russell, Betrand (2003) Analytical realism. In Stephen Mumford ed., *Russell on Metaphysics: Selections from the Writings of Bertrand Russell.* London: Routledge, 91–96. Lecture delivered, 1911.

Russell, Jeffrey (1987) *The Devil: Perceptions of Evil from Antiquity to Primitive Christianity.* Ithaca: Cornell UP.

Ryder, Richard (1975) *Victims of Science: The Use of Animals in Research.* London: Davis-Poynter.

Ryle, Gilbert (1949) *The Concept of Mind.* London: Hutchinson.

Rzepka, Charles (1986) *The Self as Mind.* Cambridge: Harvard UP.

Saeed, John (2003) *Semantics.* Oxford: Blackwell.

Sahlins, Marshall (1995) *How Natives Think. About Captain Cook, for Example.* Chicago: University of Chicago Press.

Saleilles, Raymond (1922) *De la personnalité juridique.* Paris: Rousseau.

Sartre, Jean-Paul (2007) *Existentialism is a Humanism.* New Haven: Yale UP. First published, 1945.

Saunders, Natasha (2017) *International Political Theory and the Refugee Problem.* New York: Routledge.

Saussure, Ferdinand de (1922) *Cours de linguistique générale.* Paris: Payot.

Savage-Rumbaugh, Sue and Roger Lewin (1996) *Kanzi: The Ape at the Brink of the Human Mind.* New York: Wiley.

Savage-Rumbaugh, Sue, Stuart Shanker and Talbot Taylor (1998) *Apes, Language, and the Human Mind.* New York: OUP.

Savigny, Friedrich Carl von (1840) *System des heutigen Römischen Rechts*, vol. 2. Berlin: Veit.

Schlinger, Henry (2008) Consciousness is nothing but a word. *Sceptic* 13: 58–63.

Schopenhauer, Arthur (2009) *The Two Fundamental Problems of Ethics.* Christopher Janaway, ed., Cambridge: CUP. First published, 1841.

Scott, G. E. (1990) *Moral Personhood: An Essay in the Philosophy of Moral Psychology.* Albany: SUNY Press.

Sebeok, Thomas (2001) *Signs: An Introduction to Semiotics.* 2nd edition. Toronto: University of Toronto Press.

Seed, Amanda and Michael Tomasello (2010) Primate cognition. *Topics in Cognitive Science* 2: 407–419.

Seigel, Jerrold (2005) *The Idea of the Self.* Cambridge: CUP.

Selkala, Toni and Mikko Rajavuori (2017) Traditions, myths, and utopias of personhood: an introduction. *German Law Journal* 18: 1017–1068.

Shepheard, W. (1659) *Of Corporations, Fraternities and Guilds.* London: Ward and Lock.

Shooster, Jay (2017) Legal Personhood and the positive rights of wild animals. *Wild Animal Suffering Research*, July 11, 2017, available at: was-research.org.

Siedentop, Larry (2014) *Inventing the Individual: The Origins of Western Liberalism.* London: Allen Lane.

Simon, Ariel (2006) Cows as chairs: questioning categorical legal distinctions in a non-categorical world. In Marc Hauser, Fiery Cushman and Matthew Kamen, eds., *People, Property, or Pets?* West Lafayette: Purdue UP, 3–8.

Singer, Peter (1975) *Animal Liberation.* New York: HarperCollins.

Singer, Peter (1987) Animal liberation or animal rights. *The Monist* 70: 3014.

Skeat, Walter (1912) *The Science of Etymology.* Oxford: Clarendon.

Skinner, Quentin (1999) Hobbes and the purely artificial person of the state. *The Journal of Political Philosophy* 7: 1–29.

Skrbina, David (2005) *Panpsychism in the West.* Cambridge: MIT Press.

Slaughter, Mary (1982) *Universal Languages and Scientific Taxonomy in the Seventeenth Century.* Cambridge: CUP.

Smith, Andrew (1984) Did Porphyry reject the transmigration of human souls into animals? *Rheinisches Museum für Philologie* (Neue Folge) 127: 276–284.

Smith, Bryant (1928) Legal personality. *Yale Law Journal* 37: 283–299.

Smith, Christian (2003) *Moral, Believing Animals.* Oxford: OUP.

Smith, Christian (2010) *What Is a Person?* Chicago: University of Chicago Press.

Smith, J. David (2009). The study of animal metacognition. *Trends in Cognitive Sciences* 13: 389–396.

Solum, Lawrence (1992) Legal personhood for artificial intelligences. *North Carolina LR* 70: 1231–1287.

Sommer, Benjamin (2009) *The Bodies of God and the World of Ancient Israel.* Cambridge: CUP.

Soskice, Janet (1985). *Metaphor and Religious Language.* Oxford: Clarendon.

Spaemann, Robert (2006) *Persons: The Difference between 'Someone' and 'Something'.* Oxford: OUP.

Spencer, Jane (2013) Animal feeling in the century before Darwin. In Angelique Richardson, ed., *After Darwin: Animals, Emotions, and the Mind.* Amsterdam: Rodopi, 24–50.

Spiro, Melford E. (1984) Some reflections on cultural determinism and relativism with special reference to emotion and reason. In R. A. Shweder and R A. LeVine, eds., *Culture Theory: Essays on Mind, Self, and Emotion.* Cambridge: CUP, 323–346.

Stair, James Dalrymple, Viscount of (1781) *The Institutions of the Law of Scotland Deduced from its Originals* […]. Edinburgh: Anderson.

Steffensen, Sune (2013) Human interactivity: problem-solving, solution-probing and verbal patterns in the wild. In Stephen Cowley and F. Vallée-Tourangeau, eds., *Cognition Beyond the Brain.* London: Springer, 195–222.

Steffensen, Sune (2015) Distributed language and dialogism: notes on non-locality, sense-making and interactivity. *Language Sciences* 50: 105–119.

Stetsenko, Anna and Igor Arievitch (1997) Constructing and deconstructing the self: comparing post-Vygotskian and discourse-based version of social constructivism. *Mind, Culture and Activity* 4: 159–172.

Stibbe, Arran (2001) Language, power and the social construction of animals. *Society and Animals* 9: 145–161.

Stock, Adam (2009) The organic and the mechanical. Images of man, the state and society in the eighteenth century. *Kaleidoscope* 3: 7–24.

Stone, Christopher (1972) Should trees have standing?–towards legal rights for natural objects. *Southern California LR* 45: 450–451.

Stone, Christopher (2010) *Should Trees Have Standing?* Oxford: OUP.

Stout, Daniel (2017) *Corporate Romanticism: Liberalism, Justice, and the Novel.* New York: Fordham UP.

Strawson, Peter (1996) *Individuals.* London: Routledge.

Suen, Alison (2015) *The Speaking Animal: Ethics, Language and the Human-Animal Divide.* London: Rowman and Littlefield.

Sunstein, Cass (2000) Standing for animals. *UCLA LR* 47: 1333–1368.

Sunstein, Cass and Martha Nussbaum, eds. (2004) *Animal Rights. Current Debates and New Directions.* Oxford: OUP.

Sutton, John (2004) Representation, levels, and contexts in integrational linguistics and distributed cognition. *Language Sciences* 26: 503–524.

Swinburne, Richard (1979) *The Existence of God.* Oxford: OUP.

Syrotinski, Michael (2011) From etymology (*etumos logos*) to translation, via Badiou and Paulhan. In Sean Gaston and Ian Maclachlan, eds., *Reading Derrida's* Of Grammatology. London: Continuum, 23–28.

Szabó, Zoltán Gendler (2017) Compositionality. *The Stanford Encyclopedia of Philosophy*, Edward Zalta, ed., available at: plato.stanford.edu.

Talbot, Elizabeth and Colin Wastell (2015) Corrected by reflection: the de-anthropomorphized mindset of atheism. *Journal for the Cognitive Science of Religion* 3: 113–124.

Talbot, H. Fox (1847) *English Etymologies.* London: John Murray.

Tannous, Jack (2014) In search of monotheletism. *Dumbarton Oaks Papers* 68: 29–67.

Taylor, Charles (1989) *Sources of the Self: The Making of the Modern Identity.* Cambridge: Harvard UP.

Taylor, Charles (2016) *The Language Animal.* Cambridge: Harvard UP.

Taylor, Henry and Peter Vickers (2017) Conceptual fragmentation and the rise of eliminativism. *European Journal of the Philosophy of Science* 7: 17–40.

Taylor, Paul (1986) *Respect for Nature.* Princeton: Princeton UP.

Taylor, Talbot (1997) The origin of language: why it never happened. *Language Sciences* 19: 67–77.

Taylor, Talbot and Stuart Shanker (1996) Ape linguistics (or: is Kanzi a Cartesian?). In David Cram, Andrew Linn and Elke Nowak, eds., *History of Linguistics, 1996: Traditions in Linguistics Worldwide.* Amsterdam: Benjamins, 57–68.

Teichman, Jenny (1985) The definition of person. *Philosophy* 60: 175–185.

Tellegen-Couperus, Olga (1993) *A Short History of Roman Law.* London: Routledge.

Teubner, Gunther (1988) New industrial policy and the 'essence' of the legal person. *The American Journal of Comparative Law* 36: 130–155.

Teubner, Gunther (1989) How the law thinks: toward a constructivist epistemology of law. *Law and Society Review* 23: 727–758.

Teubner, Gunther (2006) Rights of non-humans? Electronic agents and animals as new actors in politics and law. *Journal of Law and Society* 33: 497–521.
Thibault, Paul (2011) First-order languaging dynamics and second-order language: the distributed language view. *Ecological Psychology* 23: 1–36.
Thibault, Paul (2017) The reflexivity of human languaging and Nigel Love's two orders of language. *Language Sciences* 61: 74–85.
Thiel, Udo (2011) *The Early Modern Subject.* Oxford: OUP.
Thomas, Tenny (2011) Nestorianism. In John McGuckin, ed., *The Encyclopedia of Eastern Orthodox Christianity.* Wiley: Chichester, 411–414.
Thomson, Ann (2010) Animals, humans, machines and thinking matter, 1690–1707. In Charles Wolfe and Tobias Cheung, eds., *Transitions and Borders between Animals, Humans and Machines 1600–1800.* Leiden: Brill, 3–37.
Thomson, Judith (1997) People and their bodies. In Jonathan Dancy, ed., *Reading Parfit.* Oxford: Blackwell, 155–176.
Thurow, Joshua (2018) Animals with soul. *Sophia* 57: 85–101.
Tomasello, Michael and Joseph Call (1997) *Primate Cognition.* Oxford: OUP.
Tomasello, Michael and Esther Herrmann (2010) Ape and human cognition: what's the difference? *Current Directions in Psychological Science* 19: 3–8.
Toolan, Michael (1996) *Total Speech.* Durham: Duke UP.
Toolan, Michael (2009) Legal definitions. *Language and Communication* 29: 182–192.
Torchia, Joseph (2008) *Exploring Personhood: An Introduction to the Philosophy of Nature.* New York: Rowman and Littlefield.
Totten, Tyler (2015) Should elephants have standing. *Western Journal of Legal Studies* 6: 1–16.
Tønnessen, Martin (2010) The global species. *New Formations* 69: 98–110.
Trench, Richard (1853) *On the Study of Words.* Fourth revised edition. London: Parker.
Trendelenburg, Adolf (1910) A contribution to the history of the word person. *The Monist* 20: 336–363.
Tribe, Laurence (2001) Ten lessons our constitutional experience can teach us about the puzzle of animal rights: the work of Steven M. Wise. *Animal Law* 7: 1–8.
Tuck, Richard (1989) *Hobbes.* Oxford: OUP.
Turcescu, Lucian (1997) Prosopon and hypostasis in Basil of Caesarea's 'Against Eunomius' and the Epistles. *Vigiliae Christianae* 51: 374–395.
Turcescu, Lucian (2005) *Gregory of Nyssa and the Concept of Divine Persons.* Oxford: OUP.
Turkle, Sherry (2004) *The Second Self: Computers and the Human Spirit.* Cambridge: MIT press. First published, 1984.
Turner, Ryan (2013), Do animals have selves? *Studies in Symbolic Interaction* 40: 425–460.
Tylor, Edwards (1920) *Primitive Culture*, vol.1. London: Murray.
Ullmann, Stephen (1966) *Language and Style: Collected Papers.* Oxford: Blackwell.
Vaggione, Richard (2000) *Eunomius of Cyzicus and the Nicene Revolution.* Oxford: OUP.
Vaihinger, Hans (1922) *Die Philosophie des Als Ob.* 7th ed. Leipzig: Meiner.
Varner, Gary (2012) *Personhood, Ethics, and Animal Cognition: Situating Animals in Hare's Two Level Utilitarianism.* Oxford: OUP.
Vermeulen, Hans (2015) *Before Boas: The Genesis of Ethnography and Ethnology in the German Enlightenment.* Lincoln: University of Nebraska Press.
Vilaça, Guilherme Vasconcelos (2010) From Hayek's spontaneous orders to Luhmann's autopoietic systems. *Studies in Emergent Order* 3: 50–81.
Viner, Charles (1792) *A General Abridgment of Law and Equity* [...], vol 6. London.
Vinogradoff, Paul (1924) Juridical persons. *Columbia LR* 24: 594–604.

Volpicelli, Robert (2016) The varieties of impersonal experience. *Journal of Modern Literature* 39:180–186.

Wade, Richard (2004) Animal theology and ethical concerns. *Australian eJournal of Theology* 2: 1–12.

Wagman, Bruce (2010) Growing up with animal law: from courtrooms to casebooks. *Journal of Legal Education* 60: 193–208.

Waldau, Paul (2013) *Animal Studies: An Introduction*. New York: OUP.

Wandruszka, Mario (1958) Etymologie und Philosophie. *Etymologica. W. von Wartburg zum 70.Geburtstag*, Tübingen: Niemeyer, 857–871.

Warmbrōd, Ken (1974) Theoretical devices for marking semantic anomalies. *Canadian Journal of Philosophy* 3: 365–372.

Watson, Alex (2014) Who am I? The self/subject according to psychoanalytic theory. *Sage Open* 4(3): 1–14.

Watson, John (1913) Psychology as the behaviorist views it. *Psychological Review* 20: 158–177.

Watts, Alan (1957) *The Way of Zen*. London: Penguin.

Weick, Karl and Karlene Roberts (1993) Collective mind in organizations: heedful interrelating on flight decks. *Administrative Science Quarterly* 38: 357–381.

Werner, Oswald (1972) Ethnoscience 1972. *Annual Review of Anthropology* 1: 271–308.

Wetherell, Margaret and Janet Maybin (1996) The distributed self: a social constructionist perspective. In Richard Stevens, ed., *Understanding the Self.* London: Sage, 219–280.

Whapham, Theodore (2010) Pannenberg on divine personhood. *Irish Theological Quarterly* 75: 373–387.

White, Frederick (2013) Personhood: an essential characteristic of the human species. *The Linacre Quarterly* 80: 74–97.

White, Thomas I. (2007) *In Defence of Dolphins: The New Moral Frontier.* Malden: Blackwell.

White, Thomas Joseph (2015) *The Incarnate Lord*. Washington: Catholic University of America Press.

Whitehead, Hal and Luke Rendell (2014) *The Cultural Lives of Whales and Dolphins.* Chicago: University of Chicago Press.

Whitman, Walt (1902) *Leaves of Grass*. New York: Crowell.

Whorf, Benjamin Lee (1956) *Language, Thought, and Reality: Selected Writings of Benjamin Lee Whorf.* Cambridge: MIT Press.

Wierzbicka, Anna (1972) *Semantic Primes*. Frankfurt: Athenaeum.

Wierzbicka, Anna (1993) A conceptual basis for cultural psychology. *Ethos* 21: 205–231.

Wierzbicka, Anna (1997) *Understanding Cultures through Their Key Words.* Oxford: OUP.

Wierzbicka, Anna (2006) Preface. In Bert Peeters, ed., *Semantic Primes and Universal Grammar.* Amsterdam: Benjamins, 1–6.

Wierzbicka, Anna (2015) Innate conceptual primitives manifested in the languages of the world and in infant cognition. In Eric Margolis and Stephen Laurence, eds., *The Conceptual Minds.* Cambridge: MIT Press, 379–412.

Wiggins, David (1987) The person as object of science, as subject of experience and, and locus of value. In A. Peacocke and G. Gillet, eds., *Persons and Personality: A Contemporary Inquiry.* Oxford: Blackwell, 56–74.

Williams, Bernard (2005) *Descartes: The Project of Pure Inquiry.* London: Routledge.

Williams, Raymond (1983) *Keywords.* Oxford: OUP. First published, 1976.

Williams, Rowan (2008) *Dostoevsky: Language, Faith, and Fiction.* London: Continuum.

Williams, Rowan (2016) *On Augustine*. London: Bloomsbury.

Williams, Thomas and Jan Bengtsson (2018) Personalism. In Edward Zalta, ed., *The Stanford Encyclopedia of Philosophy*, available at plato.stanford.edu.

Willick, Marshall (1983) Artificial intelligence: some legal implications. *AI Magazine* 4: 5–16.

Wilkins, John (1668) *An Essay towards a Real Character, and a Philosophical Language*. London.

Wilson, Edward (1999) *Consilience: The Unity of Knowledge*. New York: Vintage.

Wise, Steven (1995) How nonhuman animals were trapped in a nonexistent universe. *Animal Law* 1: 15–45.

Wise, Steven (1996) Legal rights for nonhuman animals: the case for chimpanzees and bonobos. *Animal Law* 2: 179–186.

Wise, Steven (1998) Hardly a revolution – the eligibility of nonhuman animals for dignity-rights in liberal democracy. *Vermont LR* 22: 793–915.

Wise, Steven (2000) *Rattling the Cage: Toward Legal Rights for Animals*. Cambridge: Perseus Books.

Wise, Steven (2002a) *Rattling the Cage* defended. *Boston College LR* 43: 623–696.

Wise, Steven (2002b) *Drawing the Line: Science and the Case for Animal Rights*. Cambridge: Perseus.

Wise, Steven (2009) *An American Trilogy: Death, Slavery and Dominion Along the Banks of the Cape Fear River*. Boston: Da Capo Press.

Wishart, David (2016) Puzzling out law's person. *Indiana Journal of Global Legal Studies* 23: 743–764.

Wittgenstein, Ludwig (1981) *Tractatus Logico-Philosophicus*. London: Routledge & Kegan Paul. First published, 1922.

Wittgenstein, Ludwig (1998) *Notebooks 1914–1916*. 2nd edition. G. H. von Wright and G.E.M Anscombe, eds. Oxford: Blackwell.

Wittgenstein, Ludwig (2009) *Philosophical Investigations*. Revised 4th edition. Oxford: Blackwell.

Wolf, George (1997) Real people doing real things in real time. *Language and Communication* 17: 359–368.

Wolf, George (1999) Quine and the segregational sign. *Language and Communication* 19: 27–43.

Wolfe, Cary (2010) *What is Posthumanism?* Minneapolis: University of Minnesota Press.

Wu, Tim (2013) Machine speech. *University of Pennsylvania LR* 161: 1495–1533.

Wymyslo, Joanna (2007) Standing for endangered species: justiciability beyond humanity. *University of Baltimore Journal of Environmental Law* 15: 45–70.

Young, Merrill (1975) Did some middle Platonists deny the immortality of the soul. *The Harvard Theological Review* 68: 58–60.

Zarka, Yves Charles (1996) First philosophy and the foundation of knowledge. In Tom Sorell, ed., *The Cambridge Companion to Hobbes*. Cambridge: CUP, 62–85.

Zelman, Joanna (2012) PETA's SeaWorld slavery case dismissed by judge, February 9, 2012, available at: http://www.huffingtonpost.com/2012.

Ziesler, J. A. (1983) Soma in the Septuagint. *Novum Testamentum* 25: 133–145.

Zizioulas, John (1997) *Being as Communion: Studies in Personhood and the Church*. Crestwood: St Vladimir Seminary Press.

Zöller, Günter (1999) Schopenhauer on the self. In Christopher Janaway, ed., *The Cambridge Companion to Schopenhauer*. Cambridge: CUP, 18–43.

Zulueta, Concepción Cortés (2015) Nonhuman animal testimonies: a natural history in the first person? In Susan Nance, ed., *The Historical Animal*. Syracuse: Syracuse UP, 118–130.

Index

Note: Page numbers followed by "n" denote endnotes.

Abrams, Meyer H. 144
Agamben, Giorgio 105
agency 5, 6, 31–2, 40, 55, 57, 69, 71–80, 101, 125, 129–30, 137, 141, 147
Amadio v. Levin (1985) 142n17
animal personhood in law 105–9, 112–41
animals and humans in law 85–8
Anscombe, Elizabeth 22–3
Anthropocene 1
anthropocentricism 1–5, 32, 76, 80, 107, 116, 141, 144–8
anthropomorphism 8, 48, 57, 61, 63–5, 70, 148
anti-humanism 1–5, 34, 82, 116, 144
Aquinas, St. Thomas 9, 16
Arendt, Hannah 21
Aristotle 7, 8, 9, 15, 48, 56
Arnauld, Antoine 49
As You Like It 20
atomism 11, 48–9, 51, 52, 53–6
Augustine, St. 9, 13
authorship and the self 137–40
Ayer, Alfred J. 60

Babel 36, 37, 43, 87, 102
Bacon, Francis 36–7, 42, 56, 57, 65
Bank of the United States v. Deveaux (1809) 94
Barthes, Roland 137
Barth, Karl 5, 146
Bateson, Gregory 32, 73, 74
Bentham, Jeremy 1, 34, 104
Benveniste, Émile 21–2
Berger, Peter 30
Bertalanffy, Ludwig von 72
Blackstone, William 84, 104
Boethius 14–15, 61, 146
Bonhoeffer, Dietrich 10, 148
Boumediene v. Bush (2008) 127
Bowers v. Hardwick (1986) 130
Boyle, Robert 37
Brutus v. Cozens (1973) 144
Buber, Martin 22
Buddhism 32
Buffon, Comte de 39
Burrow-Giles Lithographic Co. v. Sarony (1883) 143n44
Byrn v. New York City Health & Hosps. Corp. (1972) 131–5

Capitalocene 2
Carnap, Rudolf 60
Cassirer, Ernst 58
category-mistake 78
Cetacean Community v. Bush (2003) 120–1
Cetacean Community v. Bush (2004) 120–1
Cherokee Nation v. State of Georgia (1831) 113–15
Chomsky, Noam 56, 70, 72, 81
Cicero 99
Citizens to End Animal Suffering and Exploitation, Inc., et al. v. The New England Aquarium et al. (1993) 119–20
Citizens United v. Federal Election Commission (2010) 96–8
cognitive linguistics 56–60
collective mind 77
Commonwealth v. Turner (1887) 111n3
componential analysis 53
compositionality 48–53
Cooley, Charles 19, 29

Corso v. Crawford Dog and Cat Hospital, Inc. (1979) 111n6, 136
Crystal, David 64
Culverwell, Nathaniel 86–7
Cummins v. Bond (1927) 138
Cupp, Richard 126, 129–30
Cuvier, Georges 39

Dalgarno, George 49
dark ecology 41
Dartmouth College v. Woodward (1819) 94
Darwin, Charles 9, 10, 28, 70, 81, 106–8, 147
Data Processing Svc. Orgs. v. Camp (1970) 141n2
Dawkins, Richard 33
deep ecology 41
Dennett, Daniel 32–4, 78, 79
Derrida, Jacques 48
Descartes, René 9, 24–6, 37, 78
Dewey, John 92, 110
dignity-rights 106–8
distributed nature of self 73–81
Douglas, Mary 75–6
Dred Scott v. Sandford (1856) 114
Duncker, Dorthe 4, 72, 73, 82, 147
Duns Scotus 5

Edwards v. Canada (1930) 103
Einstein, Albert 8
emblematic worldview 38–9
Enlightenment 28, 40
Erasmus 45
etymology 43–8

Feger v. Warwick Animal Shelter (2008) 136
Feser, Edward 62
Fichte, Johann Gottlieb 28
fiction, as an analytical category 35, 42, 60, 64, 72, 75, 82, 83, 89, 92–8
Filmer, Robert 86–7
first-order versus second-order 4, 82
Foucault, Michel 40, 105, 137
FPC v. Natural Gas Pipeline Co. (1942) 131
Francione, Gary 109, 115
Freud, Sigmund 19
Frisch, Karl von 81
Fund For Animals v. Malone (1982) 141n4

Gaia hypothesis 41
Gaius 84, 86
Geertz, Clifford 56, 74
Gellner, Ernst 52
Giddens, Anthony 31, 71
Gierke, Otto von 102
Goddard, Cliff 53–5
Goffman, Erving 20–1
Goodrich, Peter 39, 105, 140
Gray, John 2, 23, 33, 75, 105
Great Chain of Being 7, 9, 59, 105
Gregory of Nyssa 13
Grotius, Hugo 85–6
group mind 77

Harré, Rom 35
Harris, Roy: on the Adamic language 43; on Aristotle 56; on the biomechanical, macrosocial and circumstantial 68; on critique of distributed cognition 78–80; critique of Hume 65; critique of Western tradition 8; on the demythologization of linguistics 70; and Hutton 7, 56; indeterminacy 67; and the integrating mind 147; and *The Language Machine* 69; and language myth 3, 67; on the language of science 37, 110; and lay-orientation 4; on personal experience 81–2; and systems theory 81; and Taylor 45; view that there are no languageless propositions 42
Hawaiian Crow ('Alala') v. Lujan (1991) 119–20
Hayek, Friedrich von 72–3
Hazlitt, William 97
Hegel, Georg Wilhelm 28
Heidegger, Martin 48, 70, 76–7
Hercules and Leo in litigation 132–7
Hercules and Leo v. SUNY (2015) 132–7
Hinduism 32, 125
hive mind 77
Hobbes, Thomas: on defining basic terms 49; on language as misleading 56–7; and modernity 37; and the self 25–6; on state as person 98–105; on the use and abuse of language 87–8
Holmes, Oliver W. 106
Holocene 2
Humane Society v. Block (1982) 142n4
humanism 1–5, 11, 33, 34, 41, 45, 46, 68, 78, 81
Humboldt, Wilhelm von 77
Hume, David 26–7, 35, 57, 65
Husserl, Edmund 30
hypostasis 13–16, 62

impersonalism 11; and third person mode 22; and Kant's philosophy 28; and modernism 29; in the *Tractatus* 51; and God 62; and Chomskyan linguistics 72; and systems theory 147, 148
In re Goodall (1876) 102–3
In re the Administrators of Tulane Educational Fund (1992) 142n6
integrationism 3–5; and notion of the self 147–8; and systems theory 67–83
International Primate Protection League et al. v. Institute for Behavioral Research (1986) 116–17
International Primate Protection League v. Administrators of Tulane Educational Fund (1990) 117
International Primate Protection League v. Administrators of Tulane Educational Fund (1991) 141n6
In the Matter of John Storar (1981) 133
Ishiguru, Hidé 6, 35
Isidore, Bishop of Seville 45

James, William 29
Jarman v. Patterson (1828) 91
Johnson, Mark 58–60
Johnson, Samuel 7, 112
Jones, Peter 4
Joseph, John 45, 50, 52, 79–80
Jung, Carl Gustav 19

Kama the dolphin 119–20
Kant, Immanuel 12, 27–8, 32, 106, 108, 110
Kanzi the bonobo 81
Kyd, Stewart 94

Laing, Ronald D. 22
Lakoff, George 58–9
languaging 77
Latour, Bruno 37–8, 41, 76, 148
law as anthropocentric 1–2, 84–5
Lawrence v. Texas (2003) 137
Leibniz, Gottfried W. 49
Lemmon v. People (1860) 125, 133
Lévy-Bruhl, Lucien 40, 76
Lewis, Clive S. 7
Lichtenberg, Christoph 25
Linnaeus, Carl 39–40
literal meaning 22, 45, 46, 47, 50, 51, 56, 58, 59–60, 61, 63, 65, 146
Locke, John 16–18, 24, 26, 29, 31, 34, 35, 56, 65, 131
Lorenz, Konrad 81
Lovelock, James 41
Love, Nigel 4, 42, 70
Loving v. Virginia (1967) 130
Luckmann, Thomas 30
Luhmann, Niklas 34–5, 71, 73, 77, 147
Lujan v. Defenders of Wildlife (1992) 119
Luria, Alexander 74
Luther, Martin 46

Maitland, Frederick 13, 89, 97, 111
Man, Paul de 48
Manwood, Roger 93
Marais, Eugène 10, 81
Marx, Karl 19, 76
Mauss, Marcel 19
McFague, Sally 61, 63
McLuhan, Marshall 75
Mead, George H. 30
Merleau-Ponty, Maurice 73
metaphor 5, 10, 19–21, 26, 29, 39, 42, 48, 51, 56–66, 78–80, 87, 88, 92, 98–9, 102, 104, 105, 145–6
Mettrie, Julien Offray de La 9
Midgley, Mary 2, 9, 33
Miles v. City Council of Augusta, Georgia (1983) 112
Mill, John Stuart 7
Mohamad v. Palestinian Authority (2012) 91
Mohd. Salim v. State of Uttarakhand & Others, (PIL) (2014) 131
monkey selfie case 137–40
Morgan v. Kroupa (1997) 111n6
Morton, Timothy 6, 41
Mounier, Emmanuel 11
Mt. Graham Red Squirrel v. Yeutter (1991) 142n7
Müller, Friedrich Max 58, 70
Mumford, Lewis 75

Naffine, Ngaire 3, 88–9
Naruto et al v. David John Slater (2015) 138–40
Naruto the macaque 138–40
nature as bedrock term 36–41
Neurath, Otto 50
New Semantic Metalanguage 53–6
Nicole, Pierre 49
Nietzsche, Friedrich 1, 46–8
Noë, Alva 73
Nonhuman Rights Project 124–37, 140

Nonhuman Rights Project, Inc., on Behalf of Tommy, v. Patrick C. Lavery (2014) 124–37
Northern Spotted Owl v. Hodel (1988) 142n7
Northern Spotted Owl v. Lujan (1991) 142n7
Nottage v. Jackson (1883) 143n44

Obergefell v. Hodges (2015) 136, 137, 143n46
Ogden, Charles 8
Olson, Eric 22–3
Orman, Jon 69, 77–9, 81
Orwell, George 56
ousia 13–16, 146

Pablé, Adrian: and Hutton 4, 67, 69–70; on integrationism as humanism 3; and lay-orientation 4; on primacy of the self 81; on semiotics 80; speakers as language-makers 68; view that there are no languageless propositions 42
Palila v. Hawaii Dept. of Land and Natural Resources (1988) 118–19, 121
Parfit, Derek 98
Park, Robert 20
parliament of things 41
Pembina Consolidated Silver Mining Co. v. Pennsylvania (1888) 95
People for the Ethical Treatment of Animals (PETA) 116, 122, 123, 138–40
People of the State of New York ex rel. The Nonhuman Rights Project, Inc., on Behalf of Tommy, v. Patrick C. Lavery (2014) 124–37
persona/res/acta 2, 12, 109
person as bedrock term 11–23
personalism 5, 11, 62, 148
personhood 11–23; of animals 105–9, 112–41; and the corporation 92–8; and God 60–5; in law 88–92; as mask 104–5; of the state 98–102; of women 102–4
personification 11, 21, 41, 57, 58–65, 93, 102
Plato 8, 9, 43, 45
posthumanism 2
post-structuralism 31, 48, 137
Potomac Engineers v. Walser (1954) 91
Pramatha Nath Mullick v. Pradyumna Kumar Mullick (1925) 111n5
prosopon 13–16, 99
Providence Bank v. Billings (1830) 95
psychocentric surrogationalism 8, 65
Pudendorf, Samuel von 102

race psychology 77
Rahner, Karl 145–6
Rasul v. Bush (2004) 127
Real versus verbal/nominal definition 42, 45, 47, 51, 52, 54, 65, 66, 146
Reece v. Edmonton (City) (2011) 141n3
reflexivity 18, 24, 28, 30, 31, 33, 34, 65, 68
Regan, Tom 1
religious language 60–5
reocentric surrogationalism 8, 65, 80
Richards, Ivor 8
Rimbaud, Arthur 29
Rivers v. Katz (1986) 133
Roberts v. Louisiana (1977) 131
Roe v. Wade (1973) 90
Roman law 2, 12–13, 21
Romanticism 28–9, 40, 41
Romer v. Evans (1996) 134
Rowland v. California Men's Colony (1993) 91
Russell, Bertrand 50
Ryle, Gilbert 78

Saleilles, Raymond 97
Salmon v. Pacific Lumber Co. (1998) 120
Salomon v. Salomon & Co Ltd (1896) 95
Santa Clara County v. Southern Pacific Railroad Company (1886) 94
Saussure, Ferdinand de 68, 71–2, 77, 81, 83
Savigny, Friedrich Carl von 98
Schopenhauer, Arthur 32
Schütz, Alfred 30
self as bedrock term 23–35
self liberal model of 2, 16, 24; denied by system theory 35, 71, 83, 147
Sierra Club v. Morton (1972) 115–16
Silver Spring monkeys 116–18
Singer, Peter 1, 34, 108, 130
Slaughter-House Cases (1873) 123
social constructionism 30–2
Socrates 44–5
Somerset v. Stewart (1772) 125, 134
speciesism 1
Spinoza, Baruch 32
standing in law 112–16
state as person 98–102
State v. Stockton (1958) 111n3

stipulated definition 5, 22, 35, 66, 70, 72, 80, 146, 147
Stone, Christopher 113, 116
Strawson, Peter 35
structuralism 71, 77
soul as bedrock term 8–10
substantia 15
systems theory 71–83

Talbot, H. Fox 46
Taylor, Charles 24
Taylor, Talbot J. 45, 70, 81
telementation 67
Tertullian 13
Thibault, Paul 70, 73
Thurlow, Edward, First Baron 93
Tilikum et al. v. Sea World Parks & Entertainment Inc. (2012) 122–4
Tinbergen, Nikolaas 81
Tommy the chimpanzee 124–32
Toolan, Michael 7, 51, 60
translanguaging 77
Tribe, Lawrence 126–30
Trinity, doctrine of 12–16, 61–3, 101, 110, 145–8
Turner, Mark 59
Tylor, Edward 8, 9

Uexküll, Jakob von 72
Ullmann, Stephen 10, 48
Ulpian 85
Urantia Foundation v. Maaherra (1997) 140
U.S. ex rel. Standing Bear v. Crook (1879) 135
U.S. v. Amy (1859) 91
U.S. v. Brownfield (2001) 91
U.S. v. Maciel-Alcala (2010) 91

Vaihinger, Hans 145
Völkerpsychologie 77
Volksgeist 77
Volksseele 77
Vygotsky, Lev 74

Warren v. Fox Family Worldwide, Inc. (2003) 143n45
Watson, John 77
Watts, Alan 32
Weems v. U.S. (1910) 123
West Chester & P.R. Co. v. Miles (1867) 130
whales in litigation 120–4
Whitman, Walt 98
Whorf, Benjamin 52
Wierzbicka, Anna 53–6
Wiggins, David 35
Wilkins, John 48–9
Williams, Raymond 36, 41, 88, 145
Williams, Rowan 64, 145
Wise, Steven 1, 2, 105–9, 124–36
Wittgenstein, Ludwig 10, 22, 51–2, 147
Wolf, George 4, 8, 68
Wundt, Wilhelm 74

Zen Buddhism 32
Zwingli, Huldrych 46

For Product Safety Concerns and Information please contact our EU
representative GPSR@taylorandfrancis.com
Taylor & Francis Verlag GmbH, Kaufingerstraße 24, 80331 München, Germany

www.ingramcontent.com/pod-product-compliance
Ingram Content Group UK Ltd.
Pitfield, Milton Keynes, MK11 3LW, UK
UKHW022120190926
475702UK00013B/1551
* 9 7 8 1 0 3 2 0 9 3 0 9 3 *